Epiphany H
Kenwyn Churc
Kenwyn
Truro
0187285799

Journey to Priesthood

An In-depth Study of the First Women Priests
in the Church of England

HELEN THORNE

CCSRG Monograph Series 5

Centre for Comparative Studies in Religion and Gender
Department of Theology and Religious Studies
University of Bristol

2000

Published by the Centre for Comparative Studies in Religion and
Gender, 3 Woodland Road, Bristol BS8 1TB

Copyright © 2000 Centre for Comparative Studies in Religion and
Gender, Department of Theology and Religious Studies, University of
Bristol, Bristol BS8 1TB, England

1SBN 0-86292-499-5

Printed by the University of Bristol Printing Unit, Old Park Hill,
Bristol BS2 8BB

Preface to CCSRG Monograph Series

This monograph is part of a new series of publications on religion and gender which are based on research undertaken at the Centre for Comparative Studies in Religion and Gender (CCSRG) in the Department of Theology and Religious Studies at the University of Bristol. The Centre encourages innovative interdisciplinary and comparative research on inclusive gender issues in different religions, relating to women as well as men. It is the intention of this series to make the Centre's research on different religion and gender topics more widely available to others.

Research undertaken at the Centre can be grounded in different methodological paradigms; it can be primarily empirical or theoretical; it can be interdisciplinary and comparative, or focused on a single religious tradition. Or it can be applied and action- or policy-oriented with the aim to contribute to the transformation of existing gender injustices in religious and social institutions.

Besides the publication of the Research Monograph Series the Centre organises regular research seminars and encourages networking among scholars working on religion and gender issues. The Centre welcomes applications for associate membership or for postgraduate research leading to a higher degree.

This is the fifth monograph since the series was started in 1999. Whether historical, contemporary or comparative in its approach, whether dealing with doctrines, rites, symbols or people, each of these research monographs makes its own distinctive contribution to current debates about religion and gender.

Ursula King
Series Editor
University of Bristol

*In memory of my mother
Rhoda Cartwright*

ACKNOWLEDGEMENTS

There are many people who have "walked with me" on this research journey whose practical, intellectual, emotional and spiritual support has been invaluable. First, my warm appreciation and thanks to Professor Ursula King who supervised this research. Her vision initiated this project, her faith and encouragement have supported and sustained it. Throughout she has combined sensitivity and humour with a rigorous intellectual perspective for which I am profoundly grateful.

My special thanks to my Advisory Group for their helpful input: Professor Ursula King, Revd. Dr Judith Maltby, Canon June Osborne, Christina Rees, Bishop Barry Rogerson, Jane Williams and, in particular, Professor Phyllida Parsloe whose advice and helpful comments have been invaluable.

Undertaking such a large piece of research required considerable financial support, not least from the University of Bristol who provided my scholarship for the last three years. My thanks to the Alumni Foundation at the University of Bristol, WATCH, The Bishop of Bristol's Fund, Sarum St Michael's Trust, Sir Halley Stewart Trust and the Faculty of Arts Research Fund at the University of Bristol for their contribution to the additional costs of this study.

The scale and complexity of the research I have undertaken means that I am indebted to several people for their practical help and assistance: Sandra Barwise, Hugh Boulter, Tony Hughes, Norma Mckemey, Revd Ian Shield, the Department of Theology and Religious Studies at the University of Bristol, and the Centre for Comparative Studies in Religion and Gender (CCSRG).

I have benefited enormously from the emotional support of a number of people. Sheila Pregnall whose support, sisterhood and shared story-telling has been a source of great strength and encouragement. My father, Bill Cartwright, who has fostered in me a love of life-long learning and greatly encouraged me in this study. Thank you also, dad, for painstakingly compiling the mailing list for the study. And Greg, whose love, faith, belief and encouragement have sustained me through these last three years. You have provided the space in our lives to let this happen and supported me unquestioningly throughout. Thank you.

Finally my deep thanks to the women who have taken part in this study. 1247 women priests took time out of busy schedules to respond to my questionnaire and 29 gave up time to be interviewed. My hope is that this study reflects your experiences and does justice to your stories. Our journey's have been entwined, and I hope that the resulting knowledge will enhance and facilitate the future ministry of women in the Church.

CONTENTS

INTRODUCTION 1

2. THE HISTORICAL AND SOCIAL CONTEXT OF WOMEN'S ORDINATION 8

2.1	Social change in the twentieth century	8
2.2	The changing role of women in the Church of England	9
2.3	The campaign for women's ordination	11
2.4	After the vote in General Synod	16

3. THE THEOLOGICAL AND FEMINIST CONTEXT OF WOMEN'S ORDINATION 19

3.1	The rise of feminism	19
3.2	Feminist spirituality and theology	20
3.3	The theological debate about the ordination of women	26
3.4	Feminist theology and the role of women in the institutional Church	30
3.5	Gender differences and stereotypes	33

4. THE METHODOLOGICAL APPROACH OF THE RESEARCH 40

4.1	Quantitative versus qualitative methods	40
4.2	Feminism and research	42
4.3	The methodological framework of my research	47
4.4	Reflection on the interface between quantitative and qualitative methods	52

5. THE RESEARCH PROCESS 54

5.1	Gaining access	54
5.2	Interviews	55
5.3	The questionnaire	58
5.4	Evaluation of the research design	62

6. WOMEN PRIESTS - THEIR BACKGROUNDS   64

6.1   Age   65
6.2   Social class and education   65
6.3   Marital and family status   68
6.4   Employment status of women priests   74
6.5   Theological orientation   81

7. WOMEN PRIESTS - THEIR EXPERIENCES   84

7.1   Experiences of call   85
7.2   Experiences of identity   91
7.3   Experiences of the Church   93

8. WOMEN PRIESTS - THEIR ATTITUDES   100

8.1   Women priests and change   101
8.2   The role and function of the priest   108
8.3   Women priests and feminism   111

9. WOMEN PRIESTS - THEIR STORIES   119

9.1   A sense of historical significance   120
9.2   The Act of Synod   122
9.3   Gender discourse in women's accounts   125
9.4   Attitudes to change in the Church   128

10. FACING THE FUTURE - OPTIONS FOR CHANGE   134

10.1 How women can change the Church   134
10.2 How the Church can change   141

CONCLUSION   147

NOTES   154

APPENDICES   183

BIBLIOGRAPHY   200

LIST OF FIGURES AND TABLES

Figure 4a*	Positive and interpretative approaches to research	48
Figure 4b	Multi-method approach to research	48
Table 6a	Social mobility of women priests (%)	67
Figure 6b	Marital status of women priests	68
Figure 6c	Employment position by childcare responsibilities	70
Table 6d	The position of women in the Church by their age group and marital status (%)	72
Figure 6e	Employment status of women priests	75
Table 6f	Position in the Church by age group (%)	76
Figure 6g	The employment status of men and women in the Church	77
Figure 6h	Theological orientation of women priests (%)	81
Table 7a	Relationship between women priests' sense of call and vocation (%)	86
Figure 7b	Range of scores on the scale for strong sense of call	68
Table 7c	Expression of call by theological orientation (%)	87
Figure 7d	Loyalty to the Church by theological orientation (%)	92
Figure 7e	Positive scores on the factor scales for experiences in the Church	94
Figure 8a	Distribution of scores on the scale for egalitarianism	102
Figure 8b	Distribution of scores on the scale for collaboration	103
Table 8c	Collaborative approach to ministry by theological orientation (%)	105
Figure 8d	Distribution of scores on the scale for empowerment	106
Figure 8e	Distribution of scores on the scale for clericalisation	109
Figure 8f	Distribution of scores on the scale for feminism	112
Table 8g	Attitudes to feminism by theological orientation (%)	113
Figure 8h	Distribution of scores on the scale for attitudes to inclusive language	116
Table 8i	Attitude to inclusive language by age group and theological orientation (%)	117

* The numbers refer to the relevant chapters

GLOSSARY OF CHURCH OF ENGLAND TERMS[1]

This glossary contains a list of all the terms which relate to the Church of England and which have been used in this study. It provides definitions for each of the major terms which the reader may be unfamiliar with.

ARCHDEACON*   A member of the clergy, appointed by the bishop, to have administrative authority over a particular geographical part of the diocese known as an archdeanery. An archdeacon is responsible for the disciplinary supervision of clergy, the induction of incumbents, the admission of Churchwardens and the administration of Church property. There is one woman archdeacon in the Church of England.

CHAPLAIN   A member of the clergy who is employed to perform specialist duties outside of a parish, for instance in schools, hospitals, and prisons. Some chaplains are paid by the Church, others are paid by the organisations they are working for. Some individuals (the Queen and diocesan bishops) also have chaplains.

CURATE   (Also called assistant priests or ministers). Curates are licensed by the bishop to assist an incumbent in a parish setting. A curacy is generally a junior or training position, however, some retired, experienced priests also undertake curates duties.

DEACON   The diaconate is the name given to the "probationary period" for priests, which lasts for one year after ordination. When women were ordained deacon in 1987, it was initially for an indefinite period. The deacon can undertake pastoral duties, preach, teach, administer holy communion, lead worship and officiate at baptisms and funerals, but cannot preside at communion, absolve sins or bless. There are currently 111 permanent deacons.

DEACONESS   The Order of Deaconesses was created in 1861 as a formal accredited lay ministry for women. Women were ordained as deaconesses and could fulfil some elements of the ministerial role. The Order is now closed, but many women priests were originally deaconesses and some women have chosen to remain deaconesses.

---

[1] Most of the definitions in this glossary have been taken from *A Basic Church Dictionary and Compendium* by Tony Meakin (1995), Canterbury Press.

* Because of the way in which the Church of England is structured, it is difficult to give a clear organisational chart; for a general overview of its decision making structure see Appendix I. The sign * is used here to denote more senior positions in the Church.

DEAN*	The dean is the "first among equals" at a cathedral and, with the chapter, is responsible for its government. There are no women deans at present, although the position is open to women.
DIGNITARY*	A title used to denote more senior positions in the Church, for instance dean, bishop, provost, archbishop.
DIOCESAN BISHOP*	The Church of England is organised geographically into 43 dioceses (these are not generally coterminous with county boundaries in England). The episcopal ministry embraces all that a deacon or a priest does, but a bishop is also able to confirm and ordain. A diocesan bishop has responsibility for a diocese. Further legislation is required before women can be ordained to the episcopate.
DIOCESAN POST	There are a range of jobs that are linked to a diocese which may or may not be paid, and which may or may not be filled by ordained clergy. For instance, bishop's advisor on children's work, evangelism or other faiths. Some posts are held by stipendiary clergy in parish ministry who take on added responsibilities, others are specific paid posts.
FORWARD IN FAITH	A co-alition of anglo-catholic opponents to women's ministry. They are at present campaigning for a free, non-geographical, province in the Church of England which excludes women priests and their supporters. "Reform" is an evangelical organisation which opposes, amongst other things, women priests.
INCUMBENT	Incumbents are clergy who have the tenure of a benefice, which has been granted until the age of 70 and cannot be removed, except on the grounds of ill health, serious misconduct or a serious breakdown in pastoral relationships.
MOW	The Movement for the Ordination of Women was a single issue campaign group which was established in 1978 to campaign for women's priesthood. It was disbanded in 1994, after completing its objectives.
NON-STIPENDIARY MINISTERS (NSM)	An NSM is a priest or deacon who is licensed by the bishop to assist a parish. The term non-stipendiary indicates that they receive no stipend (payment) for their ministry. There is a wide variety of NSM ministry, some give only a few hours a week, while others are full-time. Some people train locally to work specifically in their home parish, they are known as LNSM or Ordained Local Ministry.

PRIEST	A priest can undertake all the duties of a deacon but can also celebrate the eucharist, solemnise a marriage and give absolution or a blessing. A priest is unable to confirm or ordain.
PRIEST IN CHARGE	A title given to priests who are either in charge of a daughter Church in a large parish, or alternatively are in charge of a Church where the priest does not have tenure, or incumbent status.
PROVOST*	Like a dean, the provost exercises leadership in a cathedral. However, this title is used in newer dioceses where the cathedral is also a parish Church. There are no women provosts at present. There is, however, one female vice-provost.
RECTOR	The title rector is now interchangeable with that of vicar unless the individual is a team rector. A team rector is the senior member of a clergy team who manages one or more team vicars in a combined parish.
RESIDENTIARY CANON*	A member of the clergy who is a permanent office holder of a cathedral, with particular responsibilities for the running of the cathedral. The residentiary canon is a member of the cathedral chapter and is a relatively senior appointment. There are a few women residentiary canons.
RURAL DEAN*	The rural dean is appointed by the bishop to act as a channel of communication between himself and the clergy and parishioners in a group of parishes known as a rural deanery. Clergy in the rural deanery meet together in a chapter which is overseen by the rural dean.
SECTOR MINISTRY	Like chaplains, sector ministers operate outside of a parish in a variety of contexts, for instance, community, education, social responsibility, and industrial mission.
STIPENDIARY MINISTER	A stipend refers to the official income given to a member of the clergy. Therefore, a stipendiary minister is paid by the Church.
SUFFRAGAN BISHOP*	A suffragan bishop is appointed to assist the diocesan bishop, to act on his behalf and with his authority. Unlike an assistant bishop, the suffragan has tenured status. There are no women assistant or suffragan bishops, as none of the positions in the episcopacy are open to women.

TEAM VICAR   Team vicars are appointed to a group of parishes, where several priests share responsibilities within the area.

THE ACT OF SYNOD   The Act of Synod was passed by General Synod in 1993, one year after the measure to ordain women had been agreed. It made provision for parishes to opt for someone other than their diocesan bishop to carry out episcopal duties in the parish. Parishes are able to request for extended episcopal oversight, normally undertaken by a provincial episcopal visitor (PEV or flying bishops).

VICAR   The term vicar denotes the priest of a parish.

WATCH   "Women and the Church" (WATCH) is the title of a group formed in 1996 to work for the inclusive ministry of women and men, lay and ordained, in the Church of England. It is campaigning for the end of discrimination against women and their supporters in the Church and is seeking the appointment of women bishops. It has recently begun to campaign for an end to the Act of Synod.

INTRODUCTION

> A cold coming we had of it,
> Just the worst time of the year
> For a journey, and such a long journey:
> The ways deep and the weather sharp,
> The very dead of winter.
> (T.S. Eliot, *The Journey of the Magi*)

On the 11th of November 1992, a cold, grey winter's day, the General Synod of the Church of England voted by the required two-thirds majority to approve legislation to ordain women as priests. As the Archbishop of Canterbury announced the vote, the crowd of supporters waiting on the steps at Church House spontaneously broke out singing "Jubilate Deo".[1] The long journey towards women's priesthood, which had taken over 100 years and had been marked by pain and joy, disappointment and hope, alienation and support, was finally over. Women could be ordained priest in the Church of England.

In Spring 1994, on 12th March, the first women were ordained in Bristol Cathedral in an historic and joyful service which ended centuries of an all-male priesthood. In the ensuing year approximately 1500 women were ordained.[2] The first women priests in the Church of England[3] are a unique and especially significant group. They are women of experience, both in Church and secular work; women of perseverance who waited many years for the chance to be priests; and women of faith and faithfulness who felt a call or vocation to serve the Church*, yet were denied access to the priesthood. Unlike other professions, where women's entry occurred gradually over many years, the Church of England suddenly at once increased its number of priests by 10% through the ordination of women, ensuring that they became a significant and immediate presence in the ranks of ordained clergy. Women's ordination was a momentous step in the development of women's ministry in the Church. My study is a rich, in-depth picture of this first group of women priests. It provides base-line research into key issues for women in the Church of England by examining the backgrounds, experiences and attitudes of this initial cohort.

The 1992 vote in General Synod occurred in a specific historical, social and theological context. It was the culmination of a long, bitter, vituperative debate in the Church of England which had accelerated since the second world war. The struggle for women's ordination in the second part of the twentieth century is well documented.[4] However, the origins of the debate, and the seed-change in attitudes to women, can be traced much further back to the nineteenth century. In the second part of the nineteenth century women became the mainstay of Anglican congregations until they out-numbered men in the Church by a ratio of two to one. At the same time their contribution to Church life began to develop, firstly in a voluntary capacity, then in paid work, and finally in ministry, culminating in the creation of the Deaconess' Order (Heeney 1988, Field-Bibb 1991, Gill 1994). At no stage was women's status in the Church equal to that of men's, but their growing involvement led to greater influence and opportunity for women within ecclesiastical structures.

---

*   The term Church is used throughout the study to describe the Church of England.

Significant advances in the status and position of women in society are often followed by a retreat. When women gained the right to vote in 1918, the popular feminist movement became dormant, and women's entry to the workplace, through the war effort, was followed by a campaign encouraging women to return to the domestic sphere. The history of Church feminism mirrors women's path in society. Although women were given opportunities to minister through the Deaconess Order in 1861, their next major advancement in the Church did not occur until 1944. The Bishop of Hong Kong, himself unable to reach Anglican communicants in occupied China, took the exceptional step of ordaining Florence Li Tim Oi, a deaconess serving in his area, to the priesthood. However, it was not until the feminist movement was rekindled in the 1960s and 1970s, that the debate about women's ministry resurfaced in the Church. In the late twentieth century women's involvement in the public, professional, and therefore economic, spheres and their increasing control and choice about fertility, contributed to a social and cultural context which, combined with the growth of feminist theological insights, created an environment where women's ordination became acceptable to society and to the Church.

The inclusion of women to the priesthood was perceived by many as a new dawn for the Church; it offered opportunities to develop new styles of ministry as women brought their different gifts and abilities to benefit the Church. There was a sense of excitement and anticipation amongst the supporters of women's ministry: excitement at the historical opportunities that were being opened up, and anticipation at the changes that women would bring to the ordained ministry. Hopes and expectations were high. Women, it was said, would bring a collaborative, egalitarian approach to ministry, they would be committed to lay empowerment and would be less concerned with hierarchical priestly status in the Church (Hoad 1984, Farrington 1994). Women, if ordained, would bring something new and essentially different to the ministry.

Yet the optimism engendered by the vote to ordain women quickly evaporated as clouds of dissent soon began to form. In order to maintain the unity of the Church, its leaders moved swiftly to limit any damage from opponents of the measure to ordain women. The House of Bishops produced legislation which was designed to safeguard the rights of those priests who found the ministry of women offensive. The Act of Synod was created in order to ensure that the Church did not split into no-go areas where women, or opponents of women's ministry, were unable to minister. The Act contained provision for opponents of women's ministry to receive alternative oversight from Provincial Episcopal Visitors. PEVs, or flying bishops as they have since become known, have no geographical province. They provide episcopal services and pastoral care to priests across the country who feel unable to accept the ministry of their diocesan bishop, because he has ordained women.

In the six years since the General Synod vote, what began as a cloud is now developing into a storm. The Act of Synod, rather than becoming a framework which allows differing factions to co-exist peacefully, has become the battle ground for further conflict. The opponents of women's ordination are continuing to ensure their voice is heard and are lobbying for a third province within the Church which would not be geographical (as Canterbury and York are), but would be a theological haven for their members. The Movement for the Ordination of Women (MOW), disbanded once the vote had been passed, has since reformed as "Women and the Church" (WATCH) in order to challenge this legislation, campaign for women bishops, and work for a more inclusive Church. The debate about women's ordination, far from receding, has gained momentum and is set to overshadow the Church's move into the twenty-first century. With falling congregational numbers and the financial insecurity of the last decade there are stormy vistas ahead for the nation's established Church.

Reflecting on the ordination of women, Sue Waldrond-Skinner stressed the historical significance of this new development:

> As we struggle from our different perceptions to interpret the significance of the ordination of women to the priesthood...one certainty eclipses all others. The knowledge that this is a moment of historical significance - that moment is now and that moment must not be somehow missed even if cannot fully be understood. (Walrond-Skinner 1994 :1)

This moment in time, the "moment" when women became priests in the Church of England, is so significant that it must not be lost, forgotten or buried as other pivotal moments for women have been. Through my study I aim to capture this "moment" in history, and use it as a source of understanding - a means to develop, to learn and to grow. There are many silent voices and invisible actors in women's social history, due largely to the fact that the majority of people who record, research and interpret past and present social orders are male. As a result many women's stories have been lost for ever.[5] Even in this supposedly post-feminist era women are rarely the sole subjects of in-depth study - women's view of the social world is far too often seen as coterminous with male experience. Women's experiences are seldom the subject of exclusive study, but are usually articulated, either in comparison to a male world-view or subsumed into the amorphous category of the general population.

This research on the first women priests in the Church of England owes its significance to the fact that it:

- is based exclusively on women's experiences and perspectives;
- investigates the lives of an historic group of women;
- focuses on an organisation where the critical mass of women increased significantly in one go;
- is representative of women priests' experiences and attitudes through an exceptional 81% response rate to the questionnaire administered during the research.

My research focuses exclusively on the stories of women priests. I do not attempt to compare their priesthood journeys with those of male clergy, nor am I studying the impact of women's ordination from a lay perspective. I am concerned solely with the backgrounds, attitudes and experiences of the women priests themselves. The picture I give in this study is from the women's own perspective, it is rooted in their experiences of priesthood which may, or may not, be identical with that of their male counterparts.

Moreover, this study is significant in both theological and social terms because it investigates the lives of a unique group of women. All of the women ordained between 1994 and 1995 had been previously ordained into the diaconate, many since 1987.[6] Some had been working in the Church for many years as parish workers, lay workers, chaplains, missionaries and deaconesses. They are the only group of women in the Church of England to have experienced the struggle for ordination, followed by the realisation of their hopes and then the reality of life as ordained priests. The journey to ordination meant that the Church ordained women in significant numbers. In one year the critical mass of women priests in the Church of England grew to 10%. This group of women has the potential to make a difference in the Church - their presence can count, and their voices be heard. As such they are an historically unique and significant group. The purpose of this research is to record their journey and to understand the implications of their experiences for the Church. The chapters which follow represent an in-depth study which look at the social, ecclesiological, pastoral, spiritual and gender aspects of the ordination of women.

My research is both descriptive and analytical. First, it records the history of the women ordinands by examining women's backgrounds, their journey into priesthood and their post-ordination experiences. Secondly, I am concerned with women's approach and attitude to ministry. Is there evidence that women are developing a less clericalised approach to ministry? Are women priests committed to collaborative, egalitarian and empowering ministry styles, or are they conforming to the "traditionally male" model of priesthood?

Women's ordination was the end of a long campaign, but only the beginning of the struggle for gender equality within the Church. Amidst the clamour for women's ordination some prophetic voices sounded a warning (Maitland 1983, Ruether 1983, Kroll 1994, Williams 1994). These voices reminded women of the dangers of joining the "male clerical club". They were fearful that women would become part of the existing power structures in the Church at the expense of developing new approaches to ministry. Sara Maitland sees the ordained ministry as inherently flawed and hierarchical as it separates the doers (the priests) from the done to (the congregation):

> By inviting some of the most able and enthusiastic women into its
> power structures institutional Christianity may be able to evade the
> more profound issues of inbuilt sexism and dualism. (Maitland
> 1983:104)

Maitland's warning should not be viewed as an argument for women to remain outside the structures of the ordained ministry,[7] but it does question women's ability to deliver the hoped-for new models of ministry. Will change be achieved in the Church by a form of clerical osmosis? Will women's presence be a source of natural transformation, because they bring different gifts and abilities? Or are they in danger of being co-opted into male clerical circles?

The Church is viewed by feminist theologians as a patriarchal institution, one which encapsulates the sexist norms of society in an hierarchical, sexist structure and which essentially favours men and disempowers women. Some feminists believe the Church can be redeemed,[8] and are committed to the regeneration of faith communities of equality and liberation. Other feminists describe themselves as post-Christian, and see the Church and the Christian religion as irredeemably male.[9] Both see feminism as an antidote to patriarchy. The feminist principles of connectedness, shared experience, campaigning and consciousness-raising are seen as the means by which women can dismantle patriarchal institutions. If indeed these elements provide women with a praxis for change, how far do women priests identify with, and are prepared to use feminist principles in their approach to sacerdotal ministry?

Just as feminist theological thought has influenced the theoretical basis of my research, so feminist insight into social research methods has contributed to my methodological approach to this study. Traditionally research is either quantitative, originating from a positivist worldview, or qualitative, based on an interpretative paradigm, in nature. Feminist researchers have heavily criticised the prevailing and preferred over-reliance on positivist, statistical methods in the study of social life (Oakley 1981, Stanley & Wise 1983). Social research has, they argue, ignored women's experience and failed to engage with, or attempt to understand, women's social world. Some feminist researchers are therefore, prescriptive about the methods they perceive as being consistent with a woman-centered perspective. Qualitative methods, such as in-depth interviewing and ethnography are a preferred source of data because they recognise and acknowledge the co-participation of respondent and researcher in the research process.

Both the traditional separation of qualitative and quantitative methods, and feminist methodological prescription, is an unnecessary and unhelpful dichotomisation in the study of the social world. In this research I have developed a methodological framework which integrates qualitative and quantitative methods and which embraces feminist research precepts - a focus on women's experience, action-oriented research and reflection on the role of the researcher. Interview data are combined with results from a large scale survey in a research framework which not only enables the methods to co-exist and complement each other, but also ensures the study is embedded in the experiences of women priests. The use of a research diary, meanwhile, has fostered reflexive research practice and contributed to my own self-awareness as a researcher. Through it I have concentrated on my personal participation in the study. The result is research which is rigorous and intellectually compelling and at the same time grounded in women's experience of priesthood.

A distinguishing hallmark of feminist research is the overt presence of the researcher in the research process. Thus it is important that I acknowledge my own personal background, involvement and investment in this study. One woman, in an interview about her priesthood, said:

> I think there was also at one point...that I had all these different
> strands to my life and I wanted somehow to bring [them] together.

My own experience resonates with the voice of this woman priest. The spiritual and professional threads of my life come together and are integrated in my research journey and, therefore, I am a participant in this study. My background and beliefs have affected my approach to research. My choice of topic and the analytical themes developed in the study are partly a response to my own thought processes and belief systems. Therefore, it is important for me to acknowledge and reflect on these elements in order to make them conscious rather than unconscious and visible rather than invisible, influences on the research.

My first degree was in the Arts, in English and Drama. I then trained and worked as a dramatherapist - a career which required high levels of personal reflection as I sought to understand my often unconscious motives and concerns. Subsequently I moved into the field of social research where I worked with users of health and social services to develop and improve new and existing services. Here, respondents were seen as participants, not as passive recipients of research. Underpinning the community development approach to the work was a belief that research is an instrument of change; it does not exist in a vacuum but should, at some level, impact upon the context in which it is located. My therapeutic background has fuelled my desire to incorporate self-reflection into my research methodology, but this is held in tension with a commitment to producing an empirical study which uses a range of research methods in order to understand the backgrounds, attitudes and experiences of women priests.

Finally, I am a Christian and, although I do not attend an Anglican Church I am a committed member of a local Community Church.[10] My Church background actively encourages women's ministry and women are involved in its leadership. However, we do not have an ordained ministry, but favour a team leadership of lay people, some of whom are employed by the Church in a full-time capacity. My understanding of, and commitment to feminism, has been partly developed by my growing awareness of gender inequality in the Church's attitude to women.[11]

All of the perspectives outlined in this section are an integral part of my approach to this research: a strong personal interest and belief in the importance of women in the Church, a desire to produce an empirical study employing a number of research methods, and a commitment to a participative approach to the research, which means at some level the study engages with the concerns and perspectives of those being studied. There is a final thread which links my journey to that of women priests. My research is carried out in the Department of Theology and Religious Studies at the University of Bristol, with a scholarship from the Faculty of Arts and with support from the Centre for Comparative Studies in Religion and Gender (CCSRG). Bristol, the site of the first ordinations of women, is also the home of this study.

The study begins in chapter 2 with a description of the social and historical context of women's ordination. It looks briefly at social change in the twentieth century which combined with the changing role of women in the Church of England to provide the right social and ecclesiological context for the debate about women's ordination. Chapter 3 outlines the theological and feminist context of women's ordination, demonstrating how feminism and feminist theology have contributed to women's advancement in the life of the Church. In this chapter I summarise the theological arguments for and against the ordination of women and draw on the philosophy of gender, and gender difference, to understand how the concept of women's ability to change the Church became entwined in the debate about their ordination.

I then focus on the empirical study of the 1547 women ordained between 1994-1995 which begins, in chapter 4, with an in-depth discussion of the methodological approaches used in my study. In particular I focus on the feminist critique of traditional research methodologies to show how I have created a methodological approach which combines qualitative and quantitative methods within a feminist research framework. In chapter 5, I outline the actual process of research before going on, in chapters 6-9, to describe in detail the research findings.[12] These chapters explore women's background, their experiences in the Church and their attitudes to ministry. Chapter 9 looks specifically at themes which arose from the analysis of the qualitative data.

The final chapters contain the conclusions from the study, offering ideas for the practical application of the research findings. Chapter 10 addresses the concept of change, looking particularly at how women can engage with the process of transformation. It describes some structural and attitudinal changes which need to take place if the Church is to fully include the ministry of women. Chapter 11 draws together the study in an overall conclusion which evaluates my research methodology and summarises my findings and interpretations.

Throughout the study I use the metaphor of a journey to describe the research, both the stories of the women priests and my own participation in the study. The concept of a journey reflects the processes by which goals are achieved, for instance the goal of women's ordination and the completion of this study. However, the idea of a journey is also a way of describing the development of knowledge, self-understanding and spirituality which are additional themes in this study. Through my research I have travelled, albeit for a brief period of time, with the first women priests in the Church of England. My hope is that I do justice to their stories and, through the critical evaluation of their experiences, contribute to opportunities for change: for women, for the Church, and for society.

CHAPTER 2

THE HISTORICAL AND SOCIAL CONTEXT OF WOMEN'S ORDINATION

Belief systems, that is the spiritual and philosophical frameworks that govern human existence, do not exist in a vacuum. Religious thought and practice are developed according to the social and cultural context in which they are embedded. Spirituality and culture are intertwined. The Christian religion, although it draws on ancient symbols and traditions, is nevertheless involved and rooted in social engagement. Religious change affects society,[1] but similarly social and cultural change provide the backdrop for unfolding spiritual truth. "The right time" is the moment in history when social conditions create a propitious environment for a paradigm shift. John Austin Baker (1984) defines this moment as an opportunity, created by God, to achieve a specific purpose. "The right time" is not about opportune, political development engendered by changing social conditions, it is the point at which spirituality and culture collide to allow new patterns of religious thought and practice to develop. The cultural and ecclesiological changes in the late nineteenth and twentieth centuries, with regards to women, created a new climate of openness and the right environment in the Church for the debate about women's ordination to take place.

Victorian religious feminism in the nineteenth century saw women engaged in social reform and social work.[2] At the same time women became increasingly involved in the life of the Church in voluntary, paid, and finally, ministerial capacities. Both these factors changed women's status in the Church and profoundly challenged male domination of ecclesiastical structures. In the second part of the twentieth century, the explosion of the women's movement and the greater involvement of women in society produced the right social context for the debate about women's ordination to emerge in full force. At the same time women's ever-growing participation in Church life, fuelled by the upsurge of feminist theology, provided the right ecclesiological environment. This was "the right time" for the debate about women's ministry, it was "the right time" for women's ordination. The question is whether the historical and theological circumstances which created the momentum for change and paved the way for women's re-emergence in Church life in the nineteenth and twentieth centuries, will also provide opportunities to explore new models and patterns of priesthood for the twenty-first century.

SOCIAL CHANGE IN THE TWENTIETH CENTURY

The social change in the twentieth century has been immense. It is only possible to touch briefly on complex social issues in order to highlight the context in which the debate about women's ordination originated. It is the changes which have affected women's role in society which are of most significance to this study. There are three main factors that have contributed to women's changing social roles: women's emergence in the work place, changing attitudes about sexuality and the family, and women's increasing contribution to economic growth and consumerism.

As the twentieth century dawned, the separation between the public and the private spheres was strongly drawn along gender lines. The workplace was a male domain whilst the domestic sphere was the realm of women. It was the two world wars which shattered this gendered delineation between the public and private. In both wars the labour shortage in Britain was so great that women were called upon to do jobs that would previously have been performed by men: ambulance drivers, factory workers and farm hands. Despite the mood of the post-war periods which discouraged women from the workplace (in order to make way for the returning men), the taboo of women in the labour market had been broken. Women could, and did, have careers. Women began to enter previously male-dominated professions, such as law, medicine and higher education, in increasing numbers. Women's growing professional involvement challenged the concept of an all-male priesthood.

The second major cultural shift for women in post-war Britain was the changing attitudes concerning sexuality and the family. In the 1960s a profound social questioning concerning many traditionally held, often Christian, values, relating to sex and the family occurred (Davie 1994). With the development of accessible contraception, and later abortion, women's sexuality was no longer irrevocably linked to child birth. This new freedom and autonomy meant that a woman's place was not necessarily in the home. As women began to consider vocations outside of motherhood and family, the concept of women's priesthood became a possibility.

Finally, in the second half of the twentieth century, changes to the economic structures of society have occurred. The growth of mass production has led to the need for a larger work force. The parallel growth of mass consumption has demanded a greater income per family unit. As a result, women's labour has become an essential part of the economic cycle. Consumerism is the final stage in the demise of the taboo about women in the work place.[3] The confidence and affirmation wrought in secular society empowered women to think seriously about their contribution to Church life - women's priesthood became more than a possibility, it became a right.

The journey towards women's priesthood was not just the result of social transformation. Chapter three focuses on the philosophical framework which accompanied these cultural changes, in particular the rise of the women's movement and the growth of feminist theological thought. However, it was also women's developing contribution to the life of the Church of England which began to encroach upon, and challenge, the idea of an all-male priesthood.

THE CHANGING ROLE OF WOMEN IN THE CHURCH OF ENGLAND

The debate about the ordination of women in the Church of England developed fully in the twentieth century and accelerated after the second world war. However, the origins of the debate and the change in attitudes to women in the Church can be traced back to the nineteenth century. Brian Heeney (1988) and Sean Gill (1994) both give detailed accounts of women's growing involvement in the Church of England: first in a voluntary capacity, then in paid work, and finally in ministry. By the late nineteenth century women were becoming the mainstay of the Victorian Church, they outnumbered men by two to one. The feminisation of the Church, coupled with women's growing involvement in Church life, began to affect theological insights. On the one hand the women's movement had difficulty establishing itself in the Church of England because of the Church's teaching on women, in particular women's perceived inferiority, and the inappropriateness of their contribution to the public sphere. On the other hand the Victorian period did see the rediscovery and incorporation of feminine qualities into the images of the Godhead as a result of women's growing visibility in the Church (Gill 1994).

For women in the Church, the legacy of the Victorian era was both constricting and empowering. Women's natural vocation was seen to be in the domestic sphere. The economic success of a family was measured by the man's ability to provide for his wife and children. In spiritual terms, women's holiness became associated with their place in the family. The Victorian Church also emphasised and spiritualised the role of the mother further underlining her vocation to domesticity (Heeney 1988, Gill 1994). However, opportunities for women's voluntary work in the Church developed as the skills associated with the home were extended to Church life. District visiting, Sunday school teaching,[4] the Mothers' Union and the Girls' Friendly Society originated as extensions of women's "natural expertise" in the domestic sphere. These opportunities provided important outlets for women's creative energy and facilitated their growing confidence in the public sphere.

The next stage in women's involvement in the Church was as paid workers: the Bible Women's Movement, Parochial Mission and the Church Army. These paid opportunities combined social work with the evangelisation of the poor. In each area women's role was to support the male clergy or Church Army officer, by working with the sick, the poor, or with other women. Women remained subordinate to men in work which was seen as an extension of their natural domestic role. However, with the growth of paid work for women came the development of further training opportunities.

Finally, in the nineteenth century women began to develop a ministerial role in the Church through their involvement in foreign missions, religious orders and eventually as deaconesses. Paid and ministerial work in the Church provided important opportunities for single women to contribute, in a formal way, to Church life. In all these roles women remained subordinate to men. Only the Deaconess was ordained into a holy order and hers was a junior role. The Church was still a long way from licensing women in a formal capacity to minister as priests.

The history of women's growing involvement in Church life is important: it shows women's concern for the marginalised in society, it highlights the problems of class division in the Church, and it demonstrates how lay movements significantly impacted on women's position in the Church. The root of women's involvement in the Church lay in the desire to create a fairer society. This philanthropic endeavour was strongly based in the class system and was, to a degree, patronising. Nevertheless, concern for the poor and a desire to improve social conditions, as an outworking of the gospel message, was a concept embedded in the origins of women's priesthood. Josephine Butler wrote:

> To the regal conception of justice, those who profess the religion of Jesus Christ must bring into public life, and into legislature, the stern practical side of the real Gospel, the religion of Christ must become again what it was when he was on earth. (Butler quoted in Webster 1994:13)

Although they are faint, the prophetic voices of liberation, which later found full voice in the women's movement and feminist theology, are heard through the stories of women's involvement in the Church.

In the late nineteenth and early twentieth centuries, social class remained a dividing factor for women in the Church (Gill 1994). Those engaged in ministry were from middle and upper classes, whilst the beneficiaries of women's endeavours were, in the main, women from poor, working class backgrounds. Contrary to the Christian theme of equality, which transcends race, class and gender, the hierarchy of secular society was reflected in women's involvement in Church life. Inherent in this class divide is the hierarchical distinction between doer (the minister) and done to (the recipient of ministry) which contradicts both a feminist and a Christian ethos.

The third distinctive factor in the history of women's re-entry into Church life was the importance and prevalence of lay movements which gave women a voice. Excluded from priestly ministry, women found expression in the Church through the development of strong lay networks. Through lay activity women gained confidence and fulfilment in the Church. The question is whether women's ordination has fostered or curtailed lay involvement in the Church. Has women's entry to the priesthood increased or diminished the wider involvement of women in the Church? Has it facilitated or hindered lay ministry and have women priests been a source of lay empowerment?

THE CAMPAIGN FOR WOMEN'S ORDINATION

The seeds of the debate about women's ordination can be traced back to the revival of the Order of Deaconesses in 1861. However, it was 131 years before those seeds could bear fruit and women could, at last, be admitted into priesthood in the Church of England. The door to women's ordination opened slowly, and sometimes unintentionally. The debate about women's ministry in the Church emerged and became focused in a vibrant campaign to ordain women, which was spearheaded by lay people. The struggle for women's ordination in the twentieth century is well summarised in the works of Furlong (1991), Armstrong (1993), and Dowell and Williams (1994). However, for a careful re-construction of the debate and legislation in the Church of England, Jacqueline Field-Bibb's book *Women Towards Priesthood* (1991) is unrivalled. Similarly, Margaret Webster's account of the Movement for the Ordination of Women, *A New Strength, A New Song,* (1994) is significant.

The revived Deaconess Order signified, and contributed to, a change in the Church's attitude to women in ministry: it affirmed and sanctioned women's ministry and allowed women to adopt elements of the professional clergy role. The legislation in 1861 concerning sisterhoods and deaconesses originated as much as a measure to curb women's involvement in the Church, as it did from a desire to promote it. The Lower House at the Convocation of Canterbury was particularly concerned to ensure that sisterhoods came under the authority and jurisdiction of the episcopate. Ironically, in an attempt to control women's growing, developing involvement in ecclesiastical structures, the Church legitimised and ratified women's ministry. The door to women's ordination opened a crack further.

The Deaconess Order was a significant step in the move towards women's ordination because it allowed women to adopt, and be identified with, elements of the priestly role. Heeney (1988) traces the professionalisation of the clergy role in the Victorian era. The signs of this professionalisation are the development of specific training in theology and pastoral work, involvement in the self-government of the Church, the production of professional literature, the development of peer identification through clerical societies, the adoption of distinctive dress and the definition of the professional priestly role (leadership in worship, preaching and pastoral care). The Order of Deaconesses enabled women to adopt and engage in some activities and clerical identifiers which had become associated with professional clergy.[5] Deaconesses had a distinctive dress, specific professional training, they became part of the Church jurisdiction, and under its authority and were set apart and licensed by bishops through a ritual of ordination. Although deaconesses were not admitted to *the* Holy Orders, they were admitted to *a* holy order, and were thus formally identified with the ministry of the Church.

The Deaconess Order was fully affirmed and recognised in the report "Ministry of Women" in 1919. This report, accepted by the Church in 1920, allowed women to prepare people for baptism and confirmation, assist in baptism (and in the cases of emergency, to baptise), to pray and give counsel to women, read morning and evening prayer, and to instruct and exhort congregations. Restrictions were placed, however, on women exhorting or preaching in consecrated places.[6] Despite this, the legislation did extend the role of women in public ministry from a purely functional role (helping the poor and working with families) to encompass spiritual, as well as practical, duties in the Church. Field-Bibb shows how the legislation concerning women constantly extended the boundaries of women's ministry whilst "contracting" or diminishing women's status in the Church (1991:79). Whilst the "Ministry of Women" report recognised women's sacred calling through the Order of Deaconesses, it clearly affirmed the priesthood as a male prerogative.

There was, however, growing lay support for the idea of women's ordination. In 1920 a document "Women and the Priesthood" was sent to the Archbishop of Canterbury. The report, originating from a group of lay and clerical members of the Church, stated that the authors could see no reason why women should not be ordained. Since women had won the right to vote, and therefore to influence the government of their country, why should they not also influence the government of their Church? In 1914 women were allowed to become members of Parish Church Councils, having initially been excluded from the measures to involve the laity in ecclesiastical government. In 1925 the Church League for Women's Suffrage became the League of the Church Militant and began campaigning for women's ordination.[7] Other campaign groups followed: the interdenominational Society for the Ministry of Women in 1929 and the Anglican Group for the Ordination of Women in 1930. Although clerics were part of these groups, the main drive and impetus for them came from the laity. Even in these early stages of debate, the pressure on the Church to change came largely from its lay members and not from its ordained ministers.

Against the backdrop of women's suffrage the pressure for women's ordination began to gain momentum and, as a result, the Church published its second report entitled "Ministry of Women" in 1935. Although the Archbishop's commission heard evidence from supporters of women's ordination, the report did not further women's ministry significantly. It reaffirmed the Order of Deaconesses as the only opportunity for women to exercise their specific, unused gifts in a ministerial role within the Church. The report emphasised the fact that the Order of Deaconesses was the Church's way of enlisting "the great gifts and special contribution of women to the varied and immense needs of the Church today".[8] Women's ministry was to be kept separate, and by implication, subordinate to men's ministry in the Church (Webster 1994). Women were deemed to have gender specific gifts that could be fully expressed through their ministry as deaconesses. The argument based on gender difference was used here to exclude women from ordination. The idea that women and men are essentially different is a theme which resonates and echoes throughout the debate about women's ordination. It is invariably used to affirm and justify an all-male priesthood, and thus exclude women from Holy Orders

By 1941 an impasse had been reached. The Order of Deaconesses was affirmed as the only holy order for women and so the priesthood remained resolutely male. At this stage history intervened. During the second world war much of China was occupied by the Japanese and was therefore inaccessible to visiting Anglican priests. Richard Hall, Bishop of Hong Kong and South China, was concerned that many communicants in his province were unable to receive the sacrament other than from a female deaconess, Florence Li Tim Oi. Hall considered it was less irregular to ordain a woman than it was to allow someone who was not a priest to preside at the eucharist. Consequently, in 1944 Bishop Hall ordained Florence Li to the priesthood. Reverend Li continued to minister as a priest for 18 months until Hall was reprimanded by a letter, supposedly from the then Archbishop, William Temple.[9] The bishop refused to suspend Florence; however, she volunteered not to function as a priest although she did not renounce her orders.[10] Bishop Hall's actions were formally condemned by the Lambeth conference in 1948.

In the post-war period, as women in society were encouraged back into the home, so women in the Church remained largely in their pews. It was a further 12 years before the Church of England responded again, and began to address the concept of women's ordination. The issue of women's role in the Church began to re-emerge at the same time as the women's movement, which was re-kindled in the 1960s in response to the civil rights movement. By this stage, however, the Church was beginning to grapple with the idea of women and the priesthood. In 1962 the report "Gender and Ministry" was presented to the Church Assembly. The report recommended that the Church examined its attitude to women's ministry in the light of changing social conditions. As a result, the Archbishops were asked to set up a commission to examine thoroughly the Church's reasons for withholding priesthood from women. In this report the concept of gender difference as a way of affirming women's calling to the priesthood was used for the first time: "Women were asking, rather, that the particular gifts of their own sexuality be brought to bear and used in the total service of the ministry of the Church." (Field-Bibb 1991:89).

In 1966 the results of the Archbishop's commission were published in the report "Women and Holy Orders". The reasons for not ordaining women were, it concluded, pragmatic rather than theological. In 1968 the Lambeth Conference asked each province in the Anglican Communion to consider the resolution that "there are no theological objections to the ordination of women". In 1971 the Anglican Consultative Council advised Bishop Gilbert Baker of Hong Kong that, with the approval of his synod and province, the council backed any decision he made to ordain women. Later that year Bishop Baker ordained Joyce Bennett and Jane Hwang to the priesthood. At the same time other Churches in, or connected with, the Anglican Communion began to follow suit.[11]

In 1975 the Church of England passed a measure agreeing that there were no theological objections to the ordination of women, although the Church voted not to remove the existing barriers to women's ordination. When the measure was returned to Synod in 1978, it was again rejected. The disappointment amongst supporters of women's ordination, at this second defeat was immense. In the silence, after the result of the vote was announced, Una Kroll's now famous cry rang out: "We asked for bread and you gave us a stone". Yet this second defeat also had the effect of galvanising proponents of women's ministry into further action. In a meeting to assess their position, the Anglican Group for the Ordination of Women met with other key campaigners (such as Una Kroll and Christian Howard) and organisations (such as the Student Christian Movement and Christian Parity) to agree a strategy for their campaign and to regroup into a nation-wide campaign organisation. At this meeting the Movement for the Ordination of Women (MOW), a single issue group campaigning for women's priesthood, was born.

MOW saw itself as a "mainstream" group, working within the structure of the Church of England to achieve change. It was, however, a broad movement embracing both radical and conservative approaches to campaigning. MOW was criticised at times for being too radical, and at other times for being too conservative in its approach. Its success was partly due to MOW's ability to hold these different approaches in tension:

> MOW was determined to try to weave together, from the very first days, different strands of conviction under an umbrella of freedom that was hard to find within the established Church...And so it has been. Some have departed, probably also giving up the church in sad despair, and a few from the more conservative end of the spectrum, but the rest of us stayed together, argued, persuaded, wept, laughed and prayed. (Webster 1994:60)

MOW's combination of a national organisation, which was able to apply pressure at high levels in the Church, with its strong grass roots membership in local and regional groups, was a powerful one. Once again lay opinion was mobilised and proved a powerful voice for change within the Church.[12]

MOW's approach to campaigning embraced feminist tenets and ideology. In particular the sense of support and connectedness fostered within MOW's structures, and its commitment to a non-hierarchical team-based structure, clearly echoed feminist ways of working. MOW did not set out to be a feminist group and may have adopted feminist principles unconsciously, rather than by design, but nevertheless it showed to the Church an alternative way of working and being:

> Organisations like the Movement for the Ordination of Women were remarkable for the degree to which they nurtured shared leadership, shared responsibility. There was no premature separating of those who would "go on" to priesthood when the time came, and those of us who would "stay behind". Working together like this has been an important experience of sisterhood for many of us, and experience of community and so an experience, importantly, of "church" for many for whom "The Church" was unable and unwilling to provide such lived examples of sharing. (Williams 1994:84)

The women who worked together and supported each other through MOW also sought to express and celebrate their spirituality together. From their position of marginalisation, women began to develop alternative worship opportunities using inclusive language, alternative symbols and new forms of prayer and imagery which included, rather than excluded, women's experience.[13] In 1987 the St Hilda Community was formed in London to develop and explore women's spirituality within the Church. Although not a formal part of MOW, the Community provided an important outlet for some of MOW's more radical members.

As the momentum for women's ordination to the priesthood grew, two events occurred in the 1980s which are of particular significance. First, the measure to allow women ordained overseas to minister in England failed. Secondly, the measure to ordain women as deacons was passed. The draft measure which allowed visiting women priests, ordained abroad, to celebrate the Eucharist was first presented to Synod in 1983. Opponents of women's ordination argued that, since the measure was deemed to be changing the service of Holy Communion, it was required to go through the full legislative procedures in the Church. It was 1986 before the measure finally came back to Synod. Although the legislation was approved by deanery and diocesan synods, it failed to reach the required two thirds majority in the Houses of Clergy and Laity and so the measure was rejected.[14] The failure of this measure is important because it illustrates how political manoeuvring, rather than theological debate, also affected and hindered the progress of women's ministry in the Church.

In 1981 a report "The Deaconess Order and the Diaconate" was presented to General Synod. This report recommended that the Church have a single Order of Deacons which was open to both men and women. The final measure to ordain women as deacons, and therefore into Holy Orders, was passed five years later in 1986. The significance of this measure was immense: it meant women could become part of the clergy and could undertake most duties undertaken by priests except preside at the eucharist, give absolution or a blessing. The Order of Deaconesses opened up the professional ministry of the Church to women, the Order of Deacons took women a step further towards priesthood. Women were able to wear the clergy uniform, hold the clergy title and undertake most, but not all, of the clergy duties. Congregations and member of the public became accustomed to the idea of women priests through their experience of women deacons. The door to women's ordination was, at last, beginning to open.

By the mid 1980s momentum began to grow at a local and national level concerning women's ordination. There was a sense that the time was right. In 1987 a report by the House of Bishops, "The Ordination of Women" was published. The report contained three parts: the theological issues involved, principles for legislation, and a framework for the legislation including safeguards for those opposed to women's ordination. It was five years before the final measure was presented to General Synod, having been passed at the diocesan and deanery synod level. During this time George Carey, a strong supporter of women's ordination, was enthroned as Archbishop of Canterbury in 1991. On November 11th 1992, in a packed chamber and following a long, tense debate, the General Synod voted, by the required two thirds majority, in each of the three houses (Bishop's, Clergy and Laity) to approve the legislation to ordain women as priests. As the vote was announced, the crowd of supporters waiting on the steps at Dean's Yard spontaneously broke out singing "Jubilate Deo". The door to women's priesthood was open:

> I went over to Church House for the announcement of the vote. It was dark and people were holding candles and crying and praying - there was a very crackling link up with the debating chamber. Then George Carey's voice came out as he announced the vote. I still cry. Then there was this joy. It was just relief and joy, I suppose it's one of my nearest experiences to what heaven will be like.[15]

Changing attitudes to women in society intertwined with a developing understanding of the gospel to provide the right time for women's ordination. There can be no doubt that MOW was a significant force in the success of the campaign for women's ordination. MOW prospered because it was a broad movement which held together different approaches under the single issue of women's ordination: the division between lay and ordained women existed in the organisation, but it was not the defining factor. MOW had strong local and regional support within a national framework which made it an effective campaign group. Finally MOW mobilised lay opinion in a vibrant movement for change: it adopted the feminist principles (albeit unconsciously) of support, connectedness and non-hierarchical structures which offered the Church an alternative model, a different way of being. The question now is whether women's ordination has enabled the Church to embrace the qualities that MOW offered, or whether it has stifled them:

> I am glad for the Church and I am glad for my friends, but I shall miss those years of camaraderie and everything they taught us. (Williams 1994:84)

AFTER THE VOTE IN GENERAL SYNOD

The legislation passed by General Synod in 1992, which enabled women to be ordained priests, also contained other clauses which protected the rights of those who were opposed to women's priesthood. The original measure exempted the Church from the Sex Discrimination Act, protected bishops who could not, within their conscience, ordain women, and provided measures for priests and parishes who could not accept the ministry of a woman priest.[16] In short, the legislation which enabled women to be priests in the Church of England did more to protect the rights of those opposed to women's ministry than it did to encourage the women hoping to enter the ministry. For those who had watched many of their sisters leave the Church in silent despair at the prevailing attitude to women, it was galling to see the generous financial compensation offered to male priests who left the Church as a result of the measure.[17]

Worse was yet to come. The initial euphoria over the vote was quickly dispelled as a prevailing mood of depression spread through the Church. The years of pain and frustration experienced by women as they journeyed towards priesthood were forgotten as the Church struggled to accommodate the despair expressed by the vociferous opponents of women's ordination. In contrast, the public appeared to embrace the measure wholeheartedly. One woman reported going into a pub in Westminster after the vote with five other women deacons:

> This guy just turned around and said "well did you do it?" and we said "yes we did" and the whole place cheered. I mean when has the Church of England, in the last century, ever had a reaction like that?[18]

In January 1993 the bishops met in Manchester and produced a statement focused at maintaining the unity of the Church by safeguarding the position of opponents and ensuring that no-go areas were not created. They also confirmed that bishops who were opposed to women's ordination would continue to be appointed. At the same time a coalition of groups opposed to women's ministry came together in an umbrella organisation "Forward in Faith". This group began to lobby strenuously amongst the bishops, where there seemed to be "an overwhelming sense of identification with the disaffected, and a feeling that something must be done to relieve their distress" (Furlong 1998:5). In June 1993 "The Bonds of Peace", a report from the House of Bishops, was produced and it provided the basis of the Act of Synod which was agreed by the General Synod in November.

Critics of the Act of Synod describe it as a "far-reaching bit of legislation, cobbled together, virtually without consultation outside the bishop's own ranks" (Furlong 1998:7). Certainly the haste with which this legislation was passed contrasts with the ponderous, painstaking approach the Church adopted when considering the measure to ordain women as priests. The Act of Synod legitimised opposition to women's ordination in what has become known as the "two integrities",[19] in order to allow opponents to remain within the Church. To accommodate opponents of women priests, two bishops were consecrated to provide alternative episcopal oversight. The Provincial Episcopal Visitors (PEVs), or "flying bishops" as they have become known, have no geographical province, but instead minister in each of the dioceses where there are clergy who are opposed to women's priesthood. The PEVs provide alternative episcopal care to priests, for whom the fact that their diocesan bishop has ordained women, makes diocesan oversight unacceptable. Far from disappearing, opposition to women's ministry is well organised, vocal and growing. Opponents are currently seeking the establishment of a third province, with a separate Archbishop, which would enable male priests to remain "untainted" from association with those who sanction women priests. At best this arrangement would lead to a church within a church, at worst there would be two Churches of England.

Opposition to the Act of Synod is growing, and there are calls to have the Act rescinded.[20] However, whilst it is still in operation, the Act of Synod has important theological, practical and philosophical implications for the Church at large, and for women's ministry in particular. In the first instance, the Act enshrines the doctrine of women as "the other", the non-man. The legislation implies that priesthood is so indelibly male, that by ordaining women, a priest's own orders are invalidated. This argument fosters a theology of "taint", for by laying hands on a woman at ordination, a bishop is himself then unacceptable to those who believe that priesthood is inimically male.

Secondly, the Act of Synod has meshed two different notions of gender difference which is both damaging, and limiting for women (Shaw, 1998). Shaw says "It seems to me that older notions of gender hierarchy have melded with notions of sexual difference to create a fairly deadly mix in which women are simultaneously thought to be *both* the "non-norm", as I have termed it, *and* different." (Shaw, 1998:21). For when the priesthood is viewed as essentially male, then the male priest becomes the norm and the female priest is defined as "the other", the inferior male. The outworking of the Act of Synod is such that the notion of "taint" also identifies a woman as so totally different from a man, that by ordaining her a bishop is himself "tainted" by her difference:

> Here, woman may be equal in all other regards but her "difference" discards her into a space which makes her sacramental ministry literally - for some - polluting. In this view, once touched by hands which have laid hands on a woman, one is tainted. (Shaw 1998:21)

The Church cannot claim to model a gospel of freedom, acceptance and inclusivity whilst it continues to legislate for, and embrace, structures that discriminate against women and affirm a, deeply rooted, sexist worldview. The Act of Synod confirms deep seated beliefs that women are inferior and subordinate to men, and I question the effect this has on the corporate psyche of the Church. It gives a clear message that it is acceptable to find women unacceptable. The legislation taps into, often unconscious, views of women which are offensive and degrading; a factor which counteracts any possibilities for change that ordaining women brought to the

Church. I believe the Act of Synod is profoundly damaging for the Church, and ultimately for wider society, because it denigrates women. However, in my research I focus particularly on the impact and effect the Act has on the ministry of women priests.

Social change, developing theological insight and women's growing involvement in Church life combined to provide "the right time" for women's ordination. The history of the debate provides important insight for today's women priests. The fact that the religious feminist movement was rooted in concern for the poor and marginalised is significant as women priests struggle to reform, not conform to, the Church hierarchy. The history of the women's movement in the Church reflects rather than challenges the class bias of the Church of England: today's priests must surely challenge this division of class hierarchy. Finally, lay involvement, throughout the long debate about women's ordination, was a powerful voice for change. Women priests must encourage, support and prepare to be challenged by ordinary people in the Church. The journey to women's ordination was slow, and even now the accompanying legislation has provided serious barriers to women's ministry. Ultimately, however, the door for women in the Church has been opened - women must continue to walk through and thus help to shape the destiny of the Church.

CHAPTER 3

THE THEOLOGICAL AND FEMINIST CONTEXT OF WOMEN'S ORDINATION

The late twentieth century provides the specific social and historical context for the debate about the ordination of women. The philosophical and theological framework for the debate is also a modern development. The rise of the feminist movement challenged patriarchal structures in society, of which institutionalised religion is one. Feminist spirituality, similarly disillusioned with institutionalised religion, but also limited by the secularisation of feminist thought, has advocated new women-centred forms of religious practice. Meanwhile feminist theology, whilst acknowledging patriarchy as the structural domination of women, states that it is the organised Church which discriminates against women, not religion itself. The debate about the ordination of women is embedded in these three strands of feminist thought.

Christianity is essentially a religion of inclusivity in which all are equal, regardless of race, class or gender. It is a movement of spiritual and physical liberation on a personal and corporate level, where human worth and dignity are central. The Christian religion is justice-seeking, anti-oppressive and non-hierarchical. It is a faith for the outcast, the marginalised and the oppressed.[1] Therefore, the central tenet for women's ordination is one of justice, for the Church cannot truly represent humanity in the twentieth century if it fails to represent women at the altar. There is no morally defensible contradiction to this argument on social grounds, so it is in the theological arena that the battle ground for the debate about women's ordination has developed. Some feminist dissidents have reminded women of the dangers of joining the "male clerical club" and called for a radical reshaping and evaluation of the concept of priesthood.

The concepts of gender and gender differences are woven into arguments for and against women's ordination. Whether or not women approach Church ministry in an inherently different way from men affects opportunities for change. If women and men are essentially different, if indeed they bring intrinsic, gender-specific gifts to priesthood, then ordaining women in sufficient numbers should bring about radical changes in the Church. Women priests will either threaten the all-male power structures of the Church or they will simply become subsumed into existing hierarchical practices.

THE RISE OF FEMINISM

Historically the development of women's involvement in public ministry in the Church is linked to the feminist movement.[2] To suggest, however, that the women's movement is cohesive and unified is misleading. Feminism is multi-faceted; its different strands inform the contrasting approaches to feminist theology and spirituality which will be outlined in section 3.2. There are broadly four types of feminism: liberal, Marxist, romantic and radical (Loades 1990, Storkey 1985). Liberal feminism focuses on achieving equal rights for women in the educational and professional spheres. It emphasises legislative change, working within the structure of society to achieve equal pay and reproductive self-determination for women. Critics of liberal feminism argue that its desire to work within "the system" fails to address the inherently patriarchal organisation of society.

Marxist feminism challenges the structures of society whereby a minority of economically powerful people (mainly men) own the majority of the means of production and therefore control the lives of most of the population, particularly women. Marxist feminism sees economic autonomy as essential in overcoming women's inequality in society. Marxism goes some way in addressing structural sexism, but economic inequality does not fully explain the differences between the position of women and men in society.

Romantic feminism is based on the concept that women are inherently different from men. It celebrates women's emotional and intuitive strengths and contrasts them positively with a male focus on the rational and technical. The structures in society, which are created and sustained by men, therefore continue to disadvantage women. For it is only when society is organised according to female strengths that women will have equality. In the reverse of patriarchy, romantic feminists view women as morally and spiritually superior to men (Ruether 1983).

Elements of romantic feminism can be found in the radical feminist movement which, as it name suggests, rejects the liberal and Marxist analysis of sexism. The world, where men are the oppressors and women the oppressed, is viewed as inherently patriarchal. Radical feminism is an eclectic movement which is easier to stereotype than to define. It can include some, or all, of the following: a belief in feminism as a central part of life, opposition to the norm of heterosexuality, and adherence to a total women-centred ideology (Storkey 1985). On the one hand radical feminism is probably the most publicly reviled facet of the women's movement,[3] and yet on the other, it has contributed important core methodological tenets to feminism which distinguish it from other political movements. First, a commitment to direct political action through non-violent campaigning, demonstrations and marches (most noticeably in England at the Greenham Common Peace Camp). Secondly, the focus on consciousness-raising, where women join together and explore, through their own stories, their experiences of powerlessness and oppression. Finally, the notion of sisterhood, where women in small, non-hierarchical groups can renew their sense of themselves and find strength for the struggle against patriarchy.

Social change and technological development have increased choice and opportunity for women. It is the feminist movement, however, which has challenged the patriarchal and androcentric structures of society. Women's emancipation can be attributed to feminist methodologies of consciousness-raising, support and non-violent campaigning (King, 1989). Women in the Church must also draw on these key elements if their ministry is to be truly integrated and accepted. Women must continue to name experiences of oppression and powerlessness in the Church, supporting and encouraging each other in all-women groups. Finally, women must continue to campaign in the Church if they are to achieve equality in its structures.

FEMINIST SPIRITUALITY AND THEOLOGY

The relationship between feminism and feminist theology has not been, and is not always, an easy one. Feminists are critical of a religion headed by a deity who is largely imaged as male, where women are apparently subjugated and their experiences ignored. Feminists see the Church as a patriarchal institution which uses exclusively male language and imagery, and which appears to condone violence against women[4] (Chester 1983, King 1989,

Trible 1990, Loades 1990). The fact that secular feminism has failed to pay sufficient attention to spiritual matters, however, has led to a growing body of feminist theological writing. Ann Loades' book *Feminist Theology: A Reader* (1990) brings together writings from key women theologians: Daly, Hampson, King, Maitland, Ruether, Schüssler Fiorenza and Trible. Loades creates a comprehensive source book of feminist theological thought in which feminist writers have sought to reclaim women's lost biblical history and to restore their place in religious expression.

Despite their uneasy relationship feminism and feminist religious thought share common themes. The split in feminism between those who wish to reform existing structures in society and those who see the need for a radical overhaul of its inherently sexist structures, is also present in feminist religious theory. Christ and Plaskow (1979) identify two strands to feminist religious thought. First the *reformist* strand, represented by those who seek to transform and reinterpret existing Jewish and Christian religious traditions - who I will define as concerned with feminist theology. Essentially the reformers are seeking equality in religious symbols, rituals and organisational structures. Secondly the *revolutionary* strand, which contains those who see existing religion as inherently sexist and are therefore looking for new women-only forms of religious expression - who I will define as concerned with feminist spirituality. In comparison to the reformers, the revolutionaries seek female ascendancy within new religious structures.

The revolutionaries, or post-Christian feminists, such as Mary Daly and Daphne Hampson, argue that it is not just the religious institutions which are patriarchal, but that it is Christianity itself, with its male deity and male saviour, which is inherently sexist and can therefore offer nothing to contemporary women (Daly 1974, Hampson 1986, 1996). Revolutionaries seek to develop a new feminist spirituality, a religion for women which sometimes draws on pre-Christian traditions, such as goddess worship, witchcraft and matriarchy groups, in an attempt to celebrate positive female energy and involvement in creation (Washbourn 1977, Starhawk 1979, King 1989). Whilst not wanting to underestimate the importance of these new forms of spirituality, I intend to focus predominantly on the reformist school of thought because my research is located firmly in the Christian tradition.

Feminist theologians such as Rosemary Radford Ruether, Janet Martin Soskice, Sara Maitland and Elisabeth Schüssler Fiorenza do not see Christian religion, in itself, as inherently sexist, but they do consider the traditions that have grown up around it as patriarchal. In her book *A Map of the New Country* (1983) Sara Maitland attributes the unconscious sexist attitudes of the early Church [5] to the dualistic worldview which underpinned Greco-Roman culture. Male experience became associated with God and the spiritual realm and was therefore identified as the norm. Female experience, on the other hand, was linked to the things-not-of-God and was therefore identified as abnormal:

> Once the divine is securely identified as male, however subconsciously, women become less divine than men; and for Christianity that also meant less human...they no longer need to be treated as though they were fully human people made in the image of God. (Maitland, 1983:8)

So it is the patriarchal institution of the Church, fuelled by a perception of women's inferiority, which has limited women's roles and experiences throughout succeeding generations. Yet within Christianity itself, all the elements of a new feminist spirituality can be found: agape love, new images of community, compassion, and peace are all integral parts of New Testament thinking (Schüssler Fiorenza 1979). In answer to the post-Christian criticism of Jesus' role as a male saviour Rosemary Radford Ruether finds the ministry of Jesus entirely compatible with feminism (1983). His ministry restored the importance of the prophetic, thus challenging existing norms in society. He renewed God-language naming God as an intimate family member and the Messiah as a servant or slave. He advocated non-hierarchical relationships and elevated the poor, weak and marginalised. Women, on the edges of society, and as symbols of the oppressed, became an integral part of the new world order which Christianity is meant to bring. Jesus' maleness is not significant; it is his role as the liberating word of God which offers hope for a new order built on equality for all. It is to biblical sources and early Christian history that feminist theologians return in order to rediscover women's biblical heritage and bring liberation for all women.

Over the past two to three decades there has been a growing body of feminist exegesis. Scholars such as Phyllis Trible, Elisabeth Schüssler Fiorenza and Mary Hayter, have revisited religious sources and rediscovered women's involvement in early Christianity. In her land mark work *In Memory of Her* (1983), Elisabeth Schüssler Fiorenza develops a feminist hermeneutic approach to New Testament studies. She does not attempt to deny post-Christian criticisms of Christianity, but advocates a rigorous examination of biblical and early Christian texts in order to rediscover women's lost participation. The argument for the ordination of women owes much to the careful, systematic rediscovery of the lost women in Jesus' ministry and in the early Church. Feminist exegesis of the Bible demonstrates that women's clear, unequivocal religious participation was counter-cultural to the social context in which Christianity originated. Feminist theologians have recovered and remembered the lives of women whose voices have become lost in the male-defined accounts of history. In doing so they have shown that women's involvement in the Church is not only valid, but essential, if it is to rediscover the liberation roots of Christianity.[6]

Feminist theology is a theology of change and challenge. It examines and discredits patriarchal religious interpretation. It rediscovers the lost or hidden elements of women's involvement in religion and uses this to counteract androcentric interpretations of religious tradition. Feminist theological thought challenges the male dominated language and symbols of Christianity, giving women-centred alternatives, and it focuses on the importance of women's experience. Finally, it is a movement of liberation in which the gospel message offers freedom and equality for all in this life, not just in the life to come. (Ruether 1983, Schüssler Fiorenza 1983, King 1989, Trible 1990). Within the context of the debate about the ordination of women, feminist theology challenges the institutionalised Church on three levels: the hierarchical power structures of the Church, the use of sexist language, symbol and ritual in worship, and the need for women's experience to be used as a source of enlightenment, truth and understanding.

The Use of Language and Symbol in Feminist Theology

> He who would valiant be, gainst all disaster
> Let him in constancy follow the master:
> There's no discouragement shall make him once relent
> His first avowed intent to be a pilgrim.[7]

When I attended an all-girls school, "To Be a Pilgrim" was our school hymn and on special occasions I sang this, along with hundreds of other girls. None of us wondered at the incongruity of singing words that appeared to refer only to men. This hymn illustrates the problem with much religious language associated with Christianity. Not only does it refer to the whole of the human race as male, but it utilises imagery associated with battle and war - not themes which resonate easily with women's experience. This persistent use of exclusively male language and imagery has led many feminists and those concerned with feminist spirituality to view Christianity as inherently sexist.[8] Feminist theologians, most noticeably Janet Morley, have worked hard to challenge this view, first, by recovering and reusing imagery and vocabulary in relation to the Divine which utilises characteristics that are traditionally associated with women. Secondly, they have done this by challenging the use of exclusive language which Janet Morley describes as the "practice of using generically (when referring to the whole of humanity) terms like 'men', 'brothers', etc." (1984:58).[9]

Language, and its use, engenders powerful emotions which operate at a subconscious level. Change in liturgy and worship produces, at best, an ambivalent response, and, at worst, aggressive opposition (Maitland 1983). This ambivalence can be seen in wider society where there has been a backlash against the perceived attempt to control language through equal opportunities legislation and awareness. Efforts to eradicate language which discriminates against people according to their gender or race have, some feel, gone too far. As a result the concept of "political correctness" has become unfashionable and the term is used derogatorily. The extremely negative reaction to change in religious language at least demonstrates the importance and significance of words and their use. More subtle, however, is the trivial response: the perception that language only matters to a small number of neurotic women, the idea that it really is not that important to the rest of society. So why is language so important? Does it affect the way in which we see ourselves, and will change in the way language is used bring about greater equality for women? Language is important because it communicates the values and norms of society; it is a basic, fundamental source of power. Exclusive language defines women as invisible or "the other"; inclusive language not only frees women, but empowers all of society.

Language has the ability to construct the way we view ourselves, our society and our faith (Morley 1984). The use of language reflects the core values of society;[10] in the same way the vocabulary used by the Church communicates the way in which it views women. The fact that God-language is almost exclusively male identifies the Divine as male and normative. The female, in contrast, is identified as alien, the non-Divine, the abnormal. Women's invisibility is further exacerbated by the use of language which identifies humanity by using exclusively male pronouns. The word "man" is used to identify everyone who is male and everyone who is not male. Women are viewed only in relation to men - they remain invisible in their own right. Once again women are on the outside of the definition of humanity. They are "the other".

The control of language is a form of oppression. Governments who wish to subdue ethnic groups within their borders, attempt to eradicate their indigenous language. Ursula King identifies the use of language as a tool for empowerment: "the power of naming is one of the most decisive human activities in constituting the world as experienced" (1989:42).[11] For generations that power has been used against women. Male-dominated language has been part of the construction of masculinity and therefore a tool for domination (Wren 1989). When the world is named according to male experience, women are silenced. In the biblical creation story the right to name the world was given to women and men. Unless women reclaim the right to name and be named in religious expression, their experiences will constantly be overlooked, their views will be marginalised and women will remain powerless.

Language and symbolism are therefore essential to feminist theology, not just as a barometer to measure the depth of change in attitudes to women, as Monica Furlong rightly states (1991), but also because they fundamentally change our view of humanity and of God. For Christianity the importance of language is more than the inclusion of female pronouns in worship. Christianity needs to reclaim the imagery of God which is associated, not with power, might and victory, but with vulnerability, openness and suffering. Imagery and metaphor which identify God with the disenfranchised, lost and the marginalised, not only reclaim women's experience, but also resonate with the experiences of other groups in society. In doing so, they touch humanity at a deep level, transcending female and male, and empowering us all. As Janet Morley points out, we need to do so not just to placate women, but because "the wholeness of our Christian community depends on it" (1984:70).

The power and beauty of inclusive language is evident from the hymn by Jan Berry sung at the inaugural WATCH service:

> Praise to God, the world's creator,
> Source of life and growth and breath,
> Cradling in her arms her children,
> Holding them from birth to death.
> In our bodies, in our living,
> Strength and truth of all we do,
> God is present working with us,
> Making us creators too.

Feminist Theology and Women's Experience

One of the core tenets of feminism is the emphasis on women's experience. In a reaction against the enlightenment praxis that all valid knowledge is external, objective and value-free, feminism emphasises and validates understanding gained through personal experience. In feminism, experience is a tool to develop feminist consciousness, and shared experiences are a source of mutual support. Where patriarchy is dominant the whole of society is conceptualised in sexist terms. As women reflect on their experiences together, they develop an alternative feminist consciousness, a consciousness which opens up a non-sexist worldview, offering freedom from the dominant structures of patriarchy, a consciousness which validates women's experiences and enables them to name the world as they see and experience it. Stanley and Wise (1983) argue that feminism is the only way of conceptualising the world in non-sexist terms:

> We need a woman's language, a language of experience; and this must necessarily come form our exploration of the personal, the everyday and what we experience - women's lived experience. (Stanley & Wise, 1983:146)

Women's experience is an important theoretical theme in feminism, but it is also a methodological tool. In the first instance, sharing experience in small non-hierarchical groups offers women support and encouragement in the all-pervading male culture. Indeed, such groups were an important part of the Christian feminist struggle.[12] Secondly, experience is an epistemological tool. Women's experience is used as a criterion against which women can critically evaluate ways of knowing. Feminist theology embraces women's experience: as a source of theological understanding and a criterion for measuring truth (Ruether 1983, Maitland 1983, Carr 1988).

From a feminist perspective, women's experience is a gauge to measure the patriarchal structures and practices of religion. Rosemary Radford Ruether argues that symbols, rituals and traditions of the Church are used and discarded according to their resonance with human experience (1983). In feminist theology women's experience is used as a plumb-line with which the symbols and traditions of the Church are authenticated - thus exposing the elements of religious practice which are formulated solely on the basis of male experience.[13] The androcentric rituals and sexist symbols which fail to resonate with women's experiences should be discarded. In their place, the Church must rediscover ways of worship which authenticate a female worldview, not at the exclusion of men, but in the search for a holistic representation of humanity.

Finally, women's experience is a source of content for the development of theological understanding and insight. We experience life outwardly through social pressures, constraints and opportunities which shape our lives, and inwardly through thoughts, feelings and emotions (King 1989). As women attempt to make sense of their experiences it not only brings important clarity of vision and insights for them as individuals and groups, but also for the Church as a whole. It is women's shared, underlying experience forged by their history of powerlessness and marginalisation which can bring new insights to the Church.

Women's experience is also seen as a tool in discerning the theological validity of women's ordination (Tanner, 1984). Since neither scripture nor tradition can produce conclusive arguments about women's priesthood, it is suggested that women's experience of being called to the priesthood (which has remained strong despite the fact it has caused conflict and is not recognised or supported by the Church) should be used to rule in favour of their ordination. However, in this argument lies the inherent conflict in the use of experience as a basis for understanding - for whose experience is valid? Opponents of women's ministry can similarly justify an all-male priesthood through their experience of not wanting women priests. For in order to validate one person's experience it is often necessary to devalue another's.

The naive use of experience as a source of understanding in feminism and feminist theology is, therefore, problematic (West 1983, Leech 1992). The concept of a universal female experience fails to acknowledge other cultural and ideological factors, apart from gender, which shape our experience: namely class, race and sexuality. To claim that the experiences of women from largely white, middle class backgrounds are synonymous with those of black women in the two-thirds world is simplistic. Since feminism is criticised for being the domain of the white middle classes,[14] its frequent failure to acknowledge the different experiences of women from other cultures is problematic.

Despite the difficulties of using experience as the only, or primary, category for knowledge development, it is a valid source of insight in the Church. However, feminist theology cannot exist in a vacuum, it has to be linked to a gospel of liberation, not just for women, but for all humanity - regardless of gender, class, race or sexual orientation. Feminist theology must be located in a universal framework of justice, and women's experience should be evaluated critically in light of other cultural and ideological factors. For as women name their experiences of oppression in patriarchal religion, they stand alongside other groups who are marginalised by society. As women use their experiences as a criterion for evaluating truth, they are able to call out prophetically against injustice. As women share their experiences, they are empowered to work for freedom from patriarchy, not only for themselves, but for other marginalised groups in society.

Feminist theology has challenged patriarchal structures in the Church, in particular the use of male-dominated language, symbol and ritual, and has reclaimed the lost voices of women in Jewish and Christian history. Feminist theologians have called upon women to reflect on their own experiences; as a measure of truth, a source to develop theological thought, and as a way of gaining support in the struggle against patriarchy. The debate about the ordination of women occurred in response to social change, and was given impetus by feminism and feminist theological thought.

THE THEOLOGICAL DEBATE ABOUT THE ORDINATION OF WOMEN

In previous generations there had been little debate about women's ministry because it was not an issue - women were not ordained. Opposition to women's ministry did not need to be justified or defended because non-ordination was the status quo. As women developed their role in society, and indeed in the Church, the issue of their ordination became pertinent. As a result, the theological arguments for and against the ordination of women developed in response to social and religious change which forced the Church to evaluate and justify its treatment of women.

The arguments for and against women's ordination are therefore inter-related, with opponents and proponents developing their arguments in parallel.[15] Both sides acknowledge that society has changed and that the debate could only have happened in the present historical and social context. Traditionalists argue that the Church should not allow culture to dictate its doctrine. In an ever-changing society the doctrinal truths of the Church remain strong as handed down through the generations, however counter-cultural they may be. Reformists lay the blame of an all-male priesthood on earlier society which mistakenly shaped Christianity to its patriarchal norms. Now that society is changing towards equality for women, the Church must allow itself to be re-shaped back to its original roots of equality (Chapman 1989, Saward 1978, Powell 1978).

Theologically, the Church of England is a broad Church taking its doctrine from scripture, tradition and reason. In reality the arguments concerning women's ordination are focused either on scripture or on tradition, depending on which wing of the Church is being represented. Dowell and Williams (1994) link the concern for ecclesiastical tradition with the "high" catholic end of the Church which views the priestly role as a sacramental one handed down from the time of Christ and which the Anglican community has no right to tamper with in isolation from the other Churches (Roman Catholic and Orthodox). The emphasis on scripture is the domain of the "low" or evangelical wing of the Church who see priesthood in practical rather than sacramental terms. Their problem with the ordination of women lies in the interpretation of specific biblical passages.

The Argument From Tradition

The first strand of the argument from tradition centres around the maleness of Christ and the sacramental role of the priest, particularly in relation to the eucharist. Since Christ was born a man, his maleness is considered theologically essential for the priesthood. The priest's role is to represent Christ to the Church, and it is therefore essential that he has one of the basic characteristics that cannot be conferred through ordination, that is Christ's maleness (Packer 1972). Norris summarises the argument by saying that Jesus actualised God-with-us by choosing to become human and choosing to become male. If the purpose of Christian ministry is to actualise God-with-us as Jesus' representative, then just as Christ's maleness was essential to his role and ministry, so is the priest's maleness essential (1984). For a woman to stand as an icon of Christ is therefore to break the thread with the historically male priesthood (Dowell and Williams 1994). Demant takes this a step further in the report to the Archbishop's Commission (1966) by arguing that Christianity was so inherently revolutionary in the context of the other world religions at the time of its origin that, had it intended to revolutionise the role of women as well, it would have done so. He argues that the maleness of Christ is not a result of chance, but is so integral to the Christian package that to tamper with it would undermine the whole religion.

One of the major flaws in this argument is that maleness was not Christ's only distinguishing feature, he was also Jewish, single, with specific hair and eye colour; yet none of these are pre-requisites for Christian ministry. It is therefore illogical to focus on sex as the key attribute for representing Christ to the church (Martin Soskice 1988). It is Christ's humanity that was the key to his redemptive role and not his maleness (Norris 1984, Hayter 1987). Christ's death, as represented in the eucharist, breaks down the barriers between God and humanity - both female and male. If the role of the priest is to represent Christ to the people and the people to Christ, it is surely essential that priests represent the totality of Christ's redemption to the whole of humanity. It is therefore not only acceptable to have a woman in the role of a priest, but essential.

Advocates of women's ordination do not see the maleness of Christ as essential to the priesthood because the sacrament of baptism not only joins a believer to the Church but also to Christ (Carey 1984). Through baptism we become one with Christ and share in his identity - this rite, the rite of entry to the Church, is open to both female and male. Therefore, it is possible for a woman to share in the identity of Christ, to represent Christ to the world, and it makes no sense to preclude women from fulfilling in ordination what they can legitimately fulfil as lay people. As Norris points out, to insist only men can represent Christ through ordination suggests that they represent a different Christ from the one identified with at baptism, which is clearly not a sustainable theology (1984).

The second strand of the tradition argument is linked to the relationship between the Anglican Communion and the Roman Catholic and Orthodox Churches. The importance of this relationship is understood to mean that the Church of England does not have the right to change essential doctrine in isolation from the other Churches. The Roman Catholic Church has declared that the divine blueprint for the Church consisted of Christ at the head of the twelve apostles, led by Peter.[16] It is this unbroken tradition of the Catholic, Orthodox and Anglican Churches that no one Church has the right to change in isolation from the other two (Hill 1988). Therefore the ordination of women to the Church of England severely challenges ecumenism, as there is no doubt that it is at odds with the core tenets of the Roman Catholic and Orthodox Churches.

In response to this argument Avis (1997) points out that Anglicanism does not see tradition in such absolutist terms, but as subject to scripture and interpreted by reason. To be locked into tradition in a way that gives no room to question or debate seems to him to stifle free-thinking within the Church. Avis argues that ordaining women is not changing doctrine, but reinterpreting and applying it - something which the Church continually does. However, the problem still remains; women's ordination poses a severe threat to ecumenical relationships between the three Churches, but as Avis points out, since neither Church recognises Anglicanism as a Christian Church, nor Anglican priestly orders, unity between the three is highly unlikely, whether or not the Church of England chooses to ordain women.

The critical appraisal of the ecumenical argument can be developed further. To view ecumenism solely in terms of three Churches (albeit large ones) limits the scope of inter-Church relationships. The Baptist and Methodist Churches have been ordaining women for many years, and there have been recent moves to merge the Methodist and Anglican Churches in England. Failing to ordain women could threaten such ecumenical developments. Indeed it could threaten internal relationships with other parts of the Anglican Communion who have already ordained women.

The cultural selectivity of the development of tradition and the interpretation of scripture also requires challenging. That is, the way in which the cultural and social context (in this case patriarchy) informs the elements of tradition which became core doctrines of the Church. So the apparent maleness of the structures (which are in themselves questionable) that Christ is said to have initiated have become immutable doctrine of the Church. In contrast, other aspects of Christ's ministry, his identification with the poor and marginalised and his criticism of power and influence, are ignored. This principle of cultural selectivity is also applied to the interpretation of scripture. The passages which refer to women are interpreted literally, whilst other passages, for instance those which talk about the redistribution of wealth (Acts 4:32), are either ignored, or viewed as valid only in the context of the early Church.

The Interpretation of Scripture

The argument for women's ordination has benefited from some excellent work by feminist theologians who have revisited scripture and early Church writings to discover a rich history of women's involvement in the ministry of Christ and in early Church life. However, the interpretation of scripture has also been a major obstacle to women's priesthood in the evangelical wing of the Church. Opponents of women's ordination argue against women's leadership, based on the doctrine of headship. The passages referred to are to be found largely in Paul's letters to the Corinthians and Timothy which appear to prohibit women from any form of public ministry including speaking and teaching (1 Corinthians 11:3-16, 1 Corinthians 14: 34-35, 1 Timothy 2: 8-15). Christ is pictured, in I Corinthians 11, as the head of the Church. Since the male/female relationship is symbolic of the relationship between a male Christ and a female church (the bride), the man is head of the woman:

> But I want you to understand that Christ is the head of every man, and the man is the head of a woman, and God is the head of Christ. (1 Corinthians 11:3)

Here the maleness of Christ is again seen as significant, not because of the central role of the eucharist, but because of the relationship between Christ and the Church. Christ is to his Church as man is to woman - this is viewed as the natural order. Just as Christ has authority over the Church, so man has authority over woman (Field 1984). Whilst evangelical Anglicans do not see the priesthood in sacramental terms, they do see it as a symbol of authority. As authority is seen to rest in men, all priests should therefore be male.

In tackling this argument proponents of women's ordination have taken two approaches: a literalist and a contextualised view of biblical sources. The literalist approach accepts the absolute authority of scripture and advocates faithful interpretation of the Bible. Proponents argue that the Greek word for head (*kephale*) has been misinterpreted to suggest a hierarchical order of creation based on authority. (Scott 1991, Storkey 1985, 1995). They suggest that the true meaning of *kephale* is non-hierarchical. Like the concept of servant or slave leadership conveyed in the Greek word *diakonos* which is used in relation to Jesus' and Paul's ministry, the word *kephale* reflects a relationship of service and love.

The literalist approach is, however, problematic. First, in adopting this stance to biblical interpretation, the literalist approach fails to adequately account for the clear anti-women statements in other parts of the New Testament. Secondly, as with the arguments from tradition, this literalist view of the Bible fails to ask key questions about why these particular passages of scripture need to be interpreted literally, when other radical passages about sharing possessions in common, appear to be overlooked or conveniently taken in context. Once again the patriarchal nature of society shapes not only the way in which religion is developed, but can also be seen to predetermine the basis on which the debate about women's ordination is held.

Within the evangelical tradition, proponents of women's ordination have advocated a wider, more contextualised interpretation of the biblical view of women's ministry (Carey 1984, Craston 1973, 1986, Tomlinson 1995, Robson, 1989). Whilst the Bible is seen as a framework for belief, it cannot be expected to give an exhaustive blueprint for the complexity of modern life. For example, the Bible gives no direct instruction on nuclear arms or ecology. These issues were not part of the social and historical context of the Biblical authors. Slavery, however, was part of the cultural context of the Old and New Testaments.[17] Yet in our current historical and social context, not to mention our understanding of the whole gospel whose essence is freedom and wholeness for humanity, slavery can be nothing but abhorrent. In the same way Paul's teaching on women must be seen in the context of the cultural setting in which he was writing. As George Carey wrote "We should not attribute omniscience to Paul. He lived within the limitations of his own culture and he could not have known the total implications of the Christian concept of humanity...The writer is addressing the needs of his own people in his own time. What we have to ask is: to what extent do instructions about first century order apply to us today" (1984:52).

Women's leadership is convincingly authenticated and validated by moving away from specific and isolated passages of scripture to look at the biblical picture as a whole.[18] Central to the message of Christianity are the concepts of creation, fall and redemption. In the creation story (Genesis 1-3) both women and men were made in God's image; in English the word female is a derivative of male, but in Hebrew they are two separate words, suggesting that men and women were created to reflect individually something of the nature of God (Carey 1984). Here there was equality, harmony and parity between the sexes. The result of the fall was to bring inequality, domination and submission in male/female relationships. The Christian message offers redemption from, and the reversal of, the fallen world order. The purpose of the Church is to represent this new order in which the intended equality between women and men is restored. This is clearly echoed in the celebratory New Testament phrase: "and there are no more distinctions between Jew and Greek, slave and free, male and female, but all of you are one in Christ Jesus." (Galatians 3:28).[19] This emphatically outlines the "mission statement" for the new Church where all, regardless of class, gender and race, are equal in Christ.

The broader, contextualised scriptural argument for the ordination of women underlines the revolutionary involvement of women in Christ's ministry and the early Church. Feminist historians have retold the stories of women who have been lost or overlooked in the patriarchal accounts of Christian history. Feminist theologians have helped to create the theological framework for women's ordination; in doing so they have challenged the patriarchal nature of the Church. Ultimately, some even question whether women should seek to join hierarchical ecclesiastical structures.

FEMINIST THEOLOGY AND THE ROLE OF WOMEN IN THE INSTITUTIONAL CHURCH

Feminist theology has revisited biblical sources to provide a convincing picture of women's involvement in the early Christian movement. In recovering women's lost history, feminist theologians have demonstrated that Christianity was a religion of inclusivity, in which women were equal partners with men. In doing so, they have given credence to women's involvement in the ministry of the Church 2,000 years later. Elisabeth Schüssler Fiorenza's concept of the "discipleship of equals" not only provides the foundation for women's ordination, but it also questions the hieratic order of the Church. Inherent in the argument for women's ordination, which is based on equality and egalitarianism, is a challenge to the patriarchal, hierarchical nature of the established Church. Can, or should, women, in their quest for priesthood, conform to structures which have the capacity to dominate and oppress others?

The Discipleship of Equals

Women's participation in Jesus' ministry and the early Church was lost, and women were subjugated when the Church became more clericalised and institutionalised. As the Church moved from the private, domestic sphere (the House Church) to the public sphere (the State Church), it came under the patriarchal structures of society (Schüssler Fiorenza 1983, Carr 1988, Edwards 1989, Torjesen 1993, Armstrong 1993). The early Church had no need for a priestly order and it was not until the second century that the concept of a hierarchical priesthood developed.[20] Priesthood has endured throughout the ensuing centuries, taking an increasingly more separatist and sacramental role. As the role of the priest developed, so the barrier between ordained and lay members of the Church grew, and women became progressively more excluded.

The notion of the priestly order is far removed from the original Christian concept of the "discipleship of equals". In her book, *In Memory of Her* (1983), Elizabeth Schüssler Fiorenza carefully constructs a picture of Jesus' ministry (the Jesus movement) and the early Church (the early Christian missionary movement) as movements of inclusivity. The Jesus movement is characterised by the symbol of "table-sharing" with the uninvited: sinners, prostitutes, beggars, tax collectors, the ritually polluted and the poor, many of whom were women, were included in this movement which proclaimed wholeness for all humanity. Women not only joined Jesus in his ministry, but were responsible for shaping the theological understanding of his followers by extending the relevance of an exclusively Jewish movement to the Gentiles. Women were also responsible for the continuation of the movement after Jesus' death, they remained constant throughout his execution and burial, and were the first to experience his resurrection (Schüssler Fiorenza 1983, Williams 1984, Storkey 1987, Edwards 1989, Armstrong 1993). The inclusive "table-sharing" of the Jesus movement, in which all were equal, created the foundation for the "discipleship of equals" in the early Christian missionary movement. Once again Schüssler Fiorenza carefully reconstructs the historical evidence to show how women were clearly involved as leaders, missionaries and apostles in the early Church.

Christianity "subverts" the patriarchal structures of society and offers hope to the poor and marginalised by presenting an alternative view of relationships, evident in the Jesus movement and the early Christian missionary movement, which are based on equality (Schüssler Fiorenza 1983:142). Through the reconstruction of Church history feminist theologians have not only legitimised and validated women's ministry, but also made it an essential part of the Christian message. Herein lies one of the core, and largely overlooked, challenges to the established Church. The structures of domination, which have subjugated women and created a priestly caste where one group exercises power over another, are challenged by the concept of the "discipleship of equals". If, as Schüssler Fiorenza has demonstrated, the symbol of "table-sharing" is implicit to the Christian message, then the community of the Church has to be egalitarian. The arguments which include women in the ministry of the Church, also open the way for a wider inclusivity, in which all elements of Church organisation are shared - including the eucharistic table-sharing. The "discipleship of equals" is, by definition, opposed to hierarchy and power as expressed in the institutional Church.

Women and Ordination: Prophetic Voices of Warning

Among those who are concerned with the ordination of women, there is a surprising lack of debate about the role and nature of priesthood.[21] There are, however, prophetic voices of caution within the boundaries of feminist theology who challenge the notion of priesthood and warn women of their involvement in the hierarchical structures of the Church (Ruether 1983, Maitland 1983, Carr 1988, Williams 1994):

> Many have come to see the clerical priesthood, the distinction between clergy and laity, and the hierarchy as it is presently structured as precisely the wider problem in the church. Thus there is argument that the admission of women to the present clerical structure would not solve but only exacerbate the contradictions of the present shape of the church. (Carr 1988:21)

To understand this concern over the Church's structures, it is helpful to draw on Rosemary Radford Ruether's appraisal of the sin of patriarchy, which she defines as not just the subjugation of women by men, but the way in which society is structured to further this relationship of dominance (1983).[22] Patriarchy is the cornerstone of society and is rooted in its legal, educational, religious and political systems. New Testament Christianity offered the opportunity to break the bondage of human rule, replacing hierarchical organisations with new communities based on mutuality and collaboration, offering an antidote to codes of domination and subjugation. In this new world order the first are last, the weak are strong, the poor are rich, and the rulers are servants. However, as the Church became more established, it re-adapted itself to the language, symbols and structures of patriarchy. Redemption from the sin of sexism comes through conversion and repentance, and it is the Church, as a liberation community, which should support this transformation and offer new models of non-hierarchical, non-sexist groupings.

Yet clearly the Church as an institution - Protestant, Catholic and Orthodox - reflects rather than rejects the patriarchal norms of society. To this end Ruether questions whether the Church can be a movement for liberation from sexism. Will the increasing involvement of women in ministry provide the alternative models of Church that humanity needs if it is to be delivered from sexism? Should women pursue entry to a clerical caste which, in itself promotes hierarchical structures of dominance in ordained/lay relationships? Sara Maitland (1983) considers the focus on women's ordination as a tactical error for, whilst the ordination of women is *an* issue, it is not *the only* issue. In the quest for the demise of patriarchy, seeking ordination without radically challenging the sexist practices of the Church, is dangerous and ineffectual. It will lead, she prophesies, to the co-option of the few to the male power structures where women's only way of surviving will be to join the male club and adopt the male-defined roles of the priesthood.

These voices are prophetic warnings to women in the Church, yet they are relatively isolated and removed from the debate about women's ordination and the continuing dialogue about women's role in the Church. For the ritual of priesthood itself can be deeply exclusive. The right to speak and to perform certain rituals, the wearing of separate, specialised clothes and the differentiation of certain roles within the Church - all elements of clerical status - do not resonate with the quest for freedom and inclusivity.[23] This is the challenge and the conflict for women seeking ordination.

Are these voices of challenge therefore arguing against the ordination of women to the priesthood? Sara Maitland does not advocate renouncing or leaving the Church, nor does she want to ignore or collude with sexism, but by staying engaged with the Church, she argues that women can choose to transform it (Maitland 1983, Carr 1988). Choice is the important concept in this argument, for women will not change the Church just by being part of it. It is only by staying connected with their roots of marginalisation and choosing to challenge existing models of dominance, that women can fulfil their calling to bring about non-hierarchical justice communities.

Ursula King argues that women need to experience and share in the outward forms of power in order to find space for freedom and self determination. Women have no problems with sacrifice, service and self-giving, it is the way in which they have experienced the world. However, women will only be able to "sacrifice" the benefits and trappings of power, when they have experienced what they are renouncing (King 1989:85). Women need the autonomy of power in order to make choices as to what to do with the trappings of power (something men have always had the opportunity to do). The first women to experience ordination in the Church of England did so with a legacy of exclusion and marginalisation. As women enter the power bases of the Church in increasing numbers, they must choose whether or not to stay connected with their experiences of being on the outside. Our faith, as feminists, is that women, from their experience of powerlessness, will chose to work for more just and inclusive structures in the Church.

GENDER DIFFERENCES AND STEREOTYPES

The notions of gender and gender differences are important to this research because they affect the extent to which the expectations that women will change the Church can be realised. If women are inherently different to men, then it can be assumed that ordaining them in enough numbers will mean that they will begin to effect change in the way the Church operates. However, if women are not different from men, there is nothing to suggest that, once they have achieved status and power, they will not abuse it in the same way that men have.

Philosophy of Gender Difference

First it is important to define the concepts of sex and gender. Traditionally sex is the word which describes the biological differences that distinguish women from men, the visible difference in genitalia related to different procreation functions. Gender, by contrast, relates to the cultural classification in which certain characteristics are attributed to each sex according to social and societal norms. The term gender applies to particular traits which describe the appropriate "masculine" and "feminine" behaviour for each sexual category. Men are perceived as "masculine" and are therefore traditionally expected to be aggressive, independent, outgoing and confident. Women are perceived as "feminine" and are therefore thought to be more sensitive, perceptive and dependent in relationships, introverted and emotional (Oakley 1972, Lober & Farrell 1991). Women and men are ascribed different social roles according to society's cultural understanding of gender. Men are physically stronger and are therefore suited to the protective role identified with the armed forces, fire and police services. The perception that men are innately competitive and aggressive makes them "naturally" suited to the business world. Women are seen as "naturally" caring and nurturing and are therefore more suitable for the pivotal role in family maintenance. If they do enter the workplace, the caring/nuturing professions such as teaching or nursing are seen as more appropriate for women. This dichotomous view of gender roles is, at one level, simplistic, yet it does represent deeply held beliefs and values.

Gendered role classifications have begun to be challenged; women have joined the armed forces, police and fire services and hold senior management positions. Men have entered the traditionally female professions of teaching and nursing. Yet, despite their greater presence in the workplace, women remain largely responsible for home making and child care. The biological function of child birth is still associated with the gendered role of child caring and herein lies the problem for women. Sex differences (apart from transsexuals) are determined at birth and are natural, gender differences are cultural and are constructed through the norms and values of society.[24] The assumption, held by many, that gender differences mirror the innate differences in the sexes, means that women's subordinate position in society is seen as part of the natural order. Society increases its social efficiency by ascribing different roles to men and women according to their perceived natural characteristics and traits (Oakley 1972, Stockard & Johnson 1992, Reskin & Padavic 1994).

Feminism challenges the way in which the norms and values of society subordinate women. However, elements of the feminist movement differ in their understanding of the causes of, and solutions to, inequality between the sexes.[25] These different approaches are echoed in feminist theology and spirituality, the former looking to redeem existing religious structures by involving women, and the latter choosing to express spirituality in all-female structures outside of what is seen as traditionally male-defined religion.[26] The concept of gender difference was an integral part of the debate about women's ordination, with both sides appropriating gender discourse to consolidate their position.

Gender Difference and the Ordination of Women

Both opponents and proponents of women's ordination argued that there are theologically significant gender differences. Opponents suggested that differences between women and men had theological implications which justified unfair treatment of women with regards to ordination. Advocates of women's ministry exploited the concept of gender difference "in order to make the case that women in virtue of their peculiar abilities or character traits are especially suitable for entry into [the Church], or, indeed, that entry of women will result in beneficial changes." (Baber 1999:120).

Opponents of women's ordination cited Jesus' all-male apostleship, the theological importance of the debate about women's ordination to the three main Churches and, in particular, the explicit differences between the sexes which make men more suited to priesthood, as theologically significant (Baber 1999):[27]

> To speak of the "equality" of women with men sounds superficially very moral and Christian, but interpreted so as to conflict with the divine plan for male-female relationships, it may prove unchristian, indeed anti-Christian. The concepts of "equality" of the sexes is in danger of destroying women's femininity and reducing them to mere substitute males. (Bruce & Duffield 1972:23)

Oddie (1984) argued that the biological differences between women and men are reflections of their different spiritual identities. Just as this difference affects the social roles each sex adopts, it is entirely appropriate that it should determine the roles that men and women have in the Church. Cooper (1972) suggests that women's skills are traditionally linked to the family, and that since men provide the link between the family and wider society, male skills are more appropriate for the priesthood. It is therefore "unnatural" for women to be priests.

Proponents of women's ordination adopted two strategies in their argument. The first sought to challenge the unhelpful, stereotypical concept of gender differences and argue for women's entry to the priesthood on the same grounds, and using the same criteria, as men (Santer 1984). The second, and preferred, strategy emphasised theologically significant gender differences to justify women's ordination. Supporters of women's ministry argued that unless women were priests, the Church would lose their gender specific gifts and abilities. Women, they suggested, would bring a less hierarchical, more collaborative approach to ministry. They would empower and involve the laity in new ways, establishing creative liturgies and new forms of worship. Women priests would create a supportive team environment rather than the competitive "one-man" ministry that had characterised the Church of England (Hoad 1984, Perberdy 1985, Furlong 1991, Kroll 1994, Farrington 1994). Indeed the main thrust of MOW's central argument for women priests was that women would bring something new and essentially different to the ministry. Professor David McClean (the author of the document on which the Synod legislation is based) said in the 1992 debate:

> For too long the special gifts of women, gifts from a generous creator God, have been under-used and under-valued. We have locked their talents away...Today, this very afternoon, may we in this room take the marvellous opportunity that we have to unlock those gifts, to enrich the church and to strengthen it in the service of God. (Quoted in Webster 1994:181)

The ordination of women, it was suggested, promised a richer, more holistic priesthood better suited to the twentieth century Church communities. Implicit in this argument is the concept that women's natural gifts and abilities would bring a new approach to ministry and therefore change the Church for the better. Only through the ordination of women, supporters argued, would the Church benefit from, and be changed by, women's "special gifts".

Martha Ice (1987) draws together basic assumptions about the differences in female and male approaches to ministry. In essence, she suggests women are less interested in power and more egalitarian, collaborative and empowering of the laity than their male colleagues. Women are more concerned with issues of social justice and less with the status of their clergy role. Whilst this is clearly an ideal type, Ice's intrinsic argument summarises many of the hopes concerning women's ministry. For if this female typology is even partly true, then the ordination of women should have a profound impact on the structures and practices of the Church of England. How far, then, are the first group of women priests contributing to change in the Church? Are they demonstrating new approaches to ministry which challenge the traditional lay/ordained divide?

Empirical Research about Gender Differences in the Ministry

It is important to draw on existing empirical research evidence to see whether there is an inherently "female" approach to ministry in the Church. On examination, the literature reveals that the evidence is, by and large, contradictory. The fact that each researcher is measuring different aspects of gender, using different research tools, is also problematic. For example, Francis (1991) uses the Eysenck personality questionnaire to establish gender difference in his study of the personality types of Anglican ordinands in the Church of England. Lehman (1993), by contrast, creates his own scale to measure gender differences in the interpersonal style, theological approach, career goals, thought forms and attitudes to power and authority of career clergy in North America. The results are inconclusive, and it is not possible to draw absolute, empirically based conclusions about gender differences in Church ministry from existing research evidence.

In her review of British and American research Nancy Nason-Clark (1987) claims that there is evidence that women are changing the face of ministry in the established Church. To quote from her study:

> As a group it appears that clergy women bring enhanced sensitivity, better pastoral care, collective leadership and a wider vision of Christian ministry to the pastorate. Whether they embrace or challenge traditional female roles, women ministers are changing some aspects of ministry, not least through their skills in counselling and their person-centred focus. (Nason-Clark, 1987:338)

Nason-Clark also concludes that women experience more obstacles than men and receive less encouragement to enter the ministry. She sees women as being more "other-centred" than men, in that they value the administration of sacraments and appreciate warm responses from parishioners. Women also find the stress of time pressure and the emotional strain of the priesthood more difficult that men. Since this is a review of other people's research, it is not possible to comment on the rigour of each element. It should be noted, however, that since women were not priested in Britain until 1994, any earlier research that compared men's experiences with women's is not comparing like with like. The role of a deacon (the only clerical position held by women until fairly recently) is very different from that of a priest.

The conclusions of Nason-Clark are partially contradicted by Ed Lehman's research. His study, *Gender and Work, The Case of the Clergy* (1993), looked at gender differences in the way in which ordained male and female clergy approach their ministry. His study focused on 517 pastors in North American Protestant denominations. The research questioned whether any differences in approach to ministry by men and women were identifiable in masculine and feminine types. It examined whether female and male clergy differed in the extent to which these types were associated with each sex. In his theoretical framework, Lehman accepted the hypothesis that women and men are inherently different. He characterised the differences in the following way: men, it was suggested, desire power over lay people, are authoritative, detached from social relationships and operate in a rational and analytic way. Theologically, men focus on the transcendence of God and they deal with ethical issues in a legalistic way. Men are characterised as being disinterested in social issues and as gaining career fulfilment from their social status. Women, on the other hand, are characterised as seeking to empower lay Church members. Women are seen to emphasise the importance of social relationships, they are characterised as egalitarian and intuitive in their approach to ministry. Theologically women are focused on the benevolence of God, are involved in social issues and find career fulfilment through other people's development.

The research found that there was diversity in the way pastors approached their work. Some described themselves in "traditionally masculine" terms and others in "traditionally feminine" terms, but this was *not* according to their sex. As a group, ministers tended to define themselves in "traditionally feminine" terms. Lehman found no evidence of systematic differences in men and women's desire for formal authority, open interpersonal style, approach to preaching, or involvement in social issues. He did find, however, that men were more likely to use power, that they preferred a rational structure and were more legalistic in their approach to ethics than women. On the other hand, women were more likely to seek to empower the congregation than men. Lehman concluded that his study raised as many questions as it answered. Differences in the ministerial styles of female and male clergy could not be attributed solely to gender, but were compounded by variations in the race, background and employment status of the respondents.

Leslie Francis' study *The Personality Characteristics of Anglican Ordinands: Feminine Men and Masculine Women* (1991) looked at the personality types of 252 ordinands - 155 men and 97 women. The Eysenck personality questionnaire was used to measure whether the ordinands' personality types differed from those of religious people in the general population. Secondly, the scale was used to compare the personality types of male and female ordinands. The results showed a clear difference in the personality types of women and men, but this contradicted the general population model. Women ordinands were more extrovert (which Eysenck defined as sociable, lively, assertive, sensation-seeking, carefree and dominant) than men. In reverse of the general population trend, male ordinands were more introverted (shy, uneasy in taking social initiatives, uncertain in leadership and reticent on public occasions). Finally, Francis found female ordinands were less neurotic than women in the general population (anxious, depressed, tense, irrational, shy, moody and emotional), but also scored less on the psychoticism scale (empathetic, unselfish, altruistic, warm and tender-hearted). Francis concludes that the characteristically masculine profile of women ordinands was largely due to the fact that they had been, and were still, engaged in the battle for ordination. Women ordinands were therefore more likely to be "tough-minded" than their male colleagues.[28]

Mandy Robbins' study *A Different Voice: A Different View* (1998) investigates the experiences and attitudes of 1239 women deacons and deaconesses in the Anglican Church. Using a self-completion questionnaire the participants were asked to respond to a series of statements which explored their perception of clergywomen compared to clergymen. The results showed that over half of the women felt that they organised their ministry more democratically than clergymen. The majority felt that they had different gifts to offer, but that these gifts were not necessarily superior to those of their male colleagues. Where women did feel that their gifts were superior, this tended to be in areas of ministry which are traditionally associated with female roles, such as leading women's groups and working with pre-school age children. Clergywomen also perceived themselves as being better at pastoral roles such as bereavement counselling. Only a small minority perceived clergywomen as better at public roles such as worship leading or preaching which are traditionally seen to be male spheres.

Robbins' comparative work is important to my research for a number of reasons. First, she draws on largely the same sample as I do. In Robbins' study the respondents were only ordained as deacons and deaconesses and were therefore unable to hold senior positions in the Church. Although some would have been in charge of parishes, or have incumbent status in sector ministry, the majority would have held junior positions in the Church. My study investigates the attitudes and experiences of women three or four years after their ordination to the priesthood, when many will have moved into positions of greater responsibility. Secondly, Robbins establishes that the women waiting for ordination to the priesthood perceived that they had different skills and abilities from their male colleagues. Implicit in this self-belief is the notion that by being ordained priest, women would bring new approaches to ministry which would, by necessity, change the Church.

Robbins self-criticism that her study is based entirely on the perception of clergy women and therefore cannot be compared to men's perceptions [29] can also be levelled at my study. However, it is important to compare the expectations of women prior to their ordination to the priesthood with their actual experiences of priestly ministry. In my study I aim to record how women clergy perceive their role and their impact on the Church. Their perceptions may, or may not, be the same as those of male clergy or the congregations who experience women's ministry. Nevertheless, women's self- perception has important implications for the Church. Whether or not women will offer new interpretations of priestly ministry depends on their view of themselves and their approach to ministry.

So the evidence concerning women in the Church is, at best, contradictory. Where existing research does confirm apparent gender differences, it is not possible to comment on whether these differences are biological, historical, cultural or individual. In his review of gender differences in religion Leslie Francis (1997) concludes that the evidence that women are more religious than men is overwhelming, for in every indicator or measure of religiosity women score higher than men. Yet despite this overwhelming evidence theorists disagree about the cause of this difference. Some researchers suggest that social and contextual influences on women explain their predisposition towards religion, whilst others argue that it is differences in personality, gender orientation and psychology which account for women's increased religiosity.

The argument comes back full circle to the philosophical debate about gender outlined at the beginning of this section. Whether the roots of gender differences are historical, cultural or biological will, I suspect, never be answered. Yet despite this, the concept of gender differences is still significant for this research. If women are inherently different from men they will, by their presence in the power bases of the Church, bring a new approach to leadership. If, as the literature suggests, women are more egalitarian, collaborative and empowering than men, women's ordination has the potential to change the patriarchal structures and sexist practices of the Church.[30]

So will women change the Church? If there are intrinsic, essential differences between the sexes women could change the Church organically. Alternatively, if there is no inherent difference in men and women's approach to ministry, women, once they have access to power, could abuse it in the same way as men - thus maintaining the status quo. I advocate a third, preferred option. There are differences between women and men which are not necessarily inherent, but have been developed through generations of women's oppression. These experiences of being marginalised, bullied and overlooked have forced women to develop new ways of working based on sisterhood, mutual support, connectedness and shared responsibility.

As women progress into positions of power, they face a choice of whether to continue in the pervading model of dominance or to stay connected with their corporate experiences of powerlessness and, in so doing, choose to change the way in which they approach ministry. This choice has to be conscious, it will not happen automatically. Through ordination, women are entering an institution which is inherently patriarchal, an institution which has, for centuries, operated as an all-male club, and an institution whose practices, structures and belief systems are defined by male experience. It is naive to expect women to change this just by their presence. Indeed, it is presumptuous to assume that all women entered the priesthood in order to change the Church. Women need to have access to power in order to decide how to deal with it. Their choice is whether to perpetuate the hierarchical structures of the Church or choose to create fairer, more egalitarian and collaborative structures. My hope is that they will choose the latter.

The debate about the ordination of women is located in a context where, challenged by the impetus of the feminist movement, women's social roles are changing. The development of feminist theological thought has not only questioned the exclusion of women in patriarchal, established religion, but has gone further to challenge the hierarchical nature of the Church and the power relationships between its ordained and lay members.

The question now is whether women's ordination can be addressed in isolation from other issues of power and inequality in the Church. Ultimately, if the Church is to be a radical liberation community reflecting the gospel message of freedom and inclusivity, then it must change. The first group of women priests in the Church of England know what it is to achieve power and autonomy, but their memories of alienation and oppression are still fresh. Will they choose to use their experiences on the margins of the Church as a catalyst for change? To do so requires a conscious act of will, born out of the feminist tenets of support, campaigning and consciousness-raising. For many women the journey towards ordination may have ended, but the struggle for a more equal community of faith has probably only just begun.

CHAPTER 4

THE METHODOLOGICAL APPROACH OF THE STUDY

Feminism, as a socio-political movement, has clearly influenced the theological thought which provides the theoretical framework for this research. In the same way feminism, and its critique of traditional social research methods, has contributed to the methodological choices that I have made in this study. Methods associated with the investigation of social life are either quantitative (concerned with the production of generalisable data which articulate social facts), or qualitative (concerned with the production of rich, in-depth data which demonstrate the way in which individuals interpret their social world). In social research, qualitative and quantitative methods have traditionally been polarised according to the paradigmatic stance of the researcher. Feminism has provided a powerful critique of ways in which the social world is measured and analysed in the social sciences. Feminist researchers have been engaged in a fast-moving debate about what, if anything, constitutes feminist research.

The research design for this study, which synthesises qualitative and quantitative methods, is both methodologically sound and congruent with feminist research principles. Quantitative and qualitative methods co-exist in a framework which uses my personal reflection and self-awareness as a means by which the interface between the two approaches to research is understood. Self-reflection, as a third form of data collection (in the form of a research diary), is used as a way of understanding this interface and of critically appraising both my methods, and my interaction with the data. It is my contention that this multi-method approach will provide data which are both rich and representative, in-depth and generalisable. My hope is, that in doing so, it will do justice to the stories of the women who have participated in this research.

QUANTITATIVE VERSUS QUALITATIVE METHODS

Social research is a process of knowledge development which attempts to make sense of the experiences, attitudes and actions of individuals or groups in society. Social research aims to analyse the social world and show how individuals construct and interpret their own experiences. There is, however, a clear philosophical and methodological split for those engaged in the investigation of social life. The paradigm debate interweaves philosophical assumptions with discussions about the nature and value of different research methods (Bryman 1988). At the heart of the debate are two conflicting worldviews. Positivism suggests that there is an external social reality which exists outside of the individual. In contrast, the interpretative paradigm assumes no such external reality, but focuses instead on the way in which individuals interpret and analyse their social contexts.

Interpretative and positivist paradigms are opposing philosophies which have affected the way in which research is conducted and have resulted in the polarisation of quantitative and qualitative methods. The essential differences in the positivist and interpretative paradigms lie in their contrasting philosophical worldviews, the use of different methods, conflicting views of the researcher in the research setting and the different outcomes from the research. (Giddens 1977, Bryman 1988, May 1993, Hammersley 1993).

The Positivist Approach

Positivist epistemology conceptualises the social world in rationalistic terms and presents human experience as external factual reality. To measure "social facts" researchers appropriate the same empirical logic of enquiry utilised in the natural sciences, and social phenomena are subject to the same natural laws as other forms of scientific discovery (Hughes 1990).[1]

Positivism is concerned with objectivity, with the measurement of social facts in a neutral, value-free research setting. Methods associated with this paradigm are empirical and are concerned with the production of accurate data. Positivist methods are quantitative in nature, producing statistical information from a representative number of cases: surveys, structured interviews, randomised and quasi-experiments. The research is often used to measure a particular theory or hypothesis which is established prior to the data collection. The researcher is independent of the data and removed from the research setting. The outcome of the research are generalisable and reliable data (Bryman, 1988, Kolakowski 1993, May 1993, Bulmer 1982).

The Interpretative Approach

The interpretative paradigm developed partly as a reaction against the orthodox, scientific positivist view of the social world (Hughes 1990). In contrast to positivism there are no external realities to be uncovered through logical empirical research in the interpretative paradigm; rather it is the way in which individuals interpret their social world and attribute meaning to their experiences which are "the starting point for objective analysis of society" (May 1993:28). The philosophy underpinning the interpretative approach concentrates on how social actors construct their ways of knowing and experiencing the world.

The methods associated with the interpretative paradigm are descriptive and are concerned with the production of in-depth data. Interpretative methods are qualitative in nature, involving small numbers of respondents in an in-depth research programme: case studies, ethnography, participant observation or unstructured interviews.[2] The knowledge resulting from qualitative research can be used to construct theory[3] and the data is rich, deep, but ungeneralisable (Glaser & Strauss 1968, May 1993, Bryman 1988, Henwood & Pidgeon 1993).

Third Paradigm Research

Traditionally research methods have been linked to opposing paradigms and in practice, the researcher focuses on either qualitative or quantitative methods (Guba & Lincoln 1988). This position has been challenged, particularly in the field of evaluation research. Cook & Reichardt (1979) have suggested that it is the research setting, rather than the philosophical background of the researcher which should suggest appropriate methods. A pragmatic approach to research means that the researcher ignores the philosophical paradigms behind the research methods and is free to work either quantitatively or qualitatively, according to the needs of the research setting. Patton (1988) argues for a Third Paradigm research where the researcher remains philosophically located in one or other of the paradigms, but is free to (and has the skills to) choose a method which is congruent with the research setting or question.

Social researchers have remained embroiled in the philosophical concerns underpinning the use of qualitative and quantitative methods. Although some have questioned the exclusive alignment of method and paradigm, most research originates from a dichotomous worldview which prescribes the use of either qualitative or quantitative methods. Feminism, however, has provided an important critique of traditional research approaches and offers an alternative framework for those engaged in the study of social life. Feminist postulates have been used to devise a methodological approach to this study in which qualitative and quantitative methods co-exist, rather than conflict, with each other.

FEMINISM AND RESEARCH

> Feminism demonstrates without any possibility of doubt, that the
> social sciences are sexist, biased, and rotten with patriarchal values.
> (Stanley & Wise 1983:12)

This stinging indictment of the way in which social life is theorised about and analysed in the social sciences, exemplifies the feminist critique of social research. To suppose, however, that feminism is unified, both in its criticisms of existing practice and its understanding of what constitutes feminist research, is a wrong assumption. Not only are there conflicting feminist viewpoints concerning research practice, but the debate about what constitutes feminist epistemology and methodology is ever-changing (Fonow & Cook 1991, Maynard & Purvis 1994, Maynard 1994).[4] Is there then a distinctly feminist research method? Are there key themes which distinguish a feminist approach from other forms of research?

The Feminist Critique of Social Research

The feminist critique of social research originates from the premise that "traditional" research has omitted, or distorted, women's experience to the extent that, whilst women are clearly present in social structures, they are rarely the focus of study. The "academic machismo" which surrounds research practice (until recently most people engaged in social research were male and their theories, methods and analyses reflected sexist interests and personalities) has meant that women's lives are invisible and their voices silent in the majority of studies into social life (Oakley 1974, Morgan 1981, Stanley & Wise 1983).[5]

For some feminists, removing discrimination against women and ensuring that they are participants in research can eliminate inequality. Feminist empiricism suggests that it is possible to eradicate sexist bias from research by making sure that women are not only included in research as subjects, but that the research questions are identified in the light of women's experiences and interests. By re-introducing women into the research process value-free, gender neutral study can be produced (Morgan 1981).

For many feminists, however, simply "adding" women into existing research practices does not address the far-researching sexist bias in research method and methodology.[6] The way in which positivist scientific study is conducted and the assumptions behind the idea of value-free or objective research conflict with the feminist worldview.[7] In particular the survey method and its production of "hard" statistical data was, and is, the target of much criticism. Quantitative research methods are perceived as anti-feminist because they present the social world in absolute factual terms, whereas in reality, large-scale studies mask, distort or ignore women's experience of the social world. The process of putting individual experience into separate categories presents, at best, a distorted view of the world. At worst, this process fails to adequately reflect social reality. The act of reducing experience into categories, in itself, constructs an alternative reality (Farren 1990, Pugh 1990):

> Much of the debate has concerned the claim that quantitative research techniques - involving the translation of individuals' experience into categories pre-defined by researchers- distorts women's experiences and result in silencing women's own voices.
> (Jayaratine & Stewart 1991:85)

Maria Mies argues that statistical, quantitative methods are themselves "instruments for structuring reality" and are therefore not suitable for feminists working to authenticate women's expression of reality (1991:60).

In the second instance quantitative methodology is criticised by feminists because of the relationship between the researcher and the researched. In the world of "hard science"[8] the researcher remains in control of the research experience, the analyses and production of information. The respondents, on the other hand, are the objects of the study and have no control over the research process. This power imbalance between the researcher and researched has the potential to be exploitative and is therefore not consistent with feminist principles (Stanley & Wise 1983, 1993, Jayaratine & Stewart 1991, Mies 1993). Ultimately quantitative methods are seen as problematic for feminists because they deal with categories rather than experience, variables rather than people, and are associated with a masculine style of control and manipulation (Millman & Moss Kanter 1975).

Adopting a qualitative methodology is seen, by some, as the answer to the problem of doing feminist research (Oakley 1981, Mies 1993). In her paper "Interviewing women: a Contradiction in Terms", Ann Oakley dissects the positivist approach to interviewing and revisits the interview from a feminist perspective (1981). The idea of the objective interviewer, controlling the interview and dis-engaging from over-familiarity with the respondent is, she argues, an anathema to feminist research. In its place Oakley suggests the interview is a shared experience, into which both interviewer and interviewee invest information about their lives. Women interviewing women in this mutual relationship is not only more feminist, but engenders greater rapport and produces richer, more in-depth data.

Whilst Oakley deals with the problem of inequality between researcher and research subject at the point of data gathering, she does not address the fact that the researcher maintains control over what is included in the analysis and the dissemination of the results. Power over the control of information and knowledge remains with the researcher and the institution they represent.[9] Other researchers suggest that alternative qualitative methods are more appropriate for feminist research. Ethnomethodological and action research approaches, in which the researcher is central to the research process and uses her own experience to develop understanding, are seen as harmonious with feminism (Stanley & Wise 1983, Mies 1993).

The equation of feminism with a particular research method (or indeed the disassociation from a particular method) is, I believe, problematic. There are clearly difficulties with the way in which quantitative methods have been mis-used and abused in the past. However, information deriving from quantitative sources, if used with integrity, can also help to achieve greater emancipation for women. Statistical data can be used to benefit women by highlighting inequality, thus contributing to fairer policy formation and resource distribution in a way that ungeneralisable qualitative data cannot.[10] The policy implications for this information could benefit the status of women on a world-wide basis in a way that ungeneralisable qualitative data could not. Similarly, traditional qualitative research methods are not necessarily "more feminist". In most qualitative research the control of knowledge and power still remain with the researcher. Qualitative methodology, like quantitative techniques, can situate the researcher on a different plane; as a detached omnipotent expert in a knowledge hierarchy over those they research (Stanley & Wise 1990, Finch 1993).

For women involved in research the concept that one method is "more feminist" than another has been unsustainable, leading to the conclusion, amongst many in the feminist community, that there is no "quintessentially feminist" method (Stanley 1990, Stanley & Wise 1993, Maynard & Purvis 1994). Sandra Harding's distinction between method, methodology and epistemology is helpful in developing feminist understanding of the research process (1987). Harding suggests that method refers to the techniques for data gathering and methodology to the theory and analysis of the research process. Epistemology is a theory of knowledge which provides a basis for understanding how knowledge is legitimised. In using the concept of method to encompass all three elements of their research women have failed to discover what is distinctly feminist about their research. The question therefore remains, is there a specifically feminist approach to research? Whilst I have shown that there is no place for prescriptive feminist dogma on methods, there are, I believe, certain key themes which distinguish feminist research from other forms of social research. It is these themes that I have attempted to incorporate into my methodological approach to this study.

Towards a Feminist Praxis

Feminism not only challenges existing research practice at a number of levels but it also offers themes, or methodological postulates, which feminist researchers need to address. The aim of traditional research is to produce "alienated knowledge", divorced from its process of production (Rose 1983). The aim of feminist research, on the other hand, is to produce "unalienated knowledge"; that is knowledge which originates from a process of shared development where the researcher's role is acknowledged, not denied. "Unalienated knowledge" also attempts to understand the act of knowing and reintegrates the research experience - so that life and thought, action and knowledge, change and research are reconnected, ultimately resulting in social change and liberation for women (Stanley 1990, Mies 1991). Whilst there are a range of different views on what constitutes feminist research, there are three main themes which run through feminist discourse: a focus on women's experience in research, a commitment to the development of action-oriented research practice, and discussion about the role of the researcher in the research process (Roberts 1981, Stanley 1990, Fonow & Cook 1991, Maynard & Purvis 1994).

Focus on Women's Experience

One of the key tenets of the feminist movement is the legitimation of women's experience; either through rediscovering the invisible lives of women from the past, or by giving voice to women's current experiences of the world. In the early stages of the debate about feminist methodology this focus on experience was perceived to be interpreted in separatist terms. The purpose of research was to give voice to women's individual experience and, as such, feminist research should concentrate on work undertaken by women, on women.[11] This position is problematic for two reasons. First, the naive focus on women's experience as a universal concept is simplistic. Whilst gender is clearly a contributory factor to the way in which women experience the world, class, race, sexual orientation, culture and economic factors are also important social criteria which determine our experience. To suggest a homogeneity of experience nullifies women's contrasting (and indeed conflicting) experiences (Harding 1987, Stanley & Wise 1993, Maynard 1994, Kelly, Burton & Regan 1994).

Secondly, the suggestion that feminist research should focus only on women is also simplistic. If feminist research is committed to ending women's oppression, then the study of how oppression is perpetuated is also of primary significance; and that will of necessity involve the study of men (Layland 1990, Stanko 1994). Feminist research should, on the other hand, be concerned with making women's lives visible and with redressing the sexist bias of academic output by investigating the social world as women experience it. This does not mean uncritically accepting women's accounts but involves engaging with how women experience the social world and how they construct their experiences of reality.

Action-oriented Research Practice

Embedded in most strands of feminist methodological thought is the notion that research should, in some way, contribute to changing women's status and position in society.[12] Some feminists argue that the research process in itself should contribute to the consciousness-raising and empowerment of individual participants (Mies 1993, Fonow & Cook 1991).[13] This concept implies that action research, in which researcher and researched work together to uncover knowledge and achieve structural change, is therefore a primary context for doing feminist research. The realities of this approach however, severely limit the scope and extent of research and the organisational settings that will accommodate it are limited.

Whilst I would not agree that the research process can, or should, seek to develop the consciousness of participants (an idea which in itself can be patronising), I do believe that the researcher must develop an ethical research approach which acknowledges the researcher's responsibility to others and where the production of knowledge is linked to social change. This does not require the researcher to be committed to an overt political agenda, but it should engender reflection on the development of the research question, the way in which research is conducted and the dissemination of the results. "Alienated knowledge" often remains the property of a few which is inaccessible to the majority - ethical, action-oriented research should address how research can, at some level, contribute to social change for women.

The Role of the Researcher in Research Practice

One of the myths of the positivist scientific approach to research is the notion that the researcher is an objective, neutral recorder of social facts. The exclusion of women from many studies of social life by so-called objective, male researchers, challenges this notion of value-free research. By ignoring women's experience, male researchers have succumbed to the pervasive sex-bias of society; a bias that is so intrinsic that it is almost invisible. Feminism has made this sexist bias visible and, in doing so, it contributed to post-modern thinking which has shattered the image of value-free, objective science (Stanley & Wise 1983, Fonow & Cook 1991, Mies 1993).

Central to a feminist research approach is the recognition of the researcher as a component in the research process and as an actor in the research setting. The values, feelings and emotions of the researcher are no longer seen as a threat to the reliability and validity of the research. Instead the researcher's examination of her participation in the research process is a key to understanding how, and why, knowledge is produced (Fonow & Cook 1991, Stanley 1990, Maynard & Purvis 1994). This personalisation of the research process not only contributes to knowledge development (the product), but enables the researcher to confront ethical issues in her relationship with her research (the process). Stanley & Wise describe this process as "intellectual autobiography" whereby the researcher sees herself as a subject of her research. As she makes explicit her personal history, the researcher ensures that the process by which her understanding and conclusions are shaped, is made visible (1990). By acknowledging and studying her involvement in the research process, the feminist researcher can address power imbalance between the researcher/researched, explore the ethics of research practice, and attempt to ensure that the resulting knowledge is not exploitative:

> Doing feminist research demands that my participation and presence - my voice - within my research project must be explicitly admitted and included in the product of that research. (Haggis 1990:72)

Ultimately there is no one research method which is more congruent with feminist principles than another. The polarisation of quantitative and qualitative methods in conflict with each other is unhelpful and is in itself reflective of a dichotomous worldview. It is not the method which the researcher uses which is feminist, but the framework in which the research is located, which distinguishes feminist research. The role of feminist research is not only to tell women's stories, but also to understand how women construct and interpret their stories in order to make sense of their social world. By adopting reflexive research practice the researcher is able to make herself visible in the research process. In doing so she goes some way to negate the power imbalance between researcher and researched. Finally a feminist framework for research is committed to producing "unalienated knowledge" which remains connected with the social world and therefore contributes to the possibility of achieving social change. In rejecting some tenets of mainstream social research feminism is not rejecting intellectual rigour. The challenge for feminists engaged in research is to develop a methodological approach which encompasses the framework I have outlined and at the same time remains intellectually compelling.

THE METHODOLOGICAL FRAMEWORK OF MY RESEARCH

The aim of the methodological framework for this research is to produce a study which is intellectually rigorous but equally grounded in the experiences of the women I am investigating. My aim is to ensure that my role as a researcher in the study is not implicit and obfuscated, but explicit. My interaction with the research, rather than threatening the reliability and validity of the study, produces greater understanding of the data, highlights potential imbalance in the researcher-researched relationship and contributes to my understanding (at least) of what it means to do feminist research.

A Synthesis of Methods

The traditional polarisation of quantitative and qualitative methods has meant researchers adopt one or other of these approaches according to their paradigmatic stance. Where qualitative and quantitative methods are combined, one is usually subservient to the other.[14] In contrast I am adopting a synthesis approach where quantitative methods (a large scale survey) and qualitative methods (in-depth interviews) co-exist, where they complement rather than conflict with each other. [15]

In feminist dialogue, the idea of a multi-method (or synthesis) approach to research is rarely muted as a viable methodology (the logistical and funding implications make it unviable for most research projects). Yet the benefits of investing in a research model which is multi-faceted are, I believe, substantial. First, the combination of survey and interview data means the research is both generalisable and authentic. It is therefore possible to make empirical statements (which have important implications for political change), whilst allowing space for the complexity of women's experiences to be explored. Secondly, the interface between the two methods; the way in which qualitative and quantitative methods interact and sometimes conflict, is in itself a source of knowledge. Understanding is developed as the researcher examines the interaction between the two methodological approaches. The differences generated from this process are ultimately likely to be as illuminating as the similarities (Maynard 1994). Finally, a synthesis methodology allows for constant checking and rechecking of the data, to ensure that the research is truly embedded in women's lives. In my research themes from the initial interviews are tested in the questionnaire and then re-visited (along with new themes) in further interviews. The different methods act as a "threshing floor" where elements of data keep returning to be checked until knowledge and understanding are developed.

In essence the methodological approach of this study is circular rather than linear. Traditional research methodologies, whether they are quantitative or qualitative in nature, take a linear approach to knowledge development (Stanley & Wise 1983). Figure 4a (see next page) shows how positivist and interpretative methodologies, although originating in separate research paradigms, both adopt a linear, essentially compartmentalised, approach to research and knowledge/theory development. Both positivist and interpretative approaches involve the researcher stepping back from, or out of, the research setting to produce "alienated knowledge". A multi-method approach to research acknowledges that the process of knowledge development is rarely so clinical or easily compartmentalised.[16] A synthesis methodology validates the process of knowledge development, it creates space for the researcher to remain in her data and in contact with participants in the research.

FIGURE 4a Positivist and Interpretative Approaches to Research.

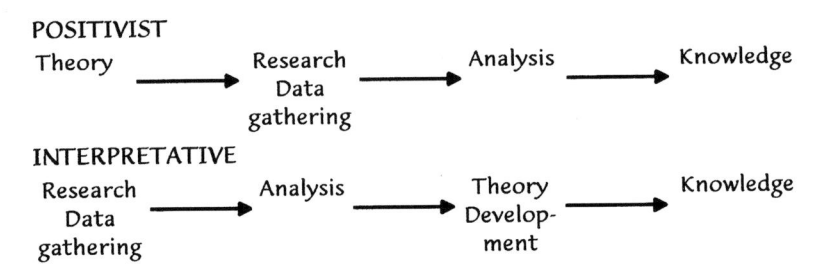

POSITIVIST
Theory → Research Data gathering → Analysis → Knowledge

INTERPRETATIVE
Research Data gathering → Analysis → Theory Development → Knowledge

Figure 4b illustrates the way in which the multi-method research design adopts a circular approach to knowledge development. In this synthesis of methods, theoretical development is organic to the research process; it does not happen in isolation, but is informed by the different stages of the study. The researcher engages with, and steps back from the research subjects, at different stages in the process, ensuring that analysis and knowledge development remain

Figure 4b Multi-method Approach to Research

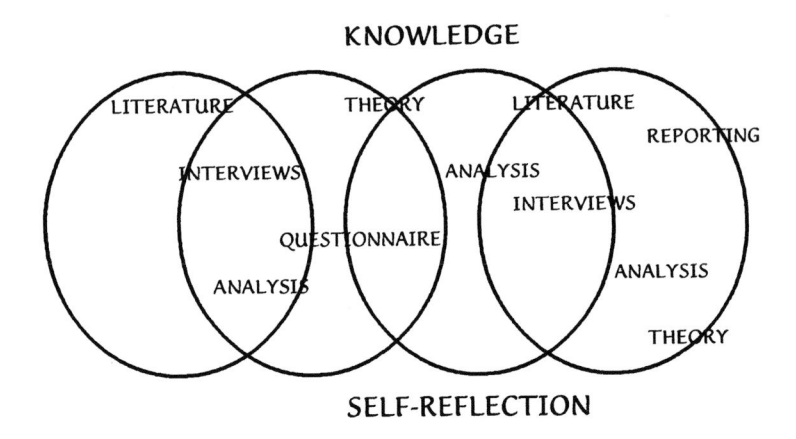

KNOWLEDGE

LITERATURE — THEORY — LITERATURE
INTERVIEWS — ANALYSIS — REPORTING
QUESTIONNAIRE — INTERVIEWS
ANALYSIS — ANALYSIS
THEORY

SELF-REFLECTION

connected with the research setting for greater periods of time. The research process in itself develops understanding. Knowledge is produced at the interface between subject, method, analysis and reflective self-understanding.

The multi-method approach, whilst it produces rich, generalisable data, also presents methodological challenges which need to be addressed. The extended fieldwork could result in a mountain of data with very little time to analyse and make sense of the results. However, the circular research design, in which analysis occurs in tandem with the data gathering process, means that the research journey is not compartmentalised. Data analysis is not left to the end of the study where it is in danger of being swamped by the volume of data.[17] The researcher is able to remain engaged with the research setting and make sense of the data in context.

A second consideration for those engaged in a multi-method approach is the temptation to make one method subservient to the other. In particular, the third stage of qualitative fieldwork could easily be sacrificed, given the already large amount of data collected through the initial interviews and the survey. This stage is, however, very important, because it acts as a balance to the reductionist tendencies of quantitative methods. Further interviews also enable the researcher to investigate themes not covered in the questionnaire and follow up issues raised in the qualitative section of the survey.

Finally, the multi-method approach can produce a lack of focus in the research. The sheer wealth of data, with its many different themes and concerns, can lead the researcher into a maze of analysis from which it is difficult to find a way out. However, at this stage, it is the literature which provides a framework for focus and theoretical understanding. This framework creates a structure which focuses the analyses but also allows space for the complexity of women's experiences to be explored. Whilst there are methodological challenges when adopting a multi-method approach, these are not insurmountable and are outweighed by the benefits of using a synthesis of qualitative and quantitative methods. The resulting knowledge is rich and concentrated. It is knowledge which is distilled by the research process but also grounded in the experience of women priests.

Incorporating Feminist Principles into the Research Model

The focus on women's experience, action-oriented research and the role of the researcher are three key principles in feminist research which I have incorporated into my research model. Kim Knott (1995), in an analysis of her own research journey, makes important methodological points which extend the feminist concept of reflecting on the role of the researcher in the research setting. Knott suggests that the research experience is transforming, not only because the resulting data has potential to change women's lives, but because the research experience offers potential personal growth for the researcher. For Knott research is not just an intellectual journey, but it is also a personal one. She argues that the process of research can be as interesting and fulfilling, for both the participant and the researcher, as the research itself. Knott's methodological reflections call on feminist researchers to move beyond an impersonal analysis of their role in the research, to a position where personal reflection, "an awareness of one's own feelings and thoughts throughout, and a consideration of their role in the research as a whole" (Knott 1995:120) are an integral part of research. Personal reflection is essential in the development of ethical and authentic research practice and is the third methodological strand of this study. A research diary, in which I recorded my thoughts and feelings about the study, enabled me to reflect on my own personal journey, my role as a researcher, and the effectiveness of my methodological approach.

The Role of the Researcher

The role of the researcher in feminist study is that of a participant, not an invisible, value-free observer. My use of a research diary meant that I could acknowledge my participation in my study. On a personal level, the diary helped to facilitate my own growth and self-understanding whilst from a methodological perspective, the use of personal reflection also developed my awareness of my interaction with the research setting. This extract from my research diary illustrates how self-reflection can make conscious what happens for all researchers, that is the way in which our belief-systems and worldviews affect the choices we make in our research:

> On a practical level I have been revisiting some of my qualitative interviews and was struck by my own personal reaction to what I was reading - those I warmed to and those I didn't. However scientific my methodology, I am again struck by my personal interaction with the data. There is a wealth of information (in the interviews) with over 128 different categories which I have abridged to 14 main themes. Even though I am being guided by the literature I have read, to some extent my own beliefs and interests will load my decisions about the way in which I proceed with the research. I don't think that is a problem if I am aware of this and am honest about what I am doing, and why.

Analysing my own participation in the research enabled me to reflect on the different roles I sub-consciously adopted as a researcher, which alerted me to feminist ethical concerns about the researcher-researched relationship. This extract shows how I participated in the interview process, and established rapport with the respondents:

> I notice when I interview people I rely heavily on empathy, on shared experiences; the commonalty of being female and committed to women's equality and emancipation in all aspects of Church life. I work hard to establish my credentials and engage with the women I am talking too. It sometimes feels like a spiritual experience. I also establish the fact that I am a Christian! Yet when I come to transcribe and analyse the texts I become the rational/external observer and quite critical of the interview participants. Our shared experience is easily sacrificed for the result. This raises questions about my (the researcher's) motivation. Is it true co-participation, or is that a role I take in order to maximise my material and gain a better response from the respondents?

Whilst rapport with the research subject produces richer, more in-depth data (Oakley 1981), my subsequent self-reflection on the interview process challenged me to ensure that the rapport I established was not mis-used or manipulative.

Self-reflection also contributes to understanding the interview process and the relationship between the researcher and the researched. In one diary extract I noticed that I had been unconsciously using a number of verbal and non-verbal empathy signals during the interviews: nodding my head, saying "mmm" or "yes". This communicated to the respondent that I had understood and agreed with what they were saying. The respondent received my empathy signal and usually moved onto another topic (leaving unfinished themes in the interview accounts which were difficult to analyse). In the first instance this reflection enabled me to improve my "interview technique", however, it also illumined the social interaction occurring in the interview:

> People appear to be explaining things to me, they are not just telling their story but constructing something which I need to understand. When I signal that I have understood it they move on to the next part of their story. This shows me something about my interview technique, but also points out the way in which people construct their stories, histories and characters.

This highlights the concept that interviews are not just factual accounts of actual events, but are also insights into the way in which people construct the accounts of their lives. The research diary also, therefore, contributed to the analytical methods and concerns of the study.

The research diary and my personal reflection on the research process enabled me to critically examine my role as a researcher; through self-reflection I was alerted to the potential power imbalance in the researcher-researched relationship. Self-analysis facilitated my personal growth as a participant in the research and my "professional" growth in the way I approach and conduct research. Through the diary I was able to make visible my otherwise invisible thoughts, feelings, and emotions, which are an integral part of research.

Focusing on Women's Experiences

The second feminist concern addressed in this methodological approach is the focus on women's experiences. Quantitative survey techniques have, in the past, been viewed as anti-feminist because they obscure or ignore women's experiences. Qualitative interviews, on the other hand, whilst they authenticate and evidence women's experiences of their social world, fail to make statements about the universality of that experience. However, in this study, survey and interview data together combined the micro and the macro levels to create a realistic account of women's experiences of priesthood. The qualitative interview data challenged over-simplified analysis of women's experience which is a danger of quantitative research, whilst statistical analysis guarded against making generalised statements about women's experiences from a small sample of respondents.

This study focuses on women's experiences in a number of ways. First, the starting point for the questionnaire (the large-scale survey tool) was in the interview data. The themes and concerns of the research were developed in response to women's accounts of their experiences as priests, as well as through the theoretical concerns expressed in the literature. It was women's stories which informed the development of the research question. Secondly, the questionnaire contained a large section in which respondents could record experiences and concerns that were not represented in the survey. This section, along with two sets of qualitative interview data, created a rich source of information reflecting women's experiences, attitudes and concerns. Finally, the themes from the survey were followed through in a series of further interviews. The circular research design illustrated in Figure 4b meant I continually returned to women's experiences in order to check and re-check the themes for analysis which enabled me to engage at several points with the experiences of the study's participants.

Action-oriented Research

The third methodological theme expressed in feminist research is the concern that research is action-oriented, that it contributes, in some way, to women's continued emancipation. The feminist researcher must address, therefore, how, and to what extent the "unalienated knowledge" produced by her research can contribute to social and political change in women's lives. Translated into my own study, as I record and analyse the experiences of the first women priests in the Church of England, I must give consideration to the way in which their stories can be heard by the wider Church.

In general there is a disparity between the research output appropriate for academic audiences and information which is of practical use to the participants of the research. Therefore, mechanisms of dissemination which are appropriate to each audience are required. The action-oriented focus of this study is being addressed in a number of ways. First, an Advisory Group to the research, made up from representatives from the Church and the Academy, are looking, amongst other things, at ways in which the study can be translated into practical outcomes for its respondents. Secondly, after the completion of this study, I am committed to producing a shorter report of the study for the Church of England. Finally I aim to disseminate a summary of the research findings to each of the participants.[18] Ultimately the researcher has little, or no control over the way in which the results of her study are received. Indeed, she can make no assumptions that her findings will be acted on in practical ways. However, the onus is still there to produce authentic knowledge which is accessible to a wide audience and which can be translated into practical action by the research participants.

REFLECTIONS ON THE INTERFACE BETWEEN QUALITATIVE AND QUANTITATIVE METHODS

To understand how quantitative and qualitative methods work together, complementing each other, it is helpful to focus on one example from the study. The original interviews showed that a sense of call or vocation was an important element in the women's accounts of their journey to the priesthood. Two approaches to this sense of call were present in the data. The first was individual, that is a clear, specific intervention from God speaking to an individual in a personal way:

> I was flicking through the alternative service looking for whatever it was and my eye just fell on a passage from the Bible and I just read it - everything just clicked...At that moment it was like an explosion in my head and I just knew that (the priesthood) was what God was calling me too.[19]

The second category relating to this call or vocation was developmental, this involved an individual growing in understanding or awareness of their call to the priesthood:

> The calling to leadership was much more by invitation from people, by encouragement, after I had done something people affirmed me and said "that's all right".[20]

Analysis of the interviews showed that women described their call as either individual or developmental, the two categories appeared mutually exclusive. In the large scale survey I included contrasting questions to discover whether women from different age groups or backgrounds (theologically and socially) expressed their sense of call in either an individual or a developmental way.[21] The results were surprising. Women priests did indeed express a strong sense of call but the results were not dichotomous. 84.5% said that God had spoken directly to them about entering the Church. However, 81% also said that they had experienced a growing sense of vocation.

Initially the analysis of the interviews suggested that individual or developmental calling were exclusive categories. The statistical results contradicted this analysis, suggesting that, for many women, their sense of call came from an individual experience of God in their lives *and* a growing, developmental sense of vocation. These two elements were not, as it had first appeared, contiguous, but in fact they were coterminous. Further interviews explored the idea of call in more depth to examine how two apparently conflicting positions could co-exist in women's accounts of their journey into priesthood (an in-depth analysis of call is included in chapter 7).

In this example qualitative and quantitative methods work together to develop understanding. The interface between the two and the apparent contradictions they contained, were significant contributory factors in the analysis. Either method alone would have produced a distorted view of women's experience of call. The circular process of checking and re-checking data through different methods refined the understanding of call and brought important analytical insights.

The aim of this study is to understand, in as comprehensive way as possible, the backgrounds, experiences and attitudes of the first women priests in the Church of England. In order to do this, my methodological approach is both large scale, but also grounded in the experiences of the women themselves. I have therefore adopted a synthesis, or multi-method approach to the research, which transcends the usual combative choice between quantitative or qualitative methods. My approach is circular, rather than linear, using interviews, survey material and written comments to check and re-check emerging themes from the data. The resulting knowledge is rich - located in women's experience of the priesthood, but it is also concerned with the "big picture", giving insight's to women's experiences on a national scale. The feminist critique of social research informed the development of the methodological approach of this study; in particular the focus on women's experience, the concern for action-oriented research, and understanding the role of the researcher in the research setting. Finally, through a research journal, I have acknowledged my own journey as part of this research. The invisible, often silent and supposedly objective researcher is made visible in this research through personal self-reflection. As I map the journey of the first women who became priests in the Church of England, I acknowledge that my journey is entwined with theirs.

CHAPTER 5

THE RESEARCH PROCESS

Research is a process of knowledge gathering, of finding and connecting different pieces of information. For the researcher it is a perilous process, as there are myriad paths that can be taken, with countless obstacles and barriers to be overcome. Yet it is also an exciting, unpredictable journey of discovery which uncovers truths and gives insight into both the lives of the research participants and the researcher - in this case, myself.[1] Indeed, as well as giving insight into the lives of women priests, this study has been a vehicle for self-exploration and a source of self-understanding.

This chapter is a description of my research journey. In it I show how I have woven together the different strands of the study, creating a research approach which is empirically rigorous, and is harmonious with the feminist methodological tenets outlined in the previous chapter. Mine is a circular, not linear, research design which reflects more accurately the actual process of research. In its re-telling, my journey can appear more sequential than it actually was. In reality many of the processes outlined in this chapter occurred concurrently. Therefore, I have separated the qualitative and quantitative elements of the study rather than present the research journey in a particular chronological order.

GAINING ACCESS

The first stage of my journey was to define the perimeters and to identify the population of my research. Since I was interested in the first group of women priests in the Church of England, I decided to include all women ordained in 1994 and 1995 in the study. Not all the women ordained in this period are classed as the "first generation", that is women who have experienced a prolonged diaconate; some will have begun training at the time of the vote in Synod and were therefore ordained alongside their male colleagues.[2] However, the majority of the women in the study had waited many years for ordination, they witnessed the vote in General Synod, and have subsequently experienced life as ordained priests. Information about all priests, whether they are stipendiary or non-stipendiary, working or retired, is in the public domain through the publication of the bi-annual Clerical Directory (*Crockfords*). I was saved the painstaking task of searching through thousands of names, looking for female first names, by the work of Reverend Ian Shield who had compiled a database from the ordination lists in the *Church Times* of all women ordained in this period.[3] My father then kindly looked up the addresses of some 1500 women in the current edition of Crockfords, from which I was able to produce a comprehensive mailing list of all women ordained in 1994-1995. I asked each of the 43 dioceses in England to update my list and, as a result, had a fairly definitive idea of the population I was studying.[4]

The next stage, having defined the population of the research, was to gain access. There is a distinction between "physical" and "social" access: the former term relates to the practical accessibility of a group of people, the latter refers to relational access - the success of which can help or hinder research (Hornsby-Smith 1993:53). Gaining "physical access" to the first group of women priests, although time-consuming and laborious, was nevertheless relatively uncomplicated. However, gaining "social access" was more complex. I began this research journey as an outsider, as I am neither priest nor Anglican (although I am female and Christian). I had no natural, social channels or connections through which to engage personally with the women I wanted to study. In order to familiarise myself with the Church of England and gain "social access" to the first group of women priests, I used a snow-balling technique which involves making and following-up contacts from a variety of sources: university, friends and acquaintances. Often these contacts would lead to further names, and so my research circle increased. This process serendipitously co-incided with the launch of WATCH, and I was able to make connections with several women priests at its inaugural meeting. Through this networking exercise I was able to arrange 17 pilot interviews with women priests.

The Advisory Group

A second consideration when negotiating "social access" to a group of people in a research setting is the credibility of the research. I found that my position as a research student was not sufficient to make women want to participate in the study, although the commitment of my supervisor, Professor Ursula King, who was known to many of the people I contacted, made my work more credible. I felt that the study needed greater input from people who were cognisant with the Church of England and its structures. I had originally intended to establish an advisory group of lay and ordained women in order to ensure greater ownership of the project and to enable me to work in a more collaborative and participative way. A pragmatic concern for greater access to and understanding of the Church led me to revise the original objectives of the group to include people, mainly women, who had a professional or academic concern for women's ministry. By necessity, therefore, I invited people whose experience and expertise meant they had senior positions in the organisations they represented.[5] In retrospect the group has been an important source of expertise and information which has helped and guided the research. Its members are well known in the Church of England and their input has given the research credibility, thus encouraging some women priests to participate.

INTERVIEWS

Interviews can be either qualitative or quantitative in nature. They range from the structured interview favoured by market researchers, to the semi-structured or open interviews used in more in-depth qualitative studies.[6] In the structured interview, the questions, and the order in which they are asked, is standardised. In the semi-structured interview the researcher asks the main questions in a standardised way, but is free to alter their sequence, and prompt or probe for further information. The unstructured or focused interview format enables the researcher to cover a range of topics with each respondent, but is free to phrase the questions, and change their order, according to the needs of the person they are interviewing (Fielding 1993).

Feminist writers emphasise research as a mutual process of knowledge development in which the researcher and researched are equal participants.[7] The focused interview is favoured by some feminist researchers because it minimises the power imbalance between researcher and respondent, and recognises their mutual participation in the research process (Oakley 1981). I chose the focused interview format for my study because it gave the maximum opportunity for women to engage with the issues and concerns which faced them in their ministry. The interview data, which were combined with feminist theological insight and my own analytical concerns provided the basis for the quantitative element of the study. The unstructured interviews, conducted before and after the quantitative data collection, enabled me to ensure that my study was rooted in women's experiences of the priesthood.

In the pilot stage of the research I undertook 17 in-depth interviews with women priests from a variety of dioceses, theological backgrounds, employment and marital status.* Each interview lasted approximately an hour and, with permission from the respondent, was taped. The tapes were transcribed verbatim[8] and then erased so that the interview data remained confidential. At the outset of each interview I emphasised that I would ensure any remarks made, or issues raised, would remain unattributable and that participants would be unidentifiable in my study. The main focus of the interview was women's journey into priesthood and, where necessary, I prompted participants to talk about their call or vocation, their ordination and first eucharist. I then asked about their experiences in the Church after ordination and whether or not they thought women would bring a different approach to ordained ministry and therefore change the Church.

I used the second round of interviews to follow up themes resulting from the quantitative data and to cover areas not included in the questionnaire. Women in chaplaincy and sector ministries felt that the survey was oriented to parish life and that it did not adequately reflect their experiences of priesthood. I therefore chose to conduct 5 of the 12 follow-up interviews with women chaplains, where I asked specifically about their experiences of ministry outside the main structures of the Church. The second round of interviews, like the pilot study, included women from a variety of backgrounds and dioceses. However, since the results from the questionnaire indicated that women with young children were experiencing considerable difficulties in the Church, I also contacted two women who were taking time out from paid ministry to care for their children. In these interviews I focused again on women's journey to priesthood, but I also asked how the participants viewed the role and function of the priest and I looked more closely at the idea of call and vocation. These were both areas of analytical interest that had arisen from the questionnaire.

Analysing the Qualitative Data

Just as there are contrasting views about the content and purpose of interviews, so there are conflicting ideas about how qualitative data should be analysed, originating from different paradigmatic approaches to research. Those operating within a positivist world view see interview data as a means of establishing social facts. By eliminating bias and maximising the validity and reliability of the research tool, the interview is a method of discovering and recording social realities. An interactionist paradigm, by contrast, views the data from interviews as evidence of ways in which participants construct their individual social reality (Silverman 1993). In my analysis of the qualitative data I was concerned not just with the content of women's accounts but also with the ways in which individual priesthood narratives were constructed.

---

*   A list of interviews is included in Appendix II

The interviews were not my only source of qualitative data. Since I was committed to giving women priests the maximum opportunity to relay issues that were pertinent to their situation, I also included a large section at the back of the questionnaire for respondents to record any further comments. This yielded over 350 pages of typed contributions which supplemented the extensive data from the interviews. For the initial analysis I took a sample of 5 interviews and 20 pages of written comments. I then assigned a number to each new category or variable in the text, which resulted in over 200 separate classifications. The next stage was to group the categories into themes for easier analysis and a total of 23 main concepts emerged.[9] All of the texts were then analysed using this coding framework, categories were discarded as they became redundant and further categories included as they became relevant in the data.

For example, attitude to campaigning became a strong theme in both the interview and qualitative data. It included 12 categories which could be divided dichotomously into a pro- or an anti-campaigning stance. Women indicated their ambivalence about direct action in the Church by expressing a fear of being seen as militant or overly feminist, through a desire to "get on with the job" and a belief that the struggle was over and there was no further need for campaigning. Some felt the time was not right to campaign for women bishops. A category which expressed a reluctance to campaign based on the view that campaigning perpetuated women's victim status proved to be a minority viewpoint and was therefore discarded. Some categories were relevant to more than one theme and they were cross referenced numerically in the coding framework.

This theme-based approach enabled me to analyse the content of women's priesthood accounts, but it also gave insight into the way in which women constructed their narratives. It highlighted particular areas which I felt required further investigation and I drew on the theory of narrative analysis to help me make sense of certain aspects in the qualitative data. The fact that I had given space in both the interviews and qualitative comments for women to tell me their stories meant that much of my data centred around women's experiences and thus fulfilled Riessman's definition of a personal narrative: "talk organised around consequential events" where the "teller in a conversation takes a listener into a past time or 'world' and recapitulates what happened then to make a point, often a moral one." (1993:3)

Narrative analysis is concerned, not directly with the content of a story, but with the way the teller constructs past events and actions. It focuses on how individuals recount their histories, what they emphasise and omit, the way in which the teller convinces the listener of authenticity, and the linguistic and cultural resources that are used to construct the story (Rosenwald & Ochberg 1992, Reissman 1993). For, "personal stories are not merely a way of telling someone (or oneself) about one's life; they are the means by which identities may be fashioned" (Rosenwald & Ochberg 1992:1).

Difficult and painful experiences are often very hard to speak, or write, about. Some events are buried so deep within an individual's consciousness that they may have difficulty even naming their experiences. Reissman suggests that one way in which people make sense of traumatic experiences is by casting them in narrative form.[10] She argues that narrators use the form of their story to make sense of their disordered experience in order to give a unity and value to events, that in their "raw" state, they did not appear to possess.[11] Narratives are not solely a way of structuring identity, they are also a tool which enables the story-teller to endow personal experiences with meaning (Skultans 1998).

Narrative analysis is normally conducted on a small number of texts. Since I had extensive qualitative data I needed to first decide how I would sample my accounts for analysis. I chose not to look at a small number of full accounts, but rather to address particular issues or anomalies raised in the research by analysing the structure of specific sections of text. Thus I was concerned with how women priests related particular aspects of their experiences in the Church. Narrative analysis was especially helpful when trying to understand apparent contradictions in the texts, or when investigating the discrepancy between qualitative and quantitative data. For instance, two strong themes which emerged from the qualitative and quantitative data were, on one hand a sense that women's ordination had received overwhelming approval by the Church, whilst on the other hand clear messages that women had experienced difficult and abusive responses to their ministry. These two apparently contradictory elements I described as "success stories" and "horror stories". I conducted a narrative analysis on a sample of these segments and the results, discussed in chapter 7, show how women priests contextualised their painful descriptions of rejection, by telling stories of success and "conversion" to their ministry. These bitter-sweet accounts enabled women to legitimate their ordination by indicating how the Church has benefited from their ministry, whilst at the same time acknowledging the traumatic events that have also dogged their journey to priesthood. As a textual device, the juxtaposition of pain and joy, of suffering and success, in the narratives enables women priests to endow their experiences with meaning.

THE QUESTIONNAIRE

The purpose of surveys are twofold: they are descriptive, in that they describe the characteristics of a certain group or population, and they are analytical in that they seek to explain particular phenomena by investigating relationships between variables or sets of variables (Hughes 1976). Self-completion questionnaires are a popular, cost-effective means of collecting data from a large, geographically dispersed, group of people (May 1993). Their use, however, is not without problems.[12] First, whilst surveys are favoured by researchers, they are not necessarily popular with research participants. Essentially questionnaires are reductionist, they investigate the commonalities of social life and do not reflect the complexity of individual experience. Unless self-completion questionnaires are compiled carefully, and are extensively piloted, they can fail to adequately encompass "real life" experience and thus alienate respondents.[13] Secondly, the impersonal nature of surveys can result in low, statistically biased, response rates. The researcher must rely on a covering letter to engage participants in the purpose and value of the research. Despite these problems, self-completion questionnaires, if used carefully, are a valuable source of information. They enable the researcher to understand the big picture and to make generalised statements about a group of people in a way which unquantifiable qualitative data does not allow.[14]

Although I chose to include a quantitative element in my study, I did not take a positivist, hypothesis-testing approach when devising the questionnaire. I did not approach the study with a rigid, theoretical model that I intended to test through the questionnaire; rather I developed the analytical framework for the study through a literature review, the analysis of the qualitative interviews, and my own intellectual concerns. As a result, the content of the questionnaire reflected the issues facing women's ministry and was embedded in the experiences of women priests.

Broadly the questionnaire set out to examine the backgrounds of the first women priests in the Church of England, understand their experiences of the Church, and investigate their approach to ministry. My study was descriptive, I was concerned with women's social, educational, theological and familial background and their experiences in the Church. It was also analytical and I was interested in women's attitude to change in the Church - whether they were demonstrating an empowering, egalitarian, collaborative approach to ministry or showing a predilection towards clericalisation. Similarly, I wanted to investigate women's attitudes to feminism and their identification with the Anglican Church. Each concept was therefore broken down into empirical indicators or variables; some, like age or marital status, were straightforward, whereas others, like clericalisation, were more complex and required a set of questions to measure one concept.[15]

The questionnaire was divided into three main parts, with the first part including a series of factual questions concerning women's personal backgrounds and history in the Church. It covered questions relating to social class, employment and educational background, marital and family status, and theological orientation. A series of questions was also asked about women's current employment status, their employment history in the Church, their ambitions for the future, and their experiences, both good and bad, of Church ministry. Finally it included questions about women's self-reported involvement in campaigning, support groups and inclusive worship. The second part of the questionnaire was a battery of attitudinal questions measured by a Likert scale.[16] This section examined women priest's approach to ministry, looking at their call, attitude to campaigning and support, and issues relating to a preferred collaborative, egalitarian and empowering approach to ministry. This section also asked about the women's experience of the diaconate, their attitudes to the second generation of women priests and their sense of historical significance as a group. The third section asked women to comment on anything they felt was not covered in the questionnaire, and to record any personal experiences more fully.

One of the limitations of self-completion questionnaires is that the researcher has no control over the respondent's interpretation of the questions. Unlike a semi-structured or focused interview, where the researcher can explain, prompt and elaborate, those engaged in survey research must rely on the thoroughness of their preparation and the unambiguity of their questioning. Therefore, in the preparation of my questionnaire, I was concerned with two key methodological concepts: the *reliability* and the *validity* of my research tool. *Reliability* refers to whether the measure used works consistently, whereas *validity* describes the extent to which a concept is being measured accurately (Gilbert 1993, Newell 1993, Proctor 1993a).

Two factors which contributed to the rigorousness and applicability of the questionnaire were its careful construction and its extensive piloting. The fact that the questionnaire was devised in response to the qualitative interviews meant that many of the concepts measured had originated from the participants in the study. Once a draft had been compiled I circulated it to a group of local women priests who completed it and commented on its structure and language. The questionnaire was then revised and sent to all the diocesan advisors on women's ministry.[17] Finally, a third draft was presented to the advisory group and then revised before the completed questionnaire was ready to be distributed. *

---

*   A copy of the questionnaire is included in Appendix III

The thorough preparation and piloting eliminated most, if not all, ambiguous and badly worded questions. It highlighted questions that were ineffectual and enabled me to ensure that the concepts I was measuring related to the experiences of women priests. I also sought to increase the accuracy of the questionnaire by using several variables to measure one concept and by presenting questions in both a positive and negative format. Someone filling in a questionnaire can become accustomed to ticking one side of a page if all the questions are worded positively. In order to break a response set it is important to present some questions in an alternative way. For instance, when measuring women's proclivity towards empowerment one of the attitudinal statements said "the easiest way to get things done is to tell people what to do", thus forcing some respondents to indicate they disagreed, rather than agreed with the question.

I chose to mail my questionnaire to all women who were ordained priest between 1994 and 1995, rather than send it to a smaller, but representative sample. Although this had budgetary implications,[18] it was important to ensure my study was as comprehensive as possible. I wanted my research to record the history of the first women priests in the Church of England and, as such, it was essential that I contacted all women who were ordained initially. The first questionnaires were sent at the beginning of November 1997 with a pre-paid reply envelope and a covering letter, explaining about the research, and signed by Professor Ursula King and myself. Each questionnaire was coded which enabled me to identify and send a second mailing to the non-respondents at the beginning of January. This proved a good time as it caught people just back from a post-Christmas break during which time little business mail would have accumulated.

There were 1547 women on my database, of whom 1247 returned the questionnaire: an 81% response rate.* This is a much higher than average response rate[19] and it can be argued that women priests were particularly motivated to respond to the questionnaire because of their own personal interest in its content. However, I believe this argument can be overstated. There have been a number of small scale studies of women priests[20] and this, coupled with intense media interest in their ordination, has caused women to be weary at being the focus of public attention. There were other factors to the study which contributed to the excellent response rate. In the first instance the questionnaire was relevant to women's experiences, and respondents were motivated to fill it in. It was a national study from a well respected university and was endorsed by a leading figure in feminist theology whilst, on a practical level, the pre-paid reply envelopes and a reminder mailing encouraged people to participate. Finally, the qualitative section enabled women to voice their own concerns and experiences rather than feel totally constrained by a box-ticking exercise.

Questionnaires, because of their anonymity, can be an important source of information when dealing with ethically or politically sensitive issues (May 1993). I certainly found that women priests used the survey, in particular the qualitative section, to record painful and difficult experiences. I was initially surprised at the levels of disclosure, until some women indicated that filling in the questionnaire, and writing down their experiences, in some cases for the first time, had been therapeutic for them. The opportunity to tell their story without being identified was an important release for some participants. The questionnaire also contained a section asking women to indicate whether or not they would be willing to be interviewed. This

---

*   The response rate by diocese is shown in Appendix IV.

received an extraordinary response, 61% of respondents said that they could be contacted for further information.[21]

Analysing the Quantitative Data

Quantitative analysis involves the use of statistical techniques to manipulate numerical data in order to investigate any underlying patterns. It seeks to discover whether there are relationships between variables which would explain or account for the patterns in the data (Hughes 1976). Once the data had been coded and entered onto SPSS (a statistical package for the social sciences), the next step was to produce a code book of all the basic descriptive statistics for each separate variable. I have summarised these statistics in Appendix V. They provide important information which was the basis for the more complex, multivariate analysis: cross-tabulation, elaboration, factor analysis and summated scales.

Cross-tabulation is a method which allows the researcher to explore relationships between variables in order to understand whether one variable (for instance, position in the Church) is dependent on another (for instance, theological orientation). The result of cross-tabulation is a two-way table which demonstrates whether or not the distribution of one variable varies when compared with another. Although an initial look at a table reveals some information, a more objective measure for understanding whether the relationship between variables is significant is required. Chi-square is a statistical measure of association which indicates the likelihood (or probability) of an apparent relationship between two variables in a table happening by chance. SPSS then generates a chi-square figure of significance (indicated by the letter p) and if that figure is less than 0.05, it can be assumed that the null hypothesis of no association between variables can be rejected and that the relationship in the table is valid. In other words, there is only a 0.05 or less likelihood that the relationship between the variables, in the group of people surveyed, has happened by chance and therefore the findings in the table can be accepted as significant.[22]

The process of elaboration enables the researcher to understand the relationship between two variables through the simultaneous introduction of additional variables (Babbie 1989). Elaboration shows whether a relationship between variables varies according to the introduction of a third antecedent or intervening variable. An antecedent variable is one which accounts for the primary relationship between two variables. For instance, in my analysis I discovered a relationship between position in the Church and the marital status of the respondent. The introduction of a third variable, age-group, partly explained the relationship and demonstrated that younger and middle age women were more likely to be affected by the link between marital status and employment position. An intervening variable is one which explains how the primary relationship works (Proctor 1993b). Chi-square is again used as a measure of association in elaboration tables.

Factor analysis is a statistical technique through which the researcher can make sense of large data sets by grouping together and exploring underlying factors which affect variation in the data. It is a form of analysis which helps reduce data by identifying a relatively small number of factors that are not directly observable, but which help to explain intrinsic patterns in the data (Kim & Mueller 1978a&b, Norusis 1991).[23] SPSS carries out a principal component factor analysis in four stages. First a correlation matrix for all the variables chosen is computed in order to identify variables which are not particularly associated. Then the factor extraction identifies the number of factors necessary to adequately explain the variation in the data. This is standardised and represented as an *eigenvalue*.[24] Only factors with an *eigenvalue* over one are accepted, and the researcher must choose an appropriate number of factors, which together account for a significant proportion of the variance in the data. The third stage in factor analysis is rotation, where the data is rotated in order to make the factors more interpretable. SPSS then calculates and assigns a score to respondents for each factor. I used factor analysis to identify underlying patterns in the data relating to women's experiences of the Church (see chapter 7).

The main method used to investigate underlying concepts in the questionnaire was summated scales. This is a method which allows the researcher to add together the scores from a set of variables to discover how strongly each individual respondent relates to a particular concept. Summated scales are a good way of understanding the strength of response to a particular set of variables. However, they must also be treated with caution since an individual who strongly agrees with some statements and strongly disagrees with others can score the same as someone who only moderately agrees with most statements (Hughes 1976).[25] I used this method to create scales from the attitudinal section of the questionnaire, but it also enabled me to combine questions relating to attitude with reported behaviour identifiers. I had also intended to use factor analysis on the attitudinal variable set, however it did not reveal any significant factors which were not already covered by the summated scales.

To produce summated scales I first identified all the variables which related to a particular concept I wanted to analyse and asked SPSS to compute a score for each respondent, based on the summated scores from the composite variables. It was important to ensure that all variables were coded in the same way, so that, because the number 1 was used to indicate strong agreement, those that had a low score on the scales showed a strong affiliation with a particular concept.[26] I then looked at the distribution of the scores on the scale to see how strongly women priests, as a group, agreed or disagreed with the particular concept being measured. For use in further analysis the scores on each new variable were recoded into smaller categories, in most cases into dichotomous groupings of "tend to agree", and "tend to disagree". The framework for deciding these condensed categories originated from the theoretical content of the scales and not the distribution of the data.

EVALUATION OF THE RESEARCH DESIGN

My research combined quantitative and qualitative methods in order to produce an in-depth study of the first group of women priests in the Church of England. By attributing equal importance to each of these methods, and refusing to allow one to be subservient to the other, I set myself a challenge. In the first instance, I needed to ensure that I approached each element of the study rigorously, making sure that I applied high standards in both the data collection and analysis. Secondly, I accumulated a wealth of data which presented me with many opportunities for analysis. I needed to allow the analytical concerns to arise from the data without becoming subsumed by the multiplicity of different themes and issues raised in the research. Finally, because of the scale of the study, I was consistently faced with the tension between data collection, analysis and writing. In short, the limitation of my research design was that I risked producing an unfocused, disparate study where the constraints of large scale data collection affected my analysis and writing.

However, it was a risk worth taking. Since I had chosen not to compartmentalise the quantitative and qualitative elements of the study I found that I was able to use the different methodological approaches to complement each other. I used the interface between the qualitative and quantitative methods to develop knowledge. I found that apparent discrepancies in the data often led to deeper understanding in a way that one method, on its own, could not have done. The circular research design meant that my analysis was not left until the end of the study and marginalised, but rather I was able to use on-going analysis to inform each stage of data collection. The different stages of the study also helped to refine the data and enabled me to focus my analytical concerns. The themes for analysis were distilled through each stage of the research process which helped, alongside the theoretical framework established by the literature review, to focus the study.

The combined methodology produced an in-depth study of the backgrounds, attitudes and experiences of women priests. Through the use of an integrated methodology I have shown that feminist research is not confined to one method, but that the principles of feminist research can be addressed through both quantitative and qualitative methods. My research journey has not always been an easy one, but it has been fruitful both personally and academically.

This study marks out a base-line for future investigation of women in the Church. My research focuses on the experiences of the first women priests in the Church of England. However, these experiences are not static, even as I write they will be changing, developing and evolving. Women who follow will probably articulate very different, contrasting, and hopefully improved, experiences of priesthood. This research provides substantial evidence on which future study can be built - it will be essential to compare and contrast the experiences of future women priests with this first, unique and significant cohort.

CHAPTER 6

WOMEN PRIESTS - THEIR BACKGROUNDS

This study is unique in that it captures women's history as it is unfolding and provides a comprehensive, detailed and thorough picture of the first group of women priests in the Church of England. There have been other, probably more significant firsts for women over the last century: the first women to receive university degrees, the first woman to enter the medical or legal professions, the first woman to become a Member of Parliament. These advances for women occurred initially on an individual basis and their significance was often left for future generations to record. In contrast, the Church of England ordained 1547 women priests in the first year, increasing its overall numbers of priests by approximately ten per cent.[1] For the first time in history a large cohort of women was admitted to the ranks of a profession in one go. In the next four chapters I will describe and discuss the results of my study - focusing initially on women's backgrounds and experiences before going on to investigate their attitudes to, and stories of, priesthood in the Church of England.

Here are a group of proficient, seasoned women ministers who are a rich source of cumulative experience for the Church. The combination of the sheer volume of their numbers and their amalgamated skill has the potential to influence the Church in a profound way. If the vision that heralded women's priesthood is to be fulfilled and women do, in fact, have the capacity to develop new, alternative models of ministry, if they can truly counteract the dehabilitating effects of patriarchy, then all of society must watch this initial cohort of women priests with great interest. For women in other organisations who have had to work individually for their positions in patriarchal structures, their progress has been more gradual and their presence at times anomalous. Sometimes bullied, isolated and belittled, these women pioneers have often had to sacrifice their will to change, using their energy to simply survive in male-dominated structures. Women priests, however, have a real opportunity to tranform hierarchical, androcentric structures in the Church. There are sufficient numbers of them to develop strong internal support structures, they have a national campaigning watchdog body (WATCH), and women priests receive widespread public affirmation. Here is a group of women whose significance is far greater than the Church. They signal to society women's potential to make a difference. As women, if we can understand them, our own capacity to be agents of transformation is illumined. We can have insight into what is required individually and corporately from women if we are to throw off the shackles of patriarchy.

Yet to suppose that, as a group, women priests are homogeneous is to over-simplify their experiences; the many hundreds of women are as complex and diverse as they are similar. Their attitudes and experiences will be informed, not just by their priestly status, but by the myriad social and cultural threads which define individual identity. Age, social class, theological orientation, employment and familial status are all elements of the internal, cultural maps which affect the way individuals think, feel and behave. Some of the categories explored here, such as age and theological orientation, are used to understand particular attitudes or experiences investigated in later chapters. Other demographic details, such as women's employment status or their family situation, have significant implications for the Church as a whole, and for women's ministry in particular, both now and in the future. My study provides a comprehensive, up-to-date picture of the first group of women priests in the Church of

England. It contains information which illumines the experiences of this unique, initial group from which it will be possible to measure women's future progress in the Church.

AGE

The age of the women who responded to the questionnaire ranged from 29 to 82, their average age was 52. The first women priests in the Church of England represent at least three generations and, as such, will have had very different experiences. Some women will have lived through a world war and seen the role of women change beyond recognition. Others will have been born into a society where a woman could become prime minister and access the highest levels of government, business and education. Age will, therefore, be an important factor when examining the different attitudes and experiences of the first group of women priests.

To examine generational difference I have distinguished three age groups: young, middle-aged and old.[2] Women in the younger group have grown up in a post-feminist era; they are likely to have more enhanced notions of women's capabilities and expect a degree of equality with men. This generation has questioned, to some extent, the traditional role of women and will probably expect to combine work with family responsibilities. Women who are middle-aged are part of the bridge generation, that is the women who have lived through the development of feminism and experienced changing expectations about their role and function in society. They are likely to have been brought up with one set of values that link women to traditional family roles, but will have seen those values change. Some will have experienced feminism and been part of the movement for women's equality. Others may have remained linked to traditionally female roles and attitudes, but all the women in this group will have experienced the impact of feminism first-hand.

Finally, the older generation are women who will have grown up in the pre-feminist era. For the majority, their formative years will have been geared towards the strong expectations that a woman's place is in the home. Women of the older generation are more likely to be conservative in their approach, particularly towards feminist ideals. These age categories are a framework for further analysis. Age and its effect on the attitudes and experiences of women priests is explored in later chapters where I examine age in relation to other variables or sets of variables.

SOCIAL CLASS AND EDUCATION

Social class is a popular concept when researching social life, but it is an extremely difficult one to clearly define and measure. The first problem, when looking at class, is who, in a family unit, determines the class of that household. Secondly, an accurate measure of class must be used: income, education and occupation are all measures of social class. The concept and measurement of social class is constantly changing, particularly in relation to women. Until recently the social class of a family unit was measured by the occupation of the male "head of the household". A woman's status was therefore defined by the status of her husband, partner or father.[3]

Since investigation into social class is not the main focus of this study, I am using the Registrar General's classification of occupation to measure the social class of women priests.[4] The main measure for class in this study is women's occupation before entering the priesthood (in conjunction with, or comparison to, their father's occupation). The occupation of women's partners and mothers was also investigated in order to explore whether or not this influenced women's status or experiences in the Church. Respondents were also asked about their highest educational qualification in order to give a clear picture of the social and educational status of women prior to their ordination to the priesthood.

The ordained women showed high levels of academic achievement, especially when one considers that many are from an older age group. 53.2% have a degree or higher degree, and a further 29.3% have a professional qualification (this is excluding any theological qualification associated with training for ordination).[5] This level of qualification is further reflected in the occupations of the respondents prior to ordination. 75.1% were in social class I or II (69% in social class II). Many of the occupations stated were of the professional caring type such as nursing, occupational and physiotherapy. However, the main occupation for women ordinands was teaching. The high numbers of teachers led me to do a separate count for them, and it was discovered that 38% of women were/are in the teaching profession. Only 4.4% classed themselves as having home responsibilities prior to ordination.

As one might expect, there are signs of upward social mobility in the women ordinands when one compares their occupations with that of their parents. 36.1% of their mothers were classed as homemakers with 25.3% in social classes I and II. 38.3% of mothers were in social class III and below compared with 16.7% of the women priests. These figures show that a quarter of women had mothers who worked in occupations associated with social class I or II. This is a high proportion given the age of the respondents, and it suggests that some women priests had female role models within their family which enforced their desire for achievement in the professional, educational and, ultimately, the ecclesiastical spheres.

The majority of women (78.9%) held occupations in social classes I and II prior to their priesthood. Table 6a compares the social class of women priests with that of their fathers and nearly two thirds of women came from households in social class I or II. However, there is also some evidence of women's upward social mobility for a third of women in social classes I and II have increased their social status in comparison to their father. Conversely half of the women in social classes III and IV have decreased their social status in relation to that of their father.[6]

When one examines the occupations of women's partners, 85.9% are in social class I or II. Once again the percentage of men in social class I is higher than the women, 20% of men have occupations in social class I which rises to 47.7% when the numbers of clergy are added in. Over a quarter of the women who were ordained in this period and are married, have clergy husbands and only 13% have partners in social class III or below. Overall, the picture is clear, the majority of women priests are connected through their occupation, their family or their partner's occupation with social classes I and II.

TABLE 6a   Social Mobility of Women Priests (%)*

		Father's Social Class		
		Social Class I & II	*Social Class III & IV*	*Social Class V & VI*
Respondent's Social Class	*Social Class I & II*	61.5	32.5	6
	Social Class III & IV	50.6	38.1	11.4
	Social Class V & VI	36.4	27.3	36.4
	Home Responsibilities	70.6	24	0
	Total	**60.2**	**33**	**6.8**

n=1125, $p \leq 0.000$

The first group of women priests are well educated and have professional backgrounds, which is an indicator of the calibre of the first women to enter the priesthood. However, the fact that their origins are predominantly middle class also raises questions about the class-structured hierarchy in the Church. Very few women have experience of manual occupations, either themselves, through their partners or through their parents, and therefore the origins and occupation of women priests reflect the essentially middle class image of the Church of England. Women's experience in professional caring jobs illustrates the wealth of potential they bring to the Church. The competencies gained through secular work which contain elements of the priestly office: concern for other people's welfare, involvement in teaching or instructing, have no doubt prepared women for their sacerdotal role. Women's standing in their professional lives has, in turn, fuelled expectancy about what they can achieve within the Church. Professional background and education has given women confidence, made them more articulate, affirmed their ambitions in the Church and given them support and encouragement on their journey to the priesthood.

However, the educational and social backgrounds of the first women priests can also be viewed as an indicator of the essentially class-based hierarchy, for which the Church of England has been criticised. Are academic and professional qualifications necessarily appropriate indicators of "good priests"? Is the fact that women clergy are predominantly middle class an indictment of the class structure in the Church which fails to represent or encourage involvement of people from working class backgrounds? Is it only women from certain professions and class structures who can compete in the male dominated hierarchy of the Church? These questions raise important considerations for the Church, not only in relation to

---

*   Tables are read across: 61.5% of women in social classes I and II had fathers in the same social classes and so on. The letter *n* denotes the number of people represented in the table. The letter *p* represents the statistical co-efficient that describes the likelihood of the relationship in the table happening by chance. If *p* is less than ($\leq$) 0.05 then the relationship in the table is accepted.

women's ministry. If Christianity is a religion which is called to transform, rather than reinforce the artificial barriers of class, race and gender, then its priestly representatives need to be drawn from a wider, less selective, social group.

MARITAL AND FAMILY STATUS

An investigation of the marital status of women priests revealed that a high proportion of women are not married. Figure 6b shows that 46% are single, divorced, widowed or in a committed relationship, but not married.[7] Only 17% of women priests have dependent children, and only 10% of women ordained in 1994-1995 have main childcare responsibilities.[8] This is partly due to the age group of those who were ordained initially, many of whom had been waiting many years for the priesthood.

FIGURE 6b   Marital Status of Women Priests

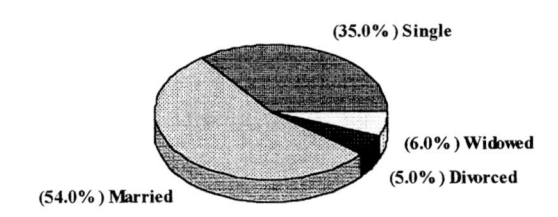

(35.0%) Single
(6.0%) Widowed
(5.0%) Divorced
(54.0%) Married

Since the average age of women ordained in this period is 52, their children are likely to have left home or be independent. However, from this initial analysis one can see that the traditional patterns for women of marriage and childcare responsibilities are not reflected in the first group of women priests. 83% of women ordained in this period have no dependent children. Whilst this can be partly attributed to the age of those waiting for ordination, it also raises questions about the compatibility of traditional female roles with priesthood. Is it something about the first group of women priests which accounts for this anomaly, or is it the nature of priesthood itself which affects women's ability to combine different social roles? Women are now adept at juggling the responsibilities of motherhood, their career and the family; what, if anything, prevents women priests from doing the same? There are important implications for the Church if women are unable to combine marital and family commitments with a traditional male priestly role. Both women and men will require a new model of priesthood, in which family and ministry are coterminous and not conflicting.

Priests with Children

The traditional priestly role is both a vocation and a profession (Krause 1971). The role of the priest is seen as a response to a call or vocation from God (in other words it is conceptualised in spiritual terms). Yet at the same time the bureaucratisation of religion (as demonstrated in the parochial system and the organisation of the Church of England's decision-making function into parliament-like synods) has contributed to the professionalisation of the clergy role. A sense of vocation and career professionalism can conflict with each other, resulting in mixed messages about the role and function of the priest.[9]

Linda Robson (1988) describes this process as "clergy double-talk". Robson draws on Wittgenstein's concept of "language games",[10] and she suggests that two conflicting "language games" are utilised in relation to the role of clergy: the "language game" of ministry and the "language game" of the professions. The "language game" of ministry is centred on three concepts: service and self-giving, a lack of worldly ambition, and a concern for pastoral issues. The "language game" of the professions has a different basis; professionalism is characterised in four main ways: a full-time occupation, specialised training institutions, professional association and a code of ethics. Robson suggests that the role of clergy differs from other occupations because it operates a system of double-talk; sometimes using the discourse of ministry and at other times the discourse of the professions.

This system of double-talk was evident in the debate about women's ordination. If women emphasised equal rights issues, utilising the language framework from the professions in their arguments for ordination, then their opponents stressed the particular nature of ministry which somehow exceeds any equal opportunity legislation. After their priesting women in Church ministry continue to be caught in the tension between the two language games, particularly in relationship to their conflicting roles as mother and priest. To what extent, then, do family responsibilities affect women's status in the Church? Why do women struggle to be both mother and priest?

Analysis of the survey shows that women with childcare responsibilities are more likely to be at junior levels in the Church than their colleagues who do not have dependent children. Figure 6c illustrates how responsibility for childcare affects a woman's position in the Church. As with other professions, the job of the priest is structured in such a way that it is hard for women with basic family commitments to participate. For women in the ministry this is compounded by the fact that the implicit supportive role designated to the wives of professionals has, in the Church, itself developed a ministerial capacity. The role of the vicar's wife has changed dramatically over the last two decades with many women working to supplement their husband's income. However, there is still some expectation among the congregation that the vicar's wife will support the functioning of the priest, and will facilitate his ministry as an unpaid co-minister. It is also still presumed that the woman will provide the main framework for the family. Women priests are caught in this conflict of expectations. They are both vicar and vicar's wife, the sustainer of family and parish. In a role which is already all-consuming, women are expected to give more. As one respondent wrote:

> I'm just about to cook chicken casserole for nine and feel people want me to be vicar and vicar's wife all at the same time. I still feel guilty having any time to myself (i.e. not Church, parish, family, husband, children).

FIGURE 6c Employment Position by Childcare Responsibilities [11]

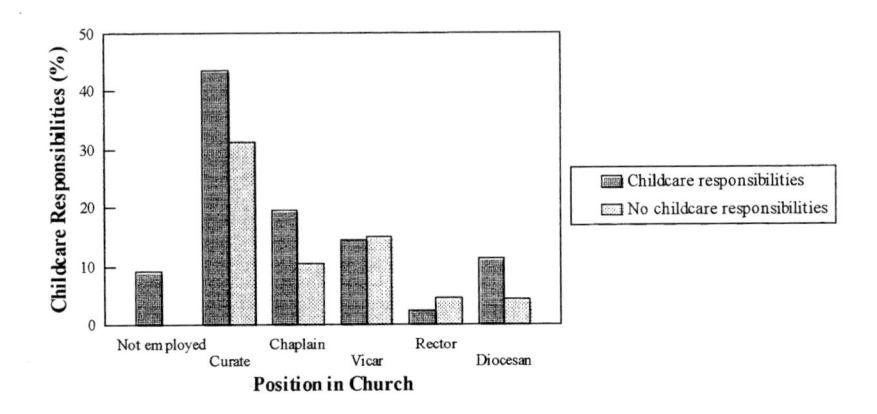

The discourse of ministry defines the clergy role in response to the needs and wants of Church congregations. The priest's job is mainly structured around the leisure time of parishioners, but it also includes many day time activities. The priest, living in the parish and often near the Church, is totally available to the parish, making it extremely difficult to organise effective childcare arrangements (particularly on low pay):

> The biggest thing I've come up against is what the Church does when a woman priest is pregnant. I had to tell the authorities what I was eligible for with regards to maternity pay or leave. I feel I'm an anomaly in the Church now - I don't fit anywhere in terms of ordained ministry.

The discourse of the profession (maternity rights and childcare) clashes with the discourse of ministry (self-giving and availability). For women with children this conflict is further exacerbated by the discourse of motherhood which, like ministry, involves self-giving, unconditional availability and the concern for the well-being of others:

> I don't think that small children should have to put up with that [constant interruption of home-life in parish ministry]. I don't really see why, when you are half way through their bed-time story you should drop it and pick the phone up. I don't really think you could operate parish ministry whilst you were caring for the children in the house, I don't think you can do two jobs well simultaneously....without having a nanny and I think you would have to pay the nanny more than you would be paid.

The discord between the "language games" of profession and ministry further disadvantages women with childcare responsibilities by sacramentalising the professional role. If the constraints of motherhood (breast-feeding or preparing a meal) impinge on the sacerdotal office of a priest, a woman finds it almost impossible to function sacramentally. The result for women is either guilt at their inability to fulfil one of their conflicting vocations, or a withdrawal from the system. As one woman wrote about her son:

> I always felt guilty, I either felt that I should be with him or I felt I should be working.

This sense of guilt is compounded for some women who are involved in a team ministry. Childcare responsibilities mean that women are unable to respond as flexibly as their male colleagues and they feel guilt at causing more work for others in the team.

Women have problems combining priesthood with motherhood because they are caught in a double bind. The priestly role has developed into a parental one where clergy are concerned for, and available to their parishioners. For men, their role as a father has clearer boundaries and, more often than not, is supported by the unconditional availability of a wife - a dynamic which is reflected in parish life. Women priests who are mothers must be accessible to both family and parish, they are expected to offer support and succour to both children and congregation. This problem is compounded by the fact that the functional role of clergy has developed in such a way that it is almost impossible for women to find and afford appropriate, flexible childcare. The time demands of priesthood, which are erratic and often based around the leisure time of the congregation, mean that it is hard to combine priesthood with family life.[12] The "language game" of ministry makes it very difficult for women to take an approach to ministry which has clear boundaries and is congruent with family life. Ministry and motherhood are seen as conflicting vocations, each demanding women to be self-giving, available and concerned for others well-being - a situation in which women can only lose:

> I think you just put yourself on hold, because what gets squeezed out at the end of the day is you. It makes it nigh on impossible to keep any friendships or any social life.

Some women have used their experiences of motherhood to challenge the structurelessness of the priestly role. Their family commitments have forced them to create boundaries in their ministerial life, and they see family responsibilities as having legitimised those limits.[13] However, for many, the demands of priesthood and motherhood are incompatible; the pressure to be successful in the former because of the novelty of women priests, and to respond to the Christian ideals in the latter, often leave women exhausted, guilty or feeling they have failed.

Women's priesthood has emphasised the inexorable difficulty of women's task - to be both mother and worker. Childcare, flexible working conditions and better pay all make it easier for women to combine work and family commitments, but they fail to address the core injustice. As long as women are expected to, and indeed take, the main responsibility for family maintenance, they will always be disadvantaged. Yes, we need new models of priesthood that are less parental and more facilitative, but we also need new values and attitudes in society. Women and men must share family commitments, part-time work and support for children if there is to be the gender revolution that is required.

Clergy Wives

18% of the women ordained in 1994-1995 are married to clergymen. Put another way, a third of married women priests are part of a clergy couple. The results of the initial interviews suggested that being married to a priest is particularly problematic for women hoping to have a career in the Church. Any priest of incumbent status is required to live within their parish boundaries; it is therefore impossible for two people of incumbent status to live in the same place.[14] This has obvious implications and difficulties for married couples. If, as the initial interviews suggested, women who are married to clergy are discriminated against, it could be expected that women in clergy couples are more likely to be non-stipendiary or at junior levels in the Church. This, however, was not the case. The percentages of non-stipendiary women priests married to clergymen is the same as non-stipendiary women married to men in secular work. Marital status does not affect women's paid employment opportunities. However, marital status does affect the position of women in the Church, particularly for those married to clergymen. Table 6d shows the way in which marital status and age affects the position that women hold in the Church.

TABLE 6d
The Position of Women in the Church by Age Group and Marital Status (%)

MARITAL STATUS		Young Age Group			Middle Age Group		
		Non Clergy	Clergy	Single	Non Clergy	Clergy	Single
POSITION IN THE CHURCH	Curate	25.2	33	22.8	34.6	27.9	30.1
	Chaplain	18	22.6	28.1	19.6	26.2	14
	Vicar	33.1	16	31.6	31.7	24.6	39
	Rector	5.8	0.9	4.4	7.1	4.9	6.6
	Diocesan	12.2	21.7	12.3	7.1	16.4	8.1
	Not employed	5.8	5.7	0.9	0	0	2.2
	Total	38.7	29.5	31.8	54.9	14	13.1
		$p \leq 0.005$			$p \leq 0.03$		

The relationship between marital status and position in the Church is significant for women who are younger or middle-aged. Younger women who are married to clergy are more likely to be curates or in a diocesan post than their colleagues who are not married to clergy or who are single. For the bridge generation (middle-age group) this relationship changes: women who are married to clergy are less likely to be curates than their younger counterparts, but they are more likely to be in a chaplaincy or sector role. This relationship suggests that the career path for clergy wives is different from that of other women in the Church. Where women are unable to have their own parish, they are able to achieve incumbent status in a chaplaincy role.[15]
Women from the bridge generation who are married to priests, are also less likely to hold senior positions in the Church and are more likely to be in diocesan posts. In short, clergy

couples have to make a choice as to whose career they will invest in, as both are unable to have full career progression in parish ministry. At the present time it appears that women are the ones who are making concessions, women's careers are second place to that of their husbands.

Women who are married to clergymen and have responsibility for childcare have fewer employment opportunities than their colleagues who have no children or who are not married to clergymen. Younger clergy wives with responsibility for childcare are five times more likely to be NSM than their counterparts with no children, and twice as likely to be NSM than their colleagues who have dependant children but who are not married to priests:

> It really is a Catch 22, the more I think about it the less I think I can [go back to work]. If my husband had a job that he could come home for those hours, or if he earned enough to pay for childcare it might be possible.

Being part of a clergy couple disadvantages women priests, particularly if they have dependent children. The qualitative data illustrate why this is the case. Some women who are married to priests fulfil their ministry through diocesan or chaplaincy/sector posts which often provide better pay and working conditions for women. However, for those wishing to operate a parish ministry there are three main problems. First, women wishing to have a separate ministry from their husbands in a different parish are unable to do so at any other than a junior level in the Church. They are required to live in their parish if they hold an incumbent status:

> I am one of those women married to a priest. I had been a deaconess for five years and a deacon for three when he was ordained. My career has had to be "cut short" because of this. At the time when my children were babies I was being offered stipendiary posts with responsibility - but felt I couldn't do justice to being a mum and a deacon in charge. Now my children are older I am told I can't have such a job because I need to live in the vicarage of the parish in which I work. I am more qualified (theologically and in years of service) than my husband but he was instituted to the parishes six weeks before my priesting.

Secondly, there are a group of women who see their ministry in the Church as a partnership with their husbands and some are willing to remain as curates or be non-stipendiary in order to ensure they can work with their partners. Yet not all dioceses are happy for couples to work together, and certainly not when both require payment. One woman reported how she completed her training curacy alongside her husband in an unpaid capacity, but was then unable to find stipendiary work:

> When we moved we looked for two jobs but were continually prejudiced against our desire to work together (even when three jobs were vacant in one team) because the Church of England had not considered this when ordaining women.

Finally, some women who are married to priests are finding difficulties in either being paid a full stipend or even being paid at all. Women priests married to clergy are more likely to be paid a part-stipend or salary than their colleagues who are single or married to non-clergy. 17.8% of women married to clergy have part-stipends, compared to 7% of those married to non clergy and 1.8% of single women. Women priests in clergy partnerships are not more likely to be non-stipendiary than their colleagues, however, there is evidence that, where they are NSM, that this is not by choice:

> We are an ordained clergy couple and therein lies a problem which makes life extremely stressful. We only receive one stipend and there are four of us...I've personally found my experience here so painful that if I could leave the Church I would do so.

For clergy couples on one stipend the situation is very difficult; one woman reported how she could not afford a second car to perform NSM duties, and paid childcare is almost impossible on one stipend.

The confusion surrounding the status of clergy couples is one example of the Church of England's fragmented approach to structural issues. Each diocese has a separate policy concerning clergy couples which appears largely to depend on the attitude of the diocesan bishop. With all the debate about the theological implications of ordaining women no planning was given to the practical employment issues that this would raise. The number of priests married to other priests will increase, but the "problem" they represent to the Church authorities will not decrease unless organisational changes are made. Even if partners share jobs, childcare, ambition and pension rights, the Church is structurally unprepared for, or able to cope with, clergy couples at this stage.

At present women priests are, in the main, the ones who suffer. Often having followed their husbands into ministry and coping with the struggles and expectations of trying to combine family life with ministry, women's careers are overlooked. Unless the Church adopts more flexible working patterns and conditions for male and female clergy, it appears that women priests who are part of a clergy couple, will be disadvantaged.

The marital and family status of the first women priests does affect the position they hold in the Church, particularly for those who have dependent children and/or who are married to other clergy. Women priests who are part of a clergy couple are unable to progress in parish ministry unless their husband is in a chaplaincy or sector role. Clergy couples must choose whose career they will pursue and, for the first group of women priests, it appears that their career is secondary to that of their husbands. Women with dependent children are caught in the conflict of discourses which operates within the Church. Priests are part of a profession which, along with responsibilities, should bring certain privileges and rights (such as maternity provision, childcare facilities and working conditions which are compatible with family life). Yet for women priests the benefits of professionalisation are mitigated by the pressures of the ministerial role. It is extremely difficult for women priests, practically and emotionally, to meet the demands that priesthood and motherhood make of them. Whether or not these expectations are internal (fuelled by unreal self expectation) or external (the projected assumptions of the Church and society) is immaterial. For many women the conflict between the two vocations is too much.

EMPLOYMENT STATUS OF WOMEN PRIESTS

One of the myths surrounding the first group of women priests in the Church of England is that they only started working for the Church at the time they were ordained priest. This "lack of experience" is seen as a reason why women should not be given preferment (promotion), for in the eyes of their critics, they have not yet proved they can do the job. In fact, many of the women ordained priest in 1994-1995 had been working for the Church of England for a number of years, and in some cases for a very long time. The average length of ministry is 15 years, which does not accurately reflect some women's much longer service.

The depth of commitment to Church ministry is illustrated by the types of paid and unpaid positions that women have held in the Church: deaconesses, parish workers, missionaries, plus a host of other unpaid lay responsibilities.[16] The first women ordained priest clearly have a wealth of Church experience and, through this, a strong identification with the Church of England and its structures. How far is this experience being utilised by the Church? Are women being given employment opportunities consistent with their experience and training, or is there a "stained glass ceiling" which is preventing women from accessing senior positions in the Church?[17]

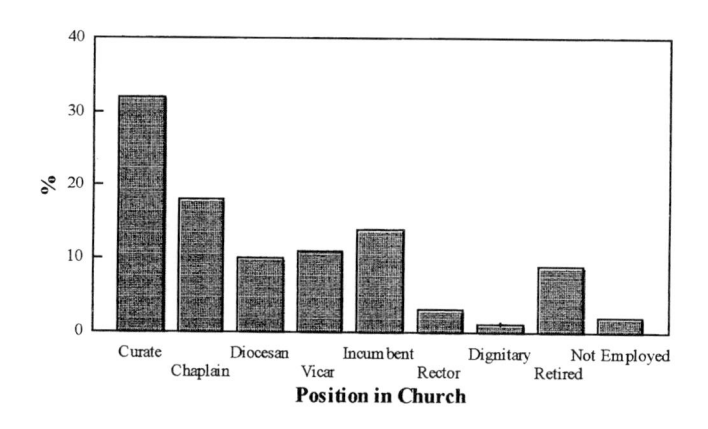

FIGURE 6e Employment Status of Women Priests

Figure 6e shows the employment status of women priests,[18] illustrating how few women are at high levels in the Church (only 4% are either rectors, archdeacons, area or rural deans, or residentiary canons). This lack of women in senior positions could be partly explained by the age of the first women priests. The fact that they waited for many years to be ordained means that this initial cohort are older and, approaching retirement age, are less likely to have been promoted after they were ordained priest. This factor was exacerbated by the fact that the Church introduced an age bar to priests entering ministry which said that no-one over 45 could hold their first stipendiary position. This rule has implications in the future for women who have family responsibilities. Women who retrain or develop careers as their children get older may then find themselves entering the ordained ministry just as the age bar comes into force. Certainly, for some women who waited a long time, ordination to the priesthood came too late for them to hold stipendiary positions:

When I was ordained as priest at the age of 56 I was told I was too old to be considered for an incumbents post. It was disappointing to say the least. So not only are there discrimination against women - but also "ageism" is creeping into the appointments procedure.

TABLE 6f Position in the Church by Age Group (%)

	\multicolumn{9}{c}{POSITION IN CHURCH}
	Curate	Chaplain	Diocesan	Vicar	Incumbent	Rector	Dignitary	Retired	Other
Young N=374	25.9	21.9	14.7	16.5	12	2.4	1.6	0.5	4.5
Middle N=463	30.9	18.2	8.4	12.3	20.1	5.8	0.6	2.1	0.8
Older N=375	37.9	9.6	6.4	5.3	9.3	1.3	1.3	24.3	0.6
$p \leq 0.000$									

Age is a factor which affects women's employment status in the Church, as Table 6f demonstrates. However, it is not, as one might expect, younger, more inexperienced women, who are at junior levels in the Church. In fact, women from the older age group are more likely to hold junior positions in the Church hierarchy. This can be accounted for by the fact that those affected by the age bar are unable to be stipendiary and are therefore at junior levels in the Church. Similarly other women from the older age group are retired, but are actively functioning as assistant priests. In contrast, younger women are more likely to be in chaplaincy or diocesan posts. Since responsibility for childcare affects the position a woman holds in the Church, and younger women are more likely to have dependent children, this relationship is partly explained by women's family responsibilities. Whilst younger women are in team vicar posts, it is members of the bridge generation, who have been in stipendiary positions for some years, who hold incumbent, rector and dignitary posts. This suggests that there is career progression for the first women priests which is based on length of service, experience and stipendiary position. Time will show if the relationship between age and diocesan/chaplaincy roles is to be permanently linked to childcare responsibilities or whether parochial ministry will develop in ways which suit younger women with family responsibilities.

The fact that women are not yet in senior positions in the Church is cause for concern and women's progress should continue to be monitored carefully.[19] However, women's status in the Church in relation to their male colleagues is even more alarming. Drawing on statistics from the Advisory Board of Ministry, Figure 6g shows a comparison of men's and women's employment status in the Church of England (1997). Women make up 14% of licensed ministers in the Church but only 4% of dignitaries are women: the majority of clergy are deployed at a parish level and yet women make up only 9% of parochial clergy. Conversely, women constitute 17% of clergy employed in a diocesan or chaplaincy post, and 31 % of those in the Church Army. However, it is the statistics concerning women's position as unpaid ministers which are most concerning, 31% of non-stipendiary posts are held by women. The picture is clear, women are more likely to be in jobs that are removed from the mainstream parochial ministry of the Church. They appear to be developing different career patterns from men in positions that are away from the centres of Church hierarchy. This is a trend which is

FIGURE 6g The Employment Status of Men and Women in the Church

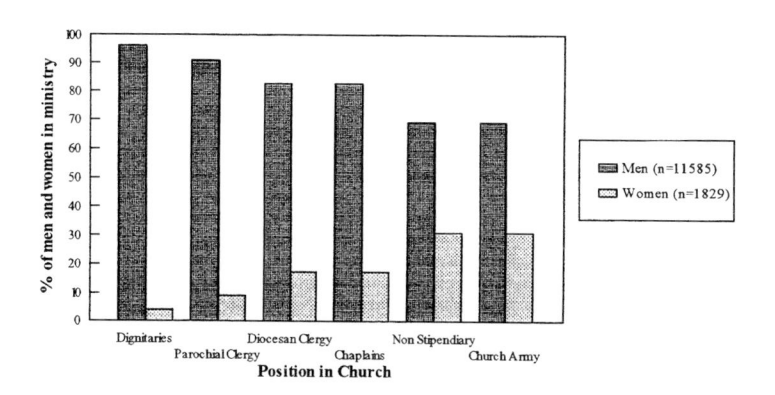

of concern, particularly if it is not the result of women's choice. Women's narratives, both in interview and written data, give a clearer account of their experiences at the margins of the Church. Their accounts of chaplaincy, sector and non-stipendiary ministry, plus their difficulties in getting jobs, reveal the extent to which some women feel marginalised in the Church.

Women in Non-stipendary Ministry

A third of women priests ordained in 1994-1995 are working for the Church in a non-stipendiary capacity (this includes women who may be paid as a chaplain by an institution whilst also acting as a non-stipendiary minister in a parish Church). Of this figure, only 12% had actually made a positive choice to be NSM: either because they preferred the freedom, did not need the money, felt called to be NSM or to remain in secular work. From the remaining 88% of non-stipendiary women priests,[20] 23% said they had not chosen to be non-stipendiary. Some women felt their diocese had implied their only option was to be NSM, others that they were finding difficulty getting a stipendiary post:

> When I first made enquiries about the possibility of ordination, an immediate assumptions was made that it would mean NSM as my three children at that stage were still fairly young. I didn't have the knowledge, awareness or confidence at the time to challenge this. The options were never made clear to me.

17% said they were non-stipendiary because it suited their family circumstances and once again women are forced to choose specific career options because of their family responsibilities:

> I trained for stipendiary ministry and worked for two years before I married - this meant a move of parish and diocese and a change to non-stipendiary ministry. I would like to have the option to return to stipendiary ministry in the future but this looks very unlikely unless I move into sector ministry.

Finally, age is a contributory factor to whether or not a woman is non-stipendiary. 43% of non-stipendiary women are either retired, but actively involved in the Church in an unpaid ministerial capacity, or too old to hold a stipendiary post. The rule which stopped priests over 45 from holding their first stipendiary post has clearly discriminated against the first group of women priests. Too old to hold a stipendiary position, many of the first women priests therefore hold junior non-stipendiary positions in the Church.

In general, women who have remained with their home parish for a number of years felt their experiences in the Church had been positive and supportive. These women have been recognised by their parish (who have supported them for ordination), have trained locally, (on the LNSM training scheme) and now work in their home parish in a non-stipendiary capacity:

> In my own parish, because I trained whilst a member of the congregation (with the local ministerial scheme) I have always felt tremendous love and support. I have been very blessed.

Where the ministry of women is owned and supported at a local level, women's experiences of being non-stipendiary are positive. However, for the majority of those in non-stipendiary ministry, they can feel overlooked, undervalued and overused by the Church:

> As a full-time NSM I share with at least one other colleague in similar circumstances a feeling of being exploited. We feel that the institutional Church of England and the universal Church of God are poles apart.

The status of non-stipendiary priests is clearly perceived as being inferior or "second-class" to stipendiary priests in the Church. Financially, unless they have an alternative source of income, women are disadvantaged. For instance, fees for funerals and weddings undertaken by NSM priests are collected into general parish finances, rather than being passed onto the priests who conducted the service. Since women are disproportionately in NSM or LNSM positions (see Figure 6g) it is clear they are disadvantaged and marginalised in Church structures. The Church of England aimed to train 245 men and 305 women as non-stipendiary ministers in 1998: so the disproportionate number of women NSM priests, compared to men, is being continued. Whether the issues experienced by women priests are gender based or not, it is clear that the Church must address the ways in which it uses non-stipendiary ministry. People willing to use their gifts and talents in an unpaid capacity for the Church are a valuable resource. The Church must ensure that non-stipendiary ministers feel supported, valued and affirmed:

> The "struggle" for me is increasingly to do with the frustrations of being non-stipendiary priest, who is under used and rather bored because her talents are no longer being developed.

Women in Chaplaincy/Sector Ministry

The qualitative analysis of interviews and written data shows clear themes relating to chaplaincy or sector ministry.[21] First, chaplaincy was seen, by many, as a positive place to work. Women felt affirmed and accepted in the workplace in a way that they did not feel in parish ministry:

> My work in the university is very liberating and empowering, but the longer I work in this sector, the more petty-minded and irrelevant the life of the Church seems to become.

Despite the fact that prisons, universities and hospitals are not generally seen as model equal opportunity employers, these secular institutions are perceived as affirming women priests in a way that the Church as an employer is not. Whilst in the Church the role of the priest is sacramental, in secular organisations the priest also fulfils a functional role, with a clear job description and line management structure:

> In hospital and other sector ministry it's been slightly different, because as far as the hospital is concerned, as long as you can do the job, it doesn't matter if you are male or female. Individual members of staff will find it difficult, individual patients will find it difficult, but the institution as a whole doesn't.

Implicit in this quotation is the notion that the Church of England, as an institution, does find the concept of women priests difficult. Therein lies the problem for women in parish ministry and the advantage, for women, of being in chaplaincy or sector ministry. The fact that gender is seen as immaterial by secular organisations, in a way that it is not by the Church, leaves women in sector ministry feeling more accepted and affirmed. This, in turn, may partly account for the higher proportion of women in chaplaincy ministry than in parochial ministry (see Figure 6g). For critics of equal opportunities legislation, it should be pointed out that one of the main differences between the Church of England and secular institutions is that the latter are subject to equal opportunity requirements through employment law, from which the former is exempt. The question for women priests, therefore, is whether they can truly be accepted within Church structures whilst they fail to be protected by employment law?

> Equal opportunity is a real issue in the hospital, but not so in the institutional Church. I feel like "me" again - a person; not a "woman deacon" or a "woman priest". I grieve that the spirit of truth and justice and equity is frequently more visible outside, than inside, the Church.

The second theme arising from the qualitative analysis focuses on the role and function of the priest in a secular institution. The sacramental role of the priest in chaplaincy ministry is limited; therefore women priests have had to develop a new understanding of their priestly role.[22] The priesthood is redefined in order to be relevant to the secular environment of chaplaincy, but also in order to distinguish the role of the priest from other support and counselling roles in the institution. In chaplaincy, the role of the priest is at the cutting edge of where life and faith meet. The chaplain explores the concept of spirituality in the market place, and women priests have demonstrated ways in which they have adapted the sacramental role of the priest within secular organisations. One woman told how she heard confession and gave absolution in a hospital corridor. A prison chaplain described how a prisoner, convicted of murdering his wife, took communion for the first time from her. As a woman in prison chaplaincy, she felt her presence offered a symbol of hope and forgiveness. Similarly the use of vestments was adapted, in another situation, to the needs of a hospital setting:

> I want to talk about a priest as a bridge builder, as an interpreter of stories and dreams, of trying to give people hope, of trying to be a symbol that God is actually involved in the mess of their lives. When I first came here, I used to robe to take communion round the wards - now I don't.... Everyone is in their pyjamas, they're sweaty and smelly and I swan in with my robes. So actually to say God comes to you in your clutter, in your mess, in your bits of broken crumbs and things, is quite important.

Whether this redefinition of priesthood is unique to women chaplains or not, I cannot tell. What I can say, however, is that in the secular market place of the hospital, the prison, the school or the university, women priests feel more affirmed and accepted. Women chaplains are seeking to understand the meaning of their sacramental role in secular institutions, they are questioning the role of the priest in modern society in a way that women in parish ministry do not appear to be doing.

Getting a Job

23% of women priests have moved diocese since being ordained. A quarter of those have done so because of difficulties with other clergy in their home diocese, or because they have experienced difficulties in getting jobs.[23] The analysis of qualitative data reveals why this might be the case. Whilst not all women have experienced difficulty getting suitable posts, clearly a number have found deployment issues problematic - something which they attribute to the fact that they are women:

> I physically looked at more than 30 posts when looking for a new job - frequently meeting either sexism, or ageism or both. I met such comments as "there are too many women in this deanery" (2 out of 8) and "I don't know how you run a house, family and do a job".

Whilst this has been the experience of some women, there is a much wider perception amongst other respondents, that women are not being given more senior posts. There is a clear feeling that a "stained glass" ceiling is in operation within the Church:

> For me personally I am now experiencing a sense of being ignored and disregarded - almost worse than overt hostility - in the matter of a senior appointment. Lip service to my ability and gifts and no chance or opportunity to exercise them, with an alarming sense of anger and frustration building again.

My research, because it is entirely based on women's perspectives, cannot investigate the truth of individual claims, but the fact that there is a strong sense among women that discrimination exists in relation to senior appointments, is an indicator of employment problems women face in the Church. The Church can argue that men also have these experiences of being overlooked, but since it is exempt from employment law, there is no official record-keeping and therefore women's claims about discrimination are difficult to refute. Proper equal opportunity monitoring would ensure a degree of transparency in Church appointments which does not presently exist. The fact that Resolutions A, B and C enable parishes to choose not to have a woman priest (in a way that no secular organisation can), suggests that women's feelings of being discriminated against are factual and not fictitious. The Church cannot counter women's claims of prejudice unless it legislates against sexist bias in appointments. At present that legislation does not exist, so the Church must listen, with humility, to women's experiences of discrimination. It must hear women's growing voices of anger and frustration.

THEOLOGICAL ORIENTATION

One of the distinguishing features of the Church of England is that it posesses a broad theological base. The three main theological positions in the Church are catholic, liberal and evangelical, but in reality, people identify their theological position in a more sophisticated way. The questionnaire asked respondents to identify their theological orientation from a choice of seven categories (see Figure 6h). This was a contentious question, and in the pilot stage of the research a number of people commented that they would have liked a mainstream Anglican category. Similarly, 3.6% of respondents chose not to answer this question, disliking to give themselves a particular theological label. However, I chose to risk leaving the question as it was, in order to force people to show a preference for their theological orientation. I feared that a mainstream Anglican category would allow people to fudge their theological preferences, and I suspected that theological orientation might well be an important variable when attempting to understand different attitudes and experiences.

FIGURE 6h Theological Orientation of Women Priests (%)

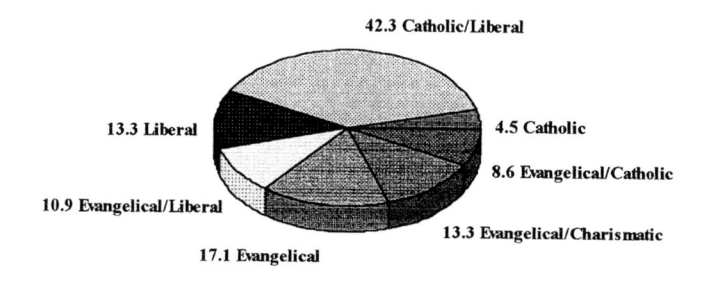

- 42.3 Catholic/Liberal
- 4.5 Catholic
- 8.6 Evangelical/Catholic
- 13.3 Evangelical/Charismatic
- 17.1 Evangelical
- 10.9 Evangelical/Liberal
- 13.3 Liberal

Figure 6h shows that 42.3% of women described themselves as catholic/liberal [24] and an overwhelming 66.2% clustered themselves around the liberal tag, including 10.5% who said they were evangelical/liberal. 40% of women described themselves as evangelical in some way; in fact, evangelical/charismatic was the second largest category with 13.3% classing themselves in this way. Only 4.5% saw themselves as anglo-catholic, but over half described their worship as containing some catholic element (evangelical/catholic and charismatic/catholic).[25] Whether or not theological orientation is a predictor of women's attitudes, approaches and experiences of ministry will be explored in the following chapters. However, the first group of women priests is evidently drawn from a broad range of theological perspectives. This suggests that an individual's call or vocation to priesthood is stronger than any internal theological arguments or obstacles. Women from different ecclesiastical traditions have been able to interpret their theological position in a way which affirms, rather than denies, women's priesthood.

Women priests are not a homogeneous group; they are diverse, complex and varied as a group and they cannot be easily labelled. Their experiences and backgrounds should not be caricatured through over-simplification, yet as I have explored the unfolding patterns and stories in the research, themes have emerged. The first group of women priests in the Church of England are women with a depth of experience in Church ministry, they bring a wealth of professional acumen, and are well educated. Despite this, there are disturbing patterns in women's employment which suggest that their ordained ministry is in danger of being marginalised by the Church. Here are a highly educated and professional group of women from largely middle class backgrounds. Having proved themselves able to succeed in the secular world, women have used these experiences to support and affirm their journey into priesthood. Yet their origins and occupations are also cause for concern. If the only women to succeed in the Church are those who can compete with men, how can women challenge the male dominated hierarchy of the Church? Where are the voices of the non-white, the working class or non-professional people? Can or will women make space for them to be heard?

Here too is a group of women with a depth of Church experience which spans three generations. Many have served the Church in a variety of roles and, though priesthood became possible in their lifetime, it was not soon enough to allow them to exercise it fully. Some women in the older generation who watched and waited, because of their age still find themselves in junior roles which are subservient to another (usually male) priest.

Finally, here is a group of women with emerging career patterns that suggest women's ministry is in danger of being overlooked in the Church. Women are disproportionately represented in chaplaincy, sector or non-stipendiary roles which are traditionally seen as separate and apart from the mainstream activity of the Church. Most disturbing is the impact that a woman's marital and family status has on her career opportunities. Clearly women with young families, or who are married to priests, are struggling to sustain mainstream careers. For women with family responsibilities these difficulties are not just structural, but arise from a deep seated conflict between the discourses of motherhood and priesthood: both demand women to be self-giving, concerned for, and available to others. If women try to do both, they do so at a cost to themselves, their family and the development of their congregations.

Ultimately women need to challenge the traditional roles they are adopting. As priests, their position of total availability can create an unhelpful, disempowering dependency in their congregations. Women must be prepared to challenge the structurelessness of parish life, to debate the role of the priest and to change the structures of the Church in order to create an egalitarian, less hierarchical, model of priesthood. Similarly, whilst women still accept the total responsibility for childcare and family maintenance, they will be the ones who must compromise in other areas of life. Unless co-parenting, part-time work and job sharing become acceptable career choices for both women and men, then women will always have to make compromises.

Finally, the emerging patterns of women's ministry need to be challenged if women are to achieve equality in the Church. However, women must ask themselves whether equal status with men is enough if it maintains the power hierarchy of the priesthood. The Church needs new models of priesthood for the twenty-first century based on equality and empowerment, models which break down barriers between lay and ordained, male and female, stipendiary and non-stipendiary, powerful and powerless. Women are in a unique position to be initiators of change. Women's memories of being on the edge, marginalised and broken, are fresh. They have entered the priesthood in sufficient numbers, so that the critical mass of women, whilst still not comparable to men, is substantial enough to begin working for change. Finally, in MOW and its daughter organisation WATCH, women priests have a framework for support and campaigning which has the capacity to operate at a local and a national level. Women priests, if they remain connected with their lay sisters, have the potential to be a powerful movement for change and development in the Church.

CHAPTER 7

WOMEN PRIESTS - THEIR EXPERIENCES

As individuals we are defined not only by our internal character and belief systems, but also by the things that happen to us. Experience affects our responses to the situations we encounter in the same way that attitudes and values do. In the previous chapter I examined the backgrounds of the first women priests in the Church of England, looking at that which they carry into priesthood: experiences from their careers, from their family lives, from their social class and from their education. In this chapter the focus is on women's experiences of priesthood. For, just as the past shapes the present reactions of women priests, so current experiences will shape the way in which they respond in the future. What happens to them now has implications, not only for the women themselves, but for the women who will follow them into ministry. A feminist approach requires that women's experiences are spoken out, that they are listened to, so that they can become part of our corporate history. The stories of women priests are recorded here. There is no doubt that what has happened to them will affect the way in which they approach their future. The challenge for the Church is to learn from these experiences so that the future for tomorrow's women can be shaped for the better.

Past experiences constitute personal history. To make sense of their history, individuals re-interpret these experiences in order to construct a narrative which they can use to retell their stories. Vieda Skultan's book *The Testimony of Lives, Narrative and Memory in Post-Soviet Latvia* (1998) claims that on one hand narratives are factual presentations of historical events, but they are also selective, individualised windows on the past. The themes, strategies and concepts used to structure individual stories are as significant as the content of the narratives. The shared devices used to structure accounts are of interest because they point to the collective elements of our past. Memories and their meanings are conveyed as much by the form of story telling as by their content.[1] As Skultans says:

> My approach does not challenge the truth of the past as witnessed, but rather investigates the cultural resources used to make sense of the past and incorporate it into a personal history. (Skultans 1998:27)

As I recount the experiences of the first group of women priests in the Church of England, I am concerned both with the content of individual narratives and with their form. Shared devices for retelling stories are highlighted here alongside mutual experiences of priesthood,[2] but there is no one universal set of experiences common to all women priests - the truth, as ever, is multi-faceted. Yet there are patterns, motifs of experience that interweave with patterns in narrative construction to form a picture of the collective whole. Themes emerged from the initial interviews with women priests, then were tested in the questionnaire and re-visited in the analysis of the qualitative comments and the further interviews. Patterns of call, patterns of identity, patterns of fulfilment and patterns of pain emerged.

First, women's experiences of their call to priesthood are examined and, in many cases, they co-exist with a sense of vocation for women. The experience of call is also an important narrative device which helps women priests to make sense of the conflict that their priesthood has engendered in the Church. Secondly, women's experiences of identity in the Church are investigated, looking at the strength of their identification with the institution of the Church and questioning the extent to which this identification will affect women's capabilities to challenge Church structures. Again, identity with the Church is a device for dealing with conflict, but it is a factor which may ultimately impinge on women's ability to challenge the very structures they identify with. Finally, women's experiences in the Church are explored. Here bitter-sweet accounts of women's stories of pain and rejection are interwoven with narratives of acceptance, love and fulfilment. My challenge is to capture the complexities of these accounts which are so often polarised in the sensationalised press reports of women's difficult experiences post-ordination. Once again the concept of individual narratives is important, as women construct their stories in a way which enables them to tell of their suffering in the context of their success. Ultimately these accounts are a rich well of information, in which the way that narratives are shaped is as significant as the stories being told.

EXPERIENCES OF CALL

Call and vocation are concepts which are interrelated; they can be interchangeable in their everyday usage - they are also heterogeneous. The differentiation between call and vocation is important: whilst both words describe a sense of higher purpose, call is associated with the "language-game" of ministry, and vocation with the "language-game" of the professions. Call relates, almost exclusively, to the religious or spiritual life and involves external affirmation from a higher being concerning an individual's direction in life.[3] Vocation also denotes a sense of call, but it describes an internal process whereby an individual develops a sense of fitness for a particular profession or ministry. Call is essentially external, it involves outside, divine endorsement which can be inversely linked to the recipient's sense of unworthiness or inability to undertake the task they are being called to. Vocation is predominantly internal affirmation, linked to a growing confirmation about the suitability of a particular path or direction in life. It is used in a religious context, but also in the professional arenas where an individual may have a vocation to nursing, teaching or medicine.

In my research the analysis of the initial interviews showed that the two concepts were used dichotomously, women priests either described their journey into priesthood as a result of a clear external call from God or because of a developing sense of internal vocation.[4] This dualistic expression of call and vocation suggested that other factors, for instance age or theological orientation, could explain the different ways in which women interpret and explain their reasons for entering the priesthood. Two opposing questions linked to call and vocation were included in the questionnaire to ascertain what factors, if any, contributed to women's differing understanding of these concepts. The results were surprising: 84.5% of respondents said that God had spoken directly to them about entering the Church, but 81% also said that their sense of vocation had developed gradually. The concepts of call and vocation were not *independent* as I had envisaged but were, for many women, *interdependent*. The discrepancy between personal experiential accounts in the interviews and self-categorisation in the questionnaire with regards to call and vocation is explored further through an analysis of narrative construction in section 7.1.2. First, I return to the statistical evidence to explore, in more depth, women's responses to call and vocation as expressed in the survey.

Experiences of Call and Vocation - A Quantitative View

The purpose of investigating women's experiences of call and vocation through the survey was to examine what factors affected women's reasons for wanting to be priests.

TABLE 7a
Relationship between Women Priests' Sense of Call and Vocation (%)

		Vocation Developed Gradually	
		Yes	*No*
Direct Call from God	Yes	78.2 (66)	21.8 (19.1)
	No	94.6 (14.5)	5.4 (0.8)

$p \leq 0.000$ n = 1199

Table 7a illustrates the strength of relationship between a direct call from God and a growing sense of vocation and shows that there is a statistical connection: 78.2% of people who had a direct call from God also had a developing sense of vocation. The figures in brackets show the percentage of the total population of the study in each category, there is a strong predilection towards both call and vocation (66% of women said they had both a strong call from God and a developing sense of vocation, only 0.8% expressed a preference for neither). From this simple cross-tabulation it is evident that call and vocation are clearly important concepts for women priests. However, a more sophisticated measure of calling was created in order to understand this issue in greater depth. A summated scale was developed which combined the responses to a set of questions relating to call, giving an overall score for each respondent. [5]

FIGURE 7b   Range of Scores on the Scale for Strong Sense of Call

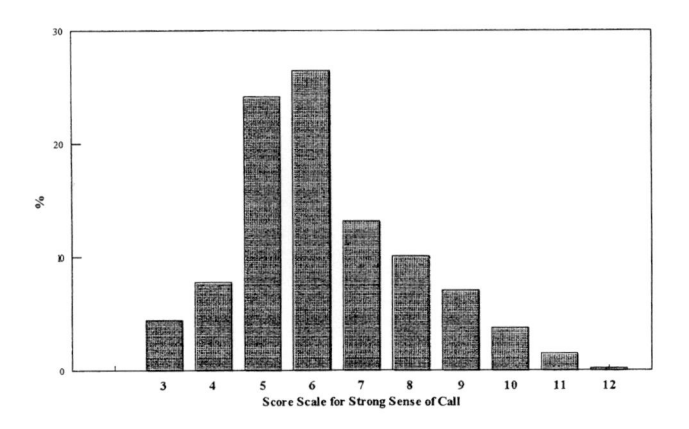

Figure 7b shows the distribution for the scale and illustrates the fact that a high proportion of women priests attribute their entry into the Church to an extrinsic intervention from God (64.3% of women identify themselves as having a strong sense of call). Clearly, for this first group of women priests their sense of call was important to them, but are there special factors which contribute to the emphasis that individual women place on their calling into the priesthood?

Age was possibly one such factor; younger women with their career expectations and access to education might be expected to express their journey into the priesthood in vocational, professional terms. This, however, was not the case: evidence showed that age had no bearing on the way in which women characterised their calling. One factor which did affect the way in which women described their entry to the priesthood was theological orientation. Women from an evangelical tradition were more likely to emphasise their calling from God than their liberal or catholic counterparts. Table 7c demonstrates that 70.7% of evangelical women described a stronger sense of call, compared to 60% of catholic and 57% of liberal women.

TABLE 7c   Expression of Call by Theological Orientation (%)

		Strong Sense of Call	*Weaker Sense of Call*
Theological Orientation	**Catholic**	60	40
	Liberal	57	43
	Evangelical	70.7	29.3

$p \leq 0.000$ n=1032

In each of the theological traditions over 50% of women expressed a strong identification with call, but for women from an evangelical heritage this tendency was accentuated. Theologically evangelicalism emphasises an individual's intimate, direct relationship with God which is established initially through personal repentance. From thereon the concept that God can intervene directly in a person's life is acceptable currency in the evangelical tradition. Women priests who express some affinity with evangelicalism are therefore more likely to experience and express their journey to priesthood as a direct response to God's intervention in their lives.

However, there is an important distinction to be made here between the concepts of experience and expression: some women have clearly experienced their call in a direct and distinct way whilst others, although they have experienced their vocation developing gradually, because of their theological background, express their call as a direct intervention from God:

> It was like a flash of light really. It happened all in one day, I can remember clearly when it was. It happened in an evening Church service...the speaker was talking about his work, sharing the faith, I just had the most extraordinary, overwhelming sense of God.

This quotation, from an evangelical woman, describes her experience of a direct call from God. In contrast, the following quotations, the first from an evangelical and the second from a catholic woman, describe a developing sense of vocation:

> I ended up teaching religious education and social studies for the next six years and it was during the latter half of that time that God started speaking about full time ministry in the Anglican Church. The way it was symbolised to me was that the desks just seemed to be getting in the way... and that's when I started exploring it with the Church that I was worshipping in.

> Slowly I began to think it was for me, I can't say I had any concrete sense of being called by God into this it was a bit like a drifting, except I knew I liked the work. Later on, when you realise that when things are enjoyable and fulfilling then, if you are not harming anyone, God's involved in it somewhere along the line.

Here, the woman from the evangelical tradition uses the expressions associated with her theological position as a way of describing her ongoing sense of vocation. The phrase "God started speaking" is more resonant with the concept of direct, divine intervention, yet it is actually relating to an indirect, developing sense of vocation. In contrast, the woman with a catholic background expresses the same sense of vocation but in functional, rather than spiritual terms, "it was a bit like drifting". It is only with hindsight that she credits this experience as being connected with God.

Theological orientation does influence the way in which women report their entry into the priesthood,[6] but it accentuates, rather than fundamentally changes, an existing relationship between calling and the first group of women priests. Women from an evangelical position already have a theological heritage which links their life-patterns with Godly intervention: for some women this heritage affects the way in which they express their calling rather than the essential way in which they experience it. Theological orientation is an indicator of how women priests describe their sense of calling and/or vocation, but it is not the only explanation. Exploring women's narratives of call in the qualitative analysis, further develops an understanding of why individual call is important to this group of women.

Narratives of Call - A Qualitative View

Call is evidently a significant, collective device in women priests' construction of their priesthood narratives. By examining the organisation of these accounts I am not denying their factual content, but through exploring women's use of call in their narratives I can better understand their experiences. Primarily, I believe that call is used as a device for dealing with the conflict that women's priesthood has brought and as a context for women's own personal suffering. Women, in general, are uncomfortable at being the source of division, their role in families (which is reflected in wider society) is often to maintain and support the equilibrium of relationships: they are perceived as carers, nurturers, healers and peace makers. The concepts of unity, harmony and self-sacrifice which, rightly or wrongly, have become associated with Christianity, further disadvantage women making it almost impossible for them to juxtapose faith and conflict in their lives, however legitimate their cause.

Secondly, call is used in narratives to consolidate women's right of entry to the priesthood, as this first group of women was seeking entrance to a position in the Church that they could not legally hold in the past. Women were asking the Church of England to change 2,000 years of deep-seated tradition, throwing relationships with two other main Christian denominations into turmoil and possibly causing division in their congregations, dioceses and the Church as a whole. It is no wonder that in women's narratives licence to seek these changes comes mainly from a Divine, not an earthly source. Whereas entry into professions such as teaching, medicine and the law concerned equity for women, entry into the Church as priests is not just a matter of equality for women, it is connected with God's will.

One woman describes her sense of call by referring to a cartoon in which a woman is speaking on the phone, a voice says "this is God calling". Her response is to reply "but I am a woman". There are faint echoes in this modern story with the Annunciation, where God speaks directly to Mary through the appearance of an angel and she responds with the question, "How can this be?". In using call as a strong theme in their narrative accounts, women priests are establishing a number of important points. First, by placing the emphasis on God speaking, women are also placing some of the responsibility for their actions with God. In some cases women's own will needed to be changed in order to be aligned to God's will, and therefore be obedient to divine call:

> The first struggle was to accept the concept (of women priests) and then eventually recover from the shock that God wanted me to be ordained. When I was made deacon in 1993 I had no sense that I should be a priest, three months later God dropped that bombshell.

This direct and lifechanging intervention from God is not something that can be argued with and, to an extent, claims a moral high ground. For whilst opponents of women's ministry can, and did, argue against the ordination of women on theological grounds, it is harder to discredit an individual account of God's intercession in their lives. In short, women recount their experience of God-affirmation in order to justify, often at an early stage in their narrative, the course they took in pursuing priesthood. In doing so, women are indicating that their motives for entering the priesthood were not selfish, but were in response to divine predication:

> After a lifetime of serving the Church with no thought of being ordained myself, but enthusiastically supporting friends I was "zapped" one Sunday morning and faced with the awesome inevitability. I could only think that Synod would vote yes if I were to start the whole process at God's command and get there before getting too old.

In this quotation the respondent indicates that her obedience to God's call was not solely a personal matter, but that her destiny was entwined with the future of women's ministry in the Church. As the narrative unfolds, it is clear that her acquiescence to God's call actually caused her personal suffering when the parish vicar refused to work with her after ordination. This animosity escalated, both for the respondent and her home parish, when members of the congregation were asked to vote about her future. The call to priesthood has clearly caused conflict for this woman priest; despite this her narrative begins with a clear affirmation of her calling in which she establishes her faithfulness to the Church, her lack of personal ambition, and finally God's unquestionable intervention in her life's purpose and plan. In this priesthood narrative call is a device by which personal suffering and the conflict that women's priesthood engendered, is contextualised and vindicated. The calling of God enables this respondent to make sense of the events leading up to, and after, her ordination, as a narrative device it signifies to the reader that the personal and corporate struggle generated by women's priesthood was a spiritual rather than an earthly concern.

Call is a source of strength and empowerment which has sustained women as they journeyed to priesthood, giving them a framework to understand their own, and other people's, resulting suffering:

> I believe I had a clear call to ministry but I didn't know what to think. The Church told me it couldn't be to the priesthood but at theological college I realised this was only because I was female. My call was the same as the men's, perhaps stronger, because despite suffering greatly from the persecution of the "antis", I couldn't give it up.

In many cases a call from God is confirmed by a respected outsider who, in some instances, recognises it before the woman herself. The presence in the narratives of a respected figure from the Church establishment, who is often male, underlines the rightness of women's priesthood. The existence of these "key others", who affirmed and spurred women towards ministry, is linked to their individual experiences of God's call and this gives credence to their ordination. Again, often situated early on in the narratives, the external affirmer, placed contiguously with the call of God, consolidates and legitimises women's position in the Church and repudiates criticism about their ordination:

> One night the minister came round and said "look how long are you going on with this (being indecisive), am I phoning the diocese tomorrow?"

> One day I plucked up courage and said to him (my vicar) "You know I would really love perhaps to be a deaconess". He said "We've all been waiting for you to see that" - it was so encouraging, it really was.

Together call and affirmation deflect the responsibility for the pain caused by women's ordination, counteract any criticism of self-promotion and demonstrate that the personal experience of God's call has been recognised by the wider Church.

I began by demonstrating that for 66% of women priests, their external experience of God's call was accompanied by a growing inner sense of vocation. Far from being dichotomous experiences, call and vocation were, for many, interdependent. In the following quotation the respondent demonstrates how vocation and calling can co-exist:

> I had a strong sense of vocation with a series of experiences of God, quite suddenly, without which it might not have occurred to me that God could ask something the Church was not saying. However it took me a turbulent time, which demanded a lot of inner growing to accept the truth of it and discern the direction.

In this quotation the external call or experience of God provides the respondent with the paradigm shift needed to embrace her growing internal process of awareness that was leading her to the priesthood. The presence of the emotional (an experience of call) and the intellectual (a developing sense of vocation) enables this woman to develop her own self-understanding and cope with the inner and outer turbulence implicated in the ordination of women. The fact that call and vocation are intrinsic elements of women's experiences of priesthood is, I believe, healthy and positive. In their pioneering, this first group of women priests, drew on internal and external, emotional and intellectual processes to discern the rightness of their cause and to gain strength for the pain their priesthood caused themselves and others.

EXPERIENCES OF IDENTITY

There is no doubt that the ordination of women has caused conflict, disunity and schism in the Church of England: the fact that the non-ordination of women also caused conflict, disunity and had the potential to cause schism is rarely alluded to. In patriarchal structures, women's oppression becomes the status quo, it incurs no comment. Women, well-schooled in the suppression of their needs and wants, have concurred with the maintenance of patriarchy through their own continued silence. In the Church this first group of priests was part of a wider movement of women whose convictions about women's ordination gave them courage to speak out, to name the injustice of their exclusion, and to work for change. We know precisely the number of male priests who have left the Church of England because women were ordained,[7] but there are no records of the women, hurt by the Church's attitude to them and disillusioned with the political wranglings about their ordination, who simply and quietly left the Church. The 1547 women who were ordained in 1994-1995 had chosen to stay. Their commitment to their Church and/or the priesthood meant there was nowhere else for them to go. A sense of calling and vocation helped women to overcome their innate discomfort at being the focus of disunity in the Church, and their identity with the Church provided women with the strength to stay engaged with its structures. However, allegiance to the Church also became a source of inner conflict as women ordinands had to experience being the cause of pain in the Church they had strong links with.

Experiences of denominational loyalty or strong identification with the Church of England are of significance for this first group of women priests: allegiance to the Church will make it difficult for women to be a source of conflict, and affiliation to the Church's structures will affect women's ability to challenge its patriarchal structures. When a scale was created for denominational loyalty [8] from the survey responses, 65% of women priests showed strong allegiance to the Church of England. The relationship between theological orientation and denominational loyalty was investigated and it was stronger for women from the catholic tradition than for women from the liberal or evangelical traditions. Figure 7d illustrates this, with 73.6% of catholic women showing strong allegiance to the Church, compared to 60% of liberals and 56.3% of evangelicals. Catholicism emphasises the importance of the Church, through the Church God's will is made known, and in it God's purposes are worked out. The relationship between Christ and the people is embodied in the person of the priest who acts as Christ's representative in the Church. In the catholic heritage the structure and practice of the Church is God-inspired and is a symbol: it speaks to the people of God and through the priest, Christ mediates between God and humanity.

FIGURE 7d
Loyalty to the Church by Theological Orientation (%)

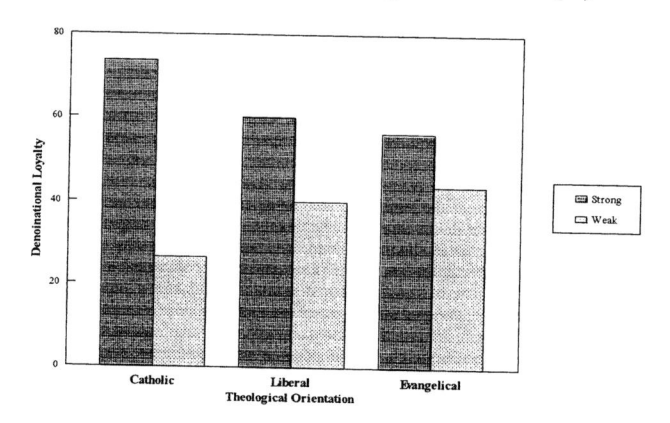

In her book *Women at the Altar,* Lavinia Byrne speaks of this symbolism as a "dynamic pattern which gives great energy and authority to those who send and those who are sent", but she also points out that because of its representative nature "the priesthood is tied into a hierarchical system of Church leadership" (1994:6). For women whose theological inheritance is captured in the symbolism of the Church, identification with, and allegiance to, that Church is fundamental. Again theological orientation accentuates an existing characteristic in this first group of women priests: it emphasises rather than changes, women's commitment to the structure and practices of the Church. Ecclesiastical allegiance and belief in Church structures has enabled women to remain loyal even though it appeared, at times, to be discounting their ministry. Faith in the Church is a source of hope which has sustained women on their long journey to the priesthood, but it was also a cause of conflict:

> My feminism and theology told me women's ordination was right, my grief at the pain in the Church on all sides meant I had difficulty being too exuberant about it.

> Women have a lot to offer the Church but many of us have been conditioned to accept whatever we are offered and be grateful and then told to keep quiet in order for the Church to see how good we are.

Denominational loyalty to the Church of England is a factor which enabled women to stay engaged with an institution which denied them access: by remaining in the organisation, either through campaigning or simply demonstrating that they could do the job, the tide turned, and women were given entry to the priesthood. However, the sense of allegiance which sustained women now has the potential to silence them. Women have experienced being the focus of disunity in a Church to which they hold a strong sense of loyalty; women's social roles are historically linked to relationship maintenance and therefore the pressure internally, and externally, for women priests is to stop fighting, stay quiet and work to reconcile the fragmentation they are perceived to have caused.[9]

Guilt sits easily on women's shoulders; it disempowers and immobilises, seeking out and manipulating areas of vulnerability. Women's identity with the Church of England, coupled with an innate fear of causing disharmony, may well immobilise and silence women priests. Patriarchy is still a dominant force in the Church, it is the true cause of the suffering, resulting from women's ordination, that the Church now feels. There is a real danger that women will take the responsibility for this suffering upon themselves. Blinded by their allegiance to the Church, women could fail to press on towards the equality they deserve. In doing so the Church may be denied the full inheritance of women's ministry.

EXPERIENCES OF THE CHURCH

Publicly the media have emphasised the personal struggles and negative effect that the ordination of women has had on the Church, with stories of abuse, employment difficulties and conflict in parishes caused by the presence of women priests.[10] Undoubtedly these sensationalist press stories reflect women's experiences in the Church, but they also obfuscate another reality for women, masking the positive effects, both personally and corporately, of their priesthood. Women's experiences of the Church cannot be simply characterised as good or bad, they are multi-layered: women priests have experienced warmth, openness, acceptance and support, but they have also been subject to bigger antagonism, oppression and abuse. Their narratives are bitter-sweet, a cacophonous interweaving of pain and joy which leave the reader confused, questioning the co-existence of rejection and affirmation, the intermingling of individual suffering and personal fulfilment in women's accounts.

So just how have women priests been received by the Church at large? This question is addressed by examining both the content and the construction of women's accounts of their experiences in the Church. Narratively painful experiences are retold in my research as "horror stories", and positive affirmation is presented in the form of "success stories". These two types of narratives have clear textual use, allowing women to speak of their suffering without diminishing their success.[11]

Experiences of the Church - A Quantitative View

It is clear that being ordained priest has had many positive personal implications for the respondents - it has brought a sense of great fulfilment, completeness and joy. Three quarters of women priests said that being able to preside at the eucharist was an important, significant benefit of their priesthood. Half the respondents felt affirmed in their vocation, and 40% felt they had gained confidence through their priesting. A third of women priests felt affirmed by the Church and members of the public, whilst 25% said they had gained authority through their ordination. Priesthood has been a source of great personal growth, development and fulfilment for this first group of women:

> Ordination to the priesthood has been a most incredible part of my own spiritual journey. I continuously feel that I am on the brink of new ground to be explored and shared. It is a great privilege to be asked to be here at this particular time in history and a great freedom is found in not having any role models.

Women were also asked in the questionnaire about their positive and negative experiences in the Church, with questions ranging from instances of positive affirmation in their role of priest through to experiences of abusive behaviour or sexual harrassment.[12] Each of the variables in this section had been identified through the initial interviews and were thus embedded in women's experiences of the Church. The resulting analysis showed a mixed reaction to women's ordination from clergy and parishioners.[13] However, the clearest response came when 91.2% of women priests said they felt that other women in the Church had gained confidence because there was a woman priest.

In order to understand more fully the implications from this set of variables, a factor analysis was carried out to see which sets of answers varied together. Three factors with *eigenvalues* over one were identified.[14] The first is institutional and it includes difficult experiences within the structures of the Church, in particular with fellow clergy. Factor two includes difficult experiences within the local Church setting, particularly with members of the public or parishioners, and factor three is again focused on the local Church setting but includes positive experiences with members of the public or parishioners. A score for individual respondents was calculated for each factor and the results in Figure 7e (see next page) show the percentage of women priests who have experienced either institutional or parish difficulties, or who have been positively affirmed at a local level.

Over half of women priests have experienced difficulties at a local Church level, but more women (58%) have also been positively affirmed locally. For women priests, their experience at a local Church level has been mixed: some parishioners have been affirming and supportive whilst others have rejected their ministry. The question, both for women priests and for the Church, is whether or not the negative attitudes expressed by parishioners and members of the public are entrenched or transitory: if former applies then there are serious implications for the integration of women into the life and structures of the Church.

FIGURE 7e Positive Scores on Factor Scales for Experiences in the Church

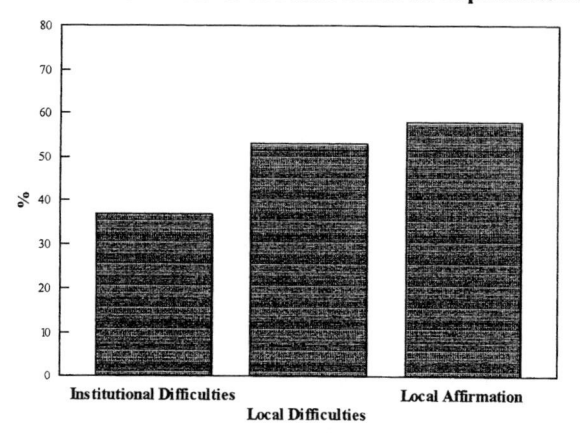

The evidence from the qualitative analysis, however, suggests that at a parish level, negative responses to women priests are circumstantial and that most opposition from the laity disintegrates as people experience the ministry of women. In both the interviews and the qualitative section of The evidence from the qualitative analysis, however, suggests that at a parish level, negative the questionnaire, stories of individual parishioner's conversion to women's ministry were prolific:

> In my present post I was informed by one couple that they did not agree with having a woman here. They said they would continue their jobs (verger and parish clerk), but that I ought to understand their stance. Thankfully, I converted them with the first funeral I took and have continued to change their opinion ever since.

> Several people have been very willing to confess their previous attitude and say how wrong they were.

Women priests have experienced the dissolution of opposition as people have encountered their ministry; similarly they report many instances of positive congregational support and affirmation, often in contrast to the negative responses from fellow clergy and the Church institution:

> I find it extremely hard to cope with the attitudes and negative behaviour of male clergy colleagues (ignoring me, patronising me, treating me like a bad smell) when I feel so affirmed by the congregation and the family.

> Generally being a woman priest in the Church has been received wonderfully by non-Church goers, more mixed by Church-goers - but no direct confrontation and generally very positive, and the bitterest, rudest reception has been from fellow clergy. "I heard you did quite well at the funeral considering you are a woman." "What do they call you then - priestess?" "You've betrayed Christ and destroyed the Church."

Statistically there is evidence of institutional difficulties for women priests (see Figure 7e) as 37% of respondents had experienced problems with fellow clergy or with the structures of the Church, a figure which is unacceptably high. Results from the questionnaire demonstrate that women's reception by the Church has been mixed: a confusion of positive congregational affirmation with institutional obstacles and local parish difficulties. However, problems at a local congregational level are more prevalent than at an institutional level, showing a discrepancy between the self-reported difficulties in the survey and the presentation of the qualitative accounts of women's experiences.

Although they are still alarmingly high, levels of institutional opposition are actually less than the reports of local, parish-based difficulties. Yet in their accounts, women priests present a different view: congregational support and public acceptance contrast with reports of rudeness, opposition and even abuse from fellow clergy. In essence both realities are true, but the effects of ecclesiastical intransigence are more powerfully felt and are contrasted with the temporary nature of lay opposition. Success stories, or accounts of individual conversions to the ministry of women, are an important narrative device in women's accounts. They legitimate women's ordination by indicating how the Church has benefited from their ministry. These stories are inspirational, they promise hope for the future and put in perspective the painful, intimidating descriptions of rejection and abuse that women have experienced within the Church.

Dealing with Opposition and Constructing Success - A Qualitative View

Intertwined in women's priesthood narratives are accounts of personal, satisfying success and painfully alienating rejection which initially contradict each other in a confusion of messages, mystifying rather than clarifying women's experiences. These narratives are a mirror to human experience; life is not compartmentalised into good and bad encounters, it is a mystery of joy and pain. Yet in their stories, women priests also draw on some of the central metaphors of Christianity: the intermingling of death and resurrection, light and darkness, joy and suffering, which ultimately find their focus in the cross. At its heart, Christ's redemptive suffering on the cross is part of the journey to wholeness and self-fulfilment for him and for the world. By retelling stories of pain, women are aligning themselves with the core symbol of the Christian faith. In the experiences of their brokenness is the opportunity for wholeness, both for themselves and for the Church. Perhaps, too, women's pain is spoken of as an atonement for the pain women feel they have caused the Church by their ordination:

> I have been given opportunities here I know other women have not been given and in a sense am privileged to suffer, in a small way, for what I believe will be an important part of the enrichment and growth of the Church as a whole.

Yet there are, we are told, two sides to every story - for every breakdown in relationship, whether it is an emotional or working partnership, two people contribute to its demise. Women have told me their stories, recounting how they have met bullying, harassment, rudeness or disrespect, but I have no power to verify them, to present the other side, to put the alternative point of view. Instead I must trust, first the numbers and range of different stories which suggest that instances of abusive behaviour on the part of male clergy do exist. Secondly, in most situations the woman is junior to her male counterpart. In the hierarchy of power she is subservient and, therefore, more likely to be the recipient of, rather than the perpetrator of, unacceptable behaviour. Thirdly, evidence from the quantitative survey confirms women's stories of the difficulties they have encountered.

Some of women's stories appear trivial but, when put together, the constant stream of disapproval erodes women's self-esteem and confidence:

> The members of my chapter have started to call each other father, even putting labels on seats to reserve them for deanery functions - mine is the one without the label. I find this trivia very irritating.

There are instances too of more profoundly offensive behaviour which constitutes emotional or physical bullying:

> But the hidden demons in our unconscious came into play: I became a monstrous threat to him [the vicar], and he came to be, for me, the one who drove me to the edge of sanity. We had some ineffectual diocesan mediation but eventually he drove me out and I resigned. The bishop and archdeacon just let it happen - after all he was the legal incumbent and I was only an NSM. Many times I wished I had never been ordained. Now I am just beginning to think that God has something else in store for the last years of my life but I feel I have lost those whom I loved and served.

This story, and others like it, are traumatic and unacceptable in any organisation, not least in one that purports to represent and reflect the love of Christ. These are painful stories to tell and to hear, but they must be listened to if the Church is to grow in understanding and develop non-discriminatory practice. "Hidden demons" and unconscious motives are something we all grapple with, but the Church is in the very real danger of further institutionalising a fundamental misogyny,[15] unless it deals openly with these issues.

The qualitative data reveal a complexity of experience for women priests which is at the same time positive and negative, both supportive and destructive, fulfilling and diminishing of women. In their accounts women polarise these experiences, accrediting the affirmation for their ministry to the laity and the opposition to women's priesthood to the clergy. Why are the instances of clergy rejection so powerful that they need to be told? Why do women choose to give credence to these occurrences in their accounts rather than reflect on the lay opposition (presuming that their choice reflects the importance with which the situation is endowed)?

The answer lies in the distribution of power in the Church. Ultimately the laity have less significance in Church structures than the clergy. In the hierarchy of power lay opposition does not have the same capacity to wound and destroy as the words and actions of ordained ministers do. In the final analysis women's future acceptance rests, not in the hands of their congregations, but in the hearts of their male colleagues, for that is where the struggle over women's ordination is occurring. Accompanying clergy opposition is a sense of intransigence and permanence which suggests that antagonism to women is somehow embedded in the very veins and sinews of the Church. In highlighting and retelling stories of deprecation women are signalling that there is a deep-rooted, structural antagonism to their ministry which is the very core of patriarchy. Can women, by their very presence, counteract the force of patriarchy or will they crumble under its potency?

If suffering, death and pain are elemental to Christian imagery, then new life, growth and resurrection are their counterparts. The central icon of the cross is twinned with the symbol of the empty tomb - for through pain there is growth and through death there is resurrection. Women priests draw on metaphors from Christianity to give meaning to their own experiences. Through their pain comes the offer of resurrection life for them and for the Church. Therefore, success is an essential part of women's priestly narratives. It is used to provide a context, putting into perspective their difficult experiences, it signals hope and justifies the rightness of their ordination. I can no more verify women's external success than I can their painful experiences of abuse, but here again their repeated occurrences in the narratives, and the confirmation of the statistical evidence, give them credence. Women's ordination is pictured, not only as a new start for the Church, but as a fulfilment of promise for women priests, for lay women and for the Church.

There are several narrative devices used in women's accounts to construct the concept of success within the context of opposition. Some women, who feel they have only encountered positive affirmation from laity and clergy begin their narratives by saying "I have been lucky", thus signalling that success is not the absolute norm for most women priests and that their experience is, therefore, abnormal. Even in these pure success stories the narrator makes reference to the disapproval towards women's ministry that they believe is prevalent in the Church. In contrast, women who have experienced difficulties in the Church use a "yes but" device which serves to put into perspective the difficulties caused by their priesthood through demonstrating their success:

> The present curate accepts women priests, for which I praise the Lord. His predecessor was against, hence a rather trying time at the commencement of my priesthood as both my vicar and curate at that time were anti. Time is a great healer - with tact and much prayer things have improved, now the same vicar is pleased to have my services. One great blessing I have had is a lot of support from the congregations of both Churches. Even those originally against the ordination of women to the priesthood now accept it - with very few exceptions.

This quotation illustrates several of the narrative devices used to construct women's priesthood narratives of their Church experience. First, the lack of affirmation from the respondent's male priestly colleagues is acknowledged, although it is down-played. What must have been an extremely difficult situation, where both senior members of staff disregarded her ministry, is described as a "rather trying time". The phrase "time is a great healer" then acts as a "yes but" link which moves the reader from the problems which have been encountered into the success of women priests which is where the respondent wants to concentrate her narrative. Finally, the account is completed by a conversion story whereby the opponents of women's ministry, which include the vicar, are won round. A passing reference is given to the few lay "exceptions" who still do not accept the ministry of a woman priest, which is in contrast to the emphasis given in the account to the negative reactions from the institution of the Church. In other words opposition, where it occurs, is portrayed as coming from the clergy in contrast to the support and affirmation from the congregation. This quotation illustrates, among other things, that women priests are tired of the focus given to the pain and problems caused by their ordination. They want to move on, and they want the Church to move on.

Linguistically, conversion stories signal that women's priesthood has been successful, but they also contain a deeper meaning. Words like "conversion", "confession" and in the previous quotation, the reference to "answered prayer", are usually linked with a particular life-changing experience of God associated with the evangelical tradition. The language used in conversion stories implies that a revelation about the propriety of women's ministry can be equated with the process of individual salvation - a theme which is echoed in Rosemary Radford Ruether's book *Sexism and God-Talk* (1983).

Ruether establishes sexism as a fundamental sin, riddled in the patriarchal structures of society which legislates women's oppression, enshrining male dominance. Redemption can only come through conversion journeys which are experienced both by women and men. Women's conversion journey entails a discovery of self and a realisation of their identity. Men require a parallel journey in which they identify and own, their part in women's oppression before standing in solidarity with them as they seek liberation. Sexism is not solely exhibited in external structures, which if changed provide a new, non-sexist world order, it is the heartbeat of patriarchy. In the Old Testament book of Ezekiel (11:19), God promises a heart of flesh in place of the stone heart. This can only happen as people face and turn away from the sin of sexism and their part in it. Conversion stories are important because they signal hope; hope in women's success as priests, but also hope that, when confronted with the reality of women's ministry, people will come face to face with a new order and turn away from patriarchy. In their confession is the hope for the Church's, and perhaps society's, redemption from sexism - when that occurs, we can truly experience resurrection life.

Through their ordination women have encountered the heart of patriarchy which has brought suffering to them as individuals and to the Church as a whole. Drawing on the metaphor of the cross in their accounts, women's pain offers the potential for redemption and healing for the Church, but, in itself, this is not enough. Individuals may have turned away from sexism, but if the Church is to truly experience resurrection life, then it must face the "hidden demons" of patriarchy. It must work to deconstruct hierarchical power bases and develop more inclusive, open ways of being. Women priests are but one step on that long journey from death to resurrection.

Patriarchy lies dormant in the structures, practices and attitudes represented by the Church of England. It is an ever present, indistinguishable factor in female/male relationships which are so distorted that they appear normal. The injustice of women's oppression is only so named when it is made evident. Women's ordination uncovered a new perspective, an alternative worldview in which women could be equal with men. The priesthood of women is a maelstrom - it has the potential to challenge patriarchy in the Church because it offers a new way of being. However for that potential to be fulfilled, women need not only to be present in Church structures, but to be actively engaged in deconstructing patriarchal structures that discriminate against them. Women's experiences of priesthood demonstrate how difficult this will be.

If women choose to challenge patriarchy then they will continue to be a source of conflict in an institution that they hold dear, within structures that they choose to identify with. Women have drawn, and will need to continue to draw, comfort and strength from their sense of calling and vocation which provides a framework through which they can make sense of the pain they have experienced and may feel they have caused. In their priesthood narratives and the self-completion questionnaire, women have painted a picture of the mixed joy and suffering that their ordination has brought - where success is a context for the pain inflicted by the cruel and sometimes abusive treatment of fellow clergy.

Ultimately, where is the outlet for this pain and sense of alienation? In the fragmented structures of the Church of England women can feel alone and unsupported, and pain, if it has no formal means of expression, can be internalised to cause depression, anxiety and stress. Women's ordination alone, although it has held a mirror to the Church and uncovered roots of sexism, is not sufficient to dismantle patriarchy in the Church. The Church must listen, not only to the content of women's priesthood narratives but to their form, in order to enable women and men to work together for justice and equality in ecclesiastical structures.

CHAPTER 8

WOMEN PRIESTS - THEIR ATTITUDES

As past experiences shape our future, so our attitudes, formed through a mixture of internal values and beliefs, and external occurrences affect the way we behave and react. Women's experiences of priesthood have shaped their reactions: their sense of call, identity with and participation in the Church have influenced women's potential to challenge and reform its patriarchal structures. Hidden in the recess of experience are the formless shapes of attitude, the internal structures of character, values and personal creed which, like experience, affect our capacity to act. The internal processes of women priests further illumine their priesthood journeys and demonstrate women's potential to shape and renew the Church.

The ordination of women was a window of promise for the Church; it implied a new start and with it came the embryonic dream of an alternative way of being, a dream where women would metamorphose the Church by renewing the male dominated organisation and transforming its patriarchal structures. This vision for women's ministry raises two important questions. First, one must ask whether or not the first group of women priests own, or identify with, the vision for ecclesiastical transformation? Did they consciously choose ordination in order to change the Church, or was the main goal for this initial cohort simply to serve the Church through priesthood? Secondly, if indeed women did identify their priesthood with opportunities for change, have they then sacrificed the dream of a new future - where equality extends to female and male, ordained and lay - for a shadowy, mirror-image of power? Women's priesthood, in itself, will not bring about the demise of patriarchy in the Church. However, when women's experiences of powerlessness, coinciding with their internal attitudes and values, come together in a conscious decision to work for change, then there is a potential for transformation.

Patriarchy is the prevailing worldview which informs the structural domination of women. It is, in essence, the air we breathe since it has become intrinsic to our ways of being and of seeing. Liberal feminists, who argue that the reconstruction of society alone has the potential to bring equality for women, have failed to acknowledge the all-pervading sexism that patriarchy brings. Patriarchal structures do not work solely by excluding women; it is the invisible characteristics permeating human organisations that have the most potent effect in society - so that even language, a core means of self-expression and communication, reflects male experience in vocabulary and imagery. Yet patriarchy is essentially damaging for both men and women; it deprives both sexes of the opportunity to explore what it is to be fully human. Women and men are oppressed by the hierarchy of power and domination which denies women's strength and men's vulnerability. Theologically, patriarchy is an anathema because it contradicts Christian principles of equality and human fulfilment:

> Because of patriarchy, men and women have inherited a truncated notion of God, skewed interpretations of human development, social alienation, and a spiritual wasteland that deprives them both of the right to grow and fail, to fail and grow. (Chittister 1998: 25)

In the Church, the priestly caste system and hierarchical organisational structure mirror patriarchal social systems. The ordination of women has unmasked some degree of misogyny in the Church, its structures and its members (both lay and ordained), but in itself, women's priesthood cannot redeem the in-built androcentric hierarchy. Women and men in the Church must live counter-culturally if the effects of patriarchy are to be reversed - they need to be collaborative, empowering and egalitarian in the way in which they work out their faith.

Feminism offers the potential for a different way of being, both for women and men. It propounds a new worldview that is a remedy for patriarchy, and it suggests an alternative methodology in order that the effects of sexism can be dismantled. Feminism is the antithesis of patriarchy because it originates in, and starts with, female rather than male experience. Feminism is organic; many aspects of feminist consciousness cannot be taught or imposed, they come only through a process of women's self-realisation. Through their shared stories, sisterhood and mutual support[1] women find the strength to counteract and contradict the patriarchal core of society - something that they must do from within its structures. Women must be priests, judges, academics, doctors and lawyers, but they can only change the organisations they belong to and work for through first identifying and naming patriarchy, then consciously choosing to work in a very different spirit, and finally by staying connected with other women. Women priests need to adopt core feminist principles if they are to be the catalyst for permanent, far-reaching change in the Church.

WOMEN PRIESTS AND CHANGE

If women priests are to change the Church, they must live counter-culturally and demonstrate that there is a new way of being. In particular there should be evidence that women are collaborative in their approach, egalitarian and empowering if we are to see the transformation that is needed in the Church. For these concepts - a concern for equality in relationships and structures, a commitment to working with people in a team setting, and the desire to release individual potential - are the antithesis of the fruits of patriarchy. If the ordination of women is to fully realise its potential, to truly be an antidote for patriarchy, then more is demanded of women priests than just their presence in the hierarchical structures of the Church. There have to be new patterns of ministry, where women demonstrate a concern for equality in Church structures, a desire to work collaboratively with the laity and with other clergy, and to establish models of working that diminish rather than emphasise the power imbalance between lay and ordained members of the Church through seeking to release individual potential.

Women Priests and Egalitarianism

Egalitarianism, a concern for equality and parity, is one hallmark of a feminist approach to spirituality and especially, I believe, of Christian spirituality. Both feminism and Christianity are essentially life-affirming and anti-oppressive (although there is much evidence to the contrary in organised religion). Although the Church has moved towards democratic structures in its government (General Synod) and to greater participation of the laity in its practice (through lay readers etc.), the real power of the Church is held by the ordained, stipendiary clergy. Will women, having entered the priesthood, work for greater parity between lay and ordained, or will they allow the power imbalance to remain?

A summated scale was created which combined the variables from the questionnaire indicating an egalitarian approach to ministry in the Church.[2] The results in Figure 8a show a normal distribution on the scale, that is the distribution of the scores is uni-modal with the mean and medium occurring contiguously. This suggests that women priests do not have an overly egalitarian approach to ministry, as the dispersal of their scores is no different from what one would expect to find in the general population.

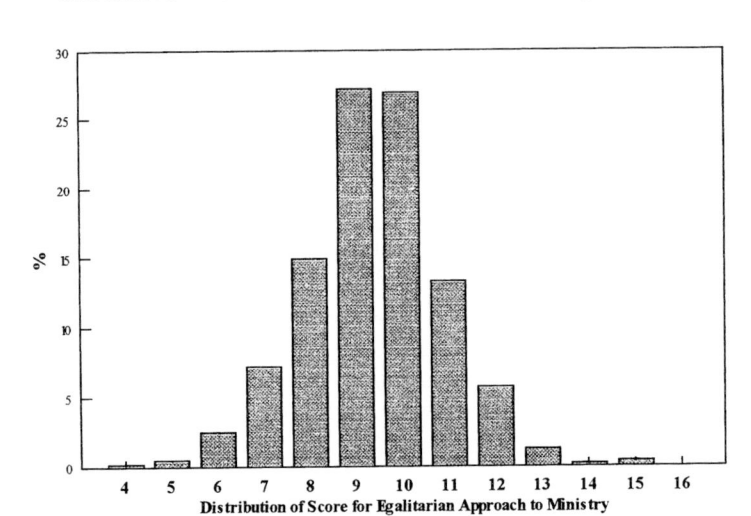

FIGURE 8a   Distribution of Scores on the Scale for Egalitarianism

These results do vary slightly when compared with theological orientation. Women from a liberal theological tradition are more likely to demonstrate a stronger affinity with a concern for equality - 64.3% of liberal women have a bias towards co-equality, compared to 57.4% of evangelicals and 44.8% of catholic women. Theological orientation is a contributory factor in attitude formation: liberalism, with its concern for equity and openness, is a seminal part of women's perspective on priesthood and their desire for an egalitarian approach to ministry.

Women Priests and Collaboration

Are women then demonstrating a more collective leadership style in the Church of England? Are they concerned with collaboration in the place of competition; with shared, inclusive ministry, as opposed to the hierarchical power-based delineation of tasks in the Church? A summated scale to measure this included attitudinal variables from the questionnaire and women's self-reported inclusion of the laity in ecclesiastical events (helping with the eucharist, preaching and pastoral work), looking for evidence that women were prepared to share the traditional elements of the priestly role with lay members of the Church.[3]

Women priests clearly demonstrated a predilection towards a collaborative leadership style in the Church. Figure 8b shows a skewed distribution of the scores with the majority of respondents revealing a strong identification with co-operative ways of working.

FIGURE 8b   Distribution of Scores on the Scale for Collaboration

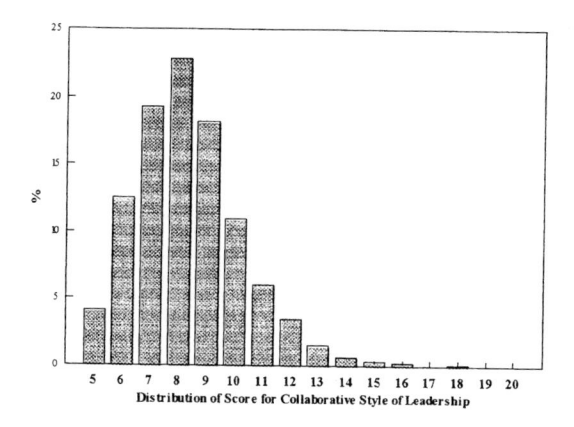

Distribution of Score for Collaborative Style of Leadership

    The results are a powerful affirmation of women's flexibility and synergistic approach to ministry. However, self-reporting can skew individual's responses because there is an internal pressure to give the "right answers" and to present oneself in a socially acceptable way. Women priests, in the face of opposition and criticism, have been concerned to emphasise their success and acceptability through their responses to my research. It is possible that the ideal of the collaborative (nurturing) priest is a strong typology that resonates, both with women's gendered self-expectations and with a priestly ideal-type, to distort responses to collaboration in my enquiry. At this stage the qualitative data served to confirm or challenge the findings from the survey. It enabled me to view women's responses through a different set of lenses and thus to distil the findings from the quantitative section of the research.

    Collaboration was a recurrent theme present in both the interview and the qualitative survey data which occurred in two forms. First, and less frequently, a cerebral commitment to a collaborative approach to the priesthood which has the literary form of a mission statement for women's ministry:

> I feel strongly that collaborative ministry is the way forward because people own what is happening and become skilled in many areas of Church life.

In this statement the respondent is outlining her internal paradigm, the map which informs the way she acts, and reacts, to priesthood. Through these mission statements women are articulating core values which apprise their approach to ministry in the Church, demonstrating that, for women, collaboration is indeed an essential element in how they work out their calling.

    Evidence of women's mutuality is also present in the qualitative data as practical, lived examples which sometimes occur when the respondent is focusing on a different issue. In the following instance the difficulties of working in a male dominated prison environment are being discussed:

> I struggle within a structure of line management and strict rules governing authority, to give our congregation as much responsibility and involvement as possible. I feel there are times when it is of great benefit to be a feminine presence in this environment and to use authority in a different way to that exercised in the disciplines around me.

Within the context of problems with prison structure the respondent indicates that she is working in a collaborative fashion with inmates in a way which contradicts the normal practice of the penal system. As a woman priest she is working counter-culturally. In this next quotation the respondent is articulating the need for women and men to work together, to complement, rather than attempt to copy, each other. Inadvertently, she indicates a co-operative, facilitating mode of working:

> Recently I organised a Lent study on prayer and met first with a male reader, a female reader and another man who has a sound knowledge of the Bible and of life. The differing opinions were invaluable in the planning and I'm sure the three groups involved will benefit from both sexes sharing the leading.

This illustrates women's co-operative approach to ministry in a number of ways: first, the respondent involves three other people early on in the organisation of the study, then she acknowledges and works with conflicting opinions in the group to create positive, rather than negative energy, and finally shares the outcomes of the group process by involving all three contributors in the leadership of the study. Both quotations are examples of how the qualitative data support evidence from the quantitative results to suggest women are not only demonstrating a collaborative approach to ministry, but that they also hold this as an essential part of their internal map, or the process by which they understand priesthood.

The pattern in the data is clear: 77% of women demonstrate a synergistic approach to their ministry. Are there, however, other factors which affect the way in which women view this element of priesthood: age, theological orientation or position in the Church? Women who are in senior positions in the Church might be expected to be less co-operative than their junior colleagues, having been socialised into a male, competitive way of being in order to gain promotion. However, this was not the case. 40.4% of women at a rector level or above showed a very strong, and 34.6% a strong, identification with team work (75%). In fact, position in the Church was not an indicator of whether or not women approach ministry collaboratively. Age does affect women's bias towards collaboration to an extent, with 25.9% of older women scoring very highly on the scale in comparison to 39.6% and 40.8% of younger and middle aged women. The strongest factor affecting women's collaborative approach to ministry is, once again, theological orientation. Table 8c shows that, of those who score very strongly on the scale, 50.5% are evangelical. In contrast, at the other end of the scale, women from a catholic persuasion are less likely to demonstrate a collaborative approach to ministry.

Evangelical theology has the potential to foster a style of working which accentuates the role of laity and diminishes the status and role of the priest. Evangelicalism emphasises the priesthood of all believers, focusing on the individual's personal relationship with God, where the priest is a facilitator for faith and not a mediator. The sacramental role of the priest does not receive the profile in evangelical theology that it does in catholicism, and therefore lay

Table 8.C Collaborative Approach to Ministry by Theological Orientation (%)

		Theological Orientation		
		Catholic	Liberal	Evangelical
	Very Strong	38.1	11.4	50.5
Collaborative Approach to Ministry	Strong	51.8	12.2	36
	Weak	50.8	16.5	32.6

$p \leq 0.000$ n=1045

people in the former tradition will have more input into the sacramental life of the Church. There is, however, the potential in the extreme evangelical position, which stresses authority, both of the scriptures and of the male head of the Church, to exercise power in an autocratic, hierarchical way contrary to the principles of co-operation and mutuality. Women priests appear to interpret their theological position in ways which affirm their inner values. Their internal commitment to collaboration finds greater expression in their ministry as a result of their external theological influences.

The evidence from my research is that women priests do approach ministry in a collaborative way, and other studies confirm these findings,[4] suggesting a gendered approach to co-operation. So why are women more collaborative than men? Is it an intrinsic gender trait or the result of a process of socialisation? One obvious explanation offered is that women's experience of motherhood, requiring them to develop skills of nurturing in order to facilitate personal growth in their children, is the cause. This process of other-realisation is then transferred into the workplace, the Church or different areas of social life.

However, this argument is ultimately too simplistic; undoubtedly women's maternal experiences profoundly affect areas of their life, yet nearly half of the women in my research had no involvement in mothering. Women have, I believe, developed new co-operative working patterns, initially in order to survive patriarchal structures in society. Eventually this alternative way of being has become a source of strength and empowerment for women - a contributory factor in their emancipation. Working collaboratively is subversive, it undermines hierarchical power structures that divide gender, race and class into the oppressors and the oppressed. It is a non-violent, empowering existence, counteracting the violence and abuse caused by autocracy, patriarchy and the love of power. Workers co-operatives, women's groups, trade and credit associations have all slowly, almost invisibly, chipped away at the monolithic power structures that oppress their members.

Collaboration is not an exclusively female trait, just as autocracy is not an intrinsically male one, but women are the forerunners, having quietly modelled new approaches to power. Their experiences of generational patriarchy have forced women to discover ways of surviving, ways of being, ways of challenging. Collaboration is the fruit of that struggle and is also, I believe, an essential, but often ignored, part of Christianity. Women, as they enter the power structures of the Church must lead us, through their actions, to the lost heart of Christianity where even God is somehow three, where trinity is unity, a Divine co-operation. Through their mutuality women prophesy new ways of being and therein lies a hope, just a flicker now, for the end of patriarchy.

Women Priests and Empowerment

The third area in which women can achieve change in the Church is through the empowerment of others. By enabling people to extend their role in the Church and in society, women can be instruments for transformation. Empowerment, collaboration and egalitarianism are inter-related concepts which are concerned with shared power, individual growth, development and consensus, but empowerment specifically addresses a way of being in which personal fulfilment is linked partly to community wholeness. An individual is not an isolated element of society, but is connected to the whole; corporate well-being is enhanced through each individual's completeness. The biblical image of the Church as a body (1 Corinthians 12) illustrates this concept well, for the strength of the body as a whole is dependent on the robustness of each individual part. The priest, as caretaker for the body, will be most successful if she can strengthen and empower its individual elements.

One model for empowering leadership in Christianity is Jesus: he worked with a small group of twelve to facilitate their individual and spiritual growth, he washed their feet, he encouraged people to find their own truth in his stories, and finally he counteracted the patriarchal power of the Roman empire through non-violence, which resulted in his trial and death. In the cross, the symbol of death giving life, God empowers humanity to be changed and to be an instrument for change. Yet empowerment has not been the way of the Church, whose structures often suppress the involvement of the majority, so that they remain the eternal children of their spiritual priestly fathers. The question is whether women priests will now become sacred mothers? Will they seek to empower lay members of the Church, encouraging spiritual independence, or will they remain stuck in an unhelpful, parental role?

A summated scale was created combining variables from the questionnaire which indicated women's attitude to empowerment.[5] The distribution of this scale (Figure 8d) is normal, suggesting that women priests are not demonstrating a particularly empowering approach to ministry, as the dispersal of their scores is similar to what one would expect to find in the general population. Having said this, over half do indicate a positive attitude to empowerment.

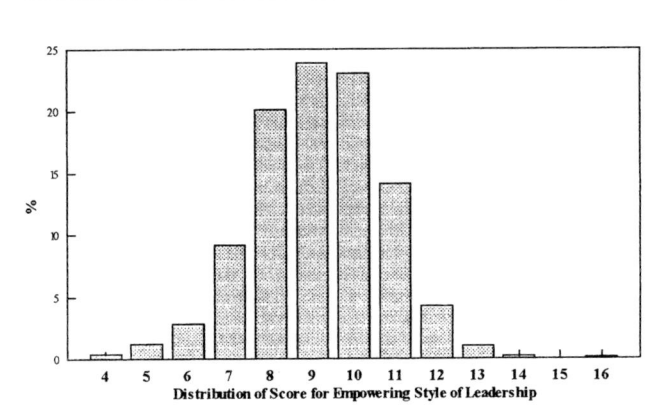

FIGURE 8d   Distribution of Scores on the Scale for Empowerment

Women from the older generation are slightly less concerned with issues relating to individual growth than younger or middle-aged women. Women from a catholic theological tradition are less likely to indicate a positive attitude to empowerment than their liberal or evangelical colleagues (51% of catholic women score positively on the scale compared to 66.7% of liberal and 63% of evangelical women). Catholic ecclesiology emphasises the sacramental elements of priesthood which justify the priest being set apart from the laity in order to fulfil specific tasks in the Church. The involvement of the laity does not have the importance in a catholic tradition that it can have in liberal and evangelical circles because of the representative role of the priest. The symbolism of the Church is maintained by making certain rites and rituals so sacrosanct that they can only be performed by ordained clergy. Therefore, the distance between lay people and priests is, to an extent, an essential element in catholic ecclesiology.

Although the statistical evidence does not demonstrate an overly strong bias towards empowerment, the importance of releasing individual potential in others is a reoccurring theme in the qualitative data, suggesting this is a significant issue for women priests. For some women, their attitude to the laity has been a source of conflict both with their congregations and with other clergy, indicating that the parental association of the priest is something which fulfils a need in both lay and ordained members of the Church. One women wrote describing a difficult situation in her parish:

> I partly put this down to the kind of ministry which I and another woman priest there encouraged - we wanted the congregation to make important decisions (they didn't), we encouraged involvement of young people and children (the congregation didn't), we experimented with worship (they preferred the way things used to be). The old "male" ways of priesthood are hard to shift and sometimes people just don't want to change.

This quotation illustrates the ambivalence in the Church to change (which was very aptly demonstrated by the long drawn-out debate about women's ordination), particularly in the parental role of the clergy.[6] Over-reliance on one's parents causes an unhealthy and inappropriate dependency. In the natural order, childhood gives way to adulthood and separation becomes an important part of growth. In a therapeutic relationship (which can partly be a secular mirror for the priest), the client's identification with the therapist should be worked through to facilitate healthy separation and autonomy. So, too, the relationship between the priest and the people needs to be one of spiritual and personal growth which ultimately leads to a sense of interdependence, not dependence, in the body of Christ. In their accounts, women are indicating a concern for lay empowerment, for autonomy not dependency: they emphasise the inter-relatedness of priest and people and are opposed to forms of clerical separatism and superiority:

> My style of ministry is about engagement, rather than detachment, accompanying others on their spiritual journeys for a while, letting people grow and go if necessary...I do not wish to "lord" it over a congregation, but to enable them to trust the glimpses of God. I wish to enable them to hear their own stories and find healing.

The discrepancy between the quantitative and qualitative data suggests a dilemma in women's approach to empowerment. This dilemma arises, in part, from an essentially patriarchal approach to power which is viewed as a limited, restricted "commodity" held by the minority, at the expense of the majority. This view of power means that once women gain the status of priesthood they are forced to choose between their new-found power and position and their desire to work in a facilitative and empowering way. However, there is an alternative feminist paradigm in which power becomes "standing with others" and "something to be multiplied and shared not accumulated." (Russell 1993:56-57). Here, power is not a finite commodity, but it is an infinite resource which can proliferate, propagate and grow. The priest's purpose is to "ferment" growth in others, and by affirming the status and role of their congregation, in the Church and in society, they are themselves affirmed in their priestly ministry.

At a time when the Church is rethinking its approach to the laity and seeking to widen the scope of involvement for non-ordained people,[7] women priests can make a significant contribution. Women's commitment to collaboration is strong, and the evidence suggests it will remain so even as women become more established in the Church. Less clear is how far women will empower the laity. Women have gained the professional and ministerial position of priesthood, but whether they are committed to developing a more inclusive approach to Church leadership, remains unresolved. Women need to make unequivocal choices to develop new forms of ministry, they need an unambivalent approach to lay empowerment if they are to fulfil the dream of transformation and the vision of a new start that their priesthood heralded.

Patriarchy is not maintained solely by men, women also collude with its structures to preserve the status quo. Power has the potential to corrupt or distort, and women have no inherent immunity against this development. They have experienced life on the margins, and as women gain ascendancy, they must choose to work differently, to offer an alternative worldview, a new way of being. Feminism, with its collective emphasis, a network of support rather than a hierarchy of power, has the capacity to enable and assist women priests to be different. In doing so, they can counteract patriarchy in the Church. Women's potential to bring change will, however, be compromised if there is evidence of their clericalisation or over-identification with priesthood.

THE ROLE AND FUNCTION OF THE PRIEST

Until the nineteenth century the priestly role was defined as much by associated social status as by spiritual function. The local standing of the parson as a "gentleman" gave him the right to be involved in the government of his parish. In the Victorian era the clergy role became professionalised, a process which was characterised by theological and pastoral education, peer support and self-government, professional literature, distinctive dress and the ring-fencing of professional activities (Heeney 1988). The clerical role now encompassed three main areas: sacramental worship, preaching, and pastoral care. Through this process of clericalisation the priest was distinguished from the lay members of the Church functionally: the catholic renewal (the Oxford Movement) and evangelical revival of the late nineteenth and early twentieth centuries provided a theological distinction between priest and people.

In catholicism the sacramental, representative role of the priest is accentuated, whilst in evangelicalism the priest as minister of God through the word is emphasised. Both theological positions set apart the ordained from the lay members of the Church in an exclusive hierarchy of relationships. Through their ordination women priests have been allowed into another hieratic level which is disconnected from the lay women who, in MOW, had engaged with their struggle for priesthood. They are set apart from the ordinary members of the Church and they are now members of the male clerical club. Have women succumbed to clerical socialisation, becoming segregated from the laity and over-connected with the Church fabric and priestly status? Or have women priests remained connected to their experiences of marginalisation through their continued association with their lay counterparts?

Women priests are clearly involving lay people in Church activities,[8] how strong, then, is their affinity with their priestly position? A summated scale for clericalisation was created.[9] The evidence in Figure 8e suggests women have a fairly strong identity with clerical status. 64.9% scored positively on the scale, the distribution of which is skewed towards a concern for priestly status.

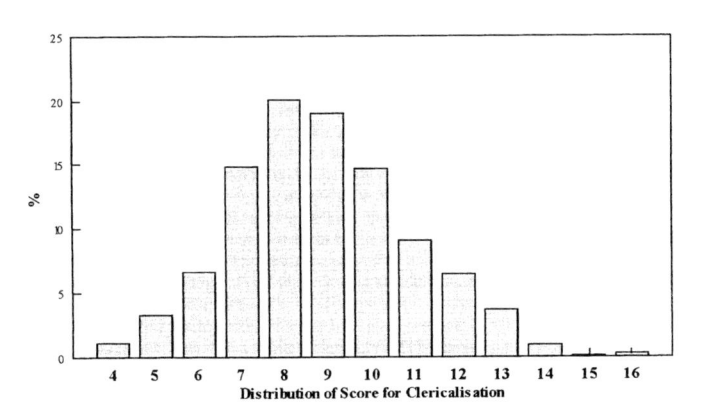

FIGURE 8e   Distribution of Scores on a Scale for Clericalisation

Women priests are working collaboratively with the laity within the constraints of Church legislation. It has become perfectly acceptable, as a result of lay training schemes, to involve parishioners in pastoral work, preaching, small group leadership and the distribution of the sacraments. However, the core elements of clerical status - dress, title, the eucharist and ordination - remain firmly linked to priesthood for this first group of women ordinands. So was priesthood the only goal for women, or was their struggle part of an overall desire to counteract the dualism of patriarchy? The binary delineation of male and female, powerful and powerless, lay and ordained is contrary to the holistic interdependence of the body-Church in Christianity. Are women priests able to combine a theological understanding of clerical status with a desire for non-hierarchical priesthood?

Rosemary Radford Ruether, in her article "The Preacher and the Priest: Two Typologies of Ministry and the Ordination of women" (1990), argues that religious traditions where ministry is associated with the word are more open to women's ordination than those which emphasise a sacramental approach. Yet the role of the preacher - the cerebral, abstract, rational minister of the word - is more sexually stereotypically male. In contrast, the role of the priest in the sacramental tradition, who "mediates the enfleshed word, the body of Christ...to the womb of the mother Church" (1990:72) belongs to a more traditionally female typology.

Ruether concludes that, in order to appropriate a maternal sacrality for themselves, men must enforce a more rigid exclusion of women. Theology, a primary indicator in the maintenance of an exclusively male priesthood, is similarly implicated in the furtherance of the separatism in lay and ordained relationships.

Certainly, in this first group of women priests, theological orientation is an indicator of clericalisation: 80% of women from a catholic theological tradition demonstrate a more clericalised approach to ministry, compared to 56.6% of liberal or 49.2% of evangelical women.[10] Ruether's association of the sacerdotal role with maternal symbolism is significant, not solely because of its identification with the female, but also in its connection of the priest with parental imagery. In the sacramental traditions the priest is gatekeeper to rites of initiation (baptism), purveyor of absolution and blessing, and mediator between God and humanity in the eucharist. Thus an adult/child relationship between priest and people, which can infantilise the laity, is established.

The qualitative data confirm the broadly theological delineation in women's understanding of the role and function of the priest. However, the nuances of the interview data suggest that, even within the confines of their theological tradition, women are attempting to approach ministry in a less clericalised way. They are exploring a philosophical framework which enables them to maintain a sacramental role whilst empowering the laity to develop independence and to grow as individuals:

> I see the role to be about the interpretation of God to the people and actually through what we are, and in a sense what we do, actually being interpreters of God.

> I think of the role of the priest as getting alongside people whoever they are, wherever they are and that the whole boundaries of class, rich or poor, shouldn't be of any importance when you are getting alongside people. This doesn't mean that other Christians don't as well, but I feel that in the eucharist one somehow offers it all up as a prayer in a very particular way.

> In the villages, you know people more and when you are saying a prayer you are holding them. The other idea of the priest being a bridge, a drainpipe between God and the people. You are enabling people to say their prayers.

In each of these three instances the priesthood is described in sacramental, but not hierarchical terms. In the first example the priest is not a representative of God, but is an interpreter, placed in a linear relationship between divine and lay. An interpreter facilitates communication between two parties and, as such, the priest is pictured as an intermediary between God and the Church. In the second quotation, the priest is seen alongside, not above, the people. In the eucharist the priest symbolically gathers together each person's experience and pain, through prayer, offering them to God. In the third extract, the priest is described as a bridge, someone who holds the people in prayer and enables individuals to develop their own spiritual life. The drainpipe image does suggest a non-linear relationship between God and the people in which the priest acts as a channel. However, the use of the word "drainpipe" is self-deprecatory, indicating a desire to counteract any possible hierarchical interpretations of this relationship. The evidence from the qualitative data suggests that, where women view the sacerdotal role in sacramental terms, they are attempting to understand a deeply held theological position in a way which facilitates growth in their congregations rather than infantilises them. Women priests are seeking to interpret and describe the separateness of certain priestly tasks and rites in a non-hierarchical way.

A dilemma exists for this first group of women priests. They have gained entry into an elite, privileged institution - do they then become part of a clerical club which perpetuates an immutable power imbalance between lay and ordained people, or do they seek to subvert hierarchical, disempowering structures of dominance? At present the scales are poised, evidence of clerical socialisation in women priests is balanced by their desire to explore sacramental priesthood within a framework of lay empowerment and self-actualisation. Women, both lay and ordained, need to enter into a debate about the role and function of the priest, searching for different theological interpretations that do not foster unhelpful co-dependence (for in the perpetuation of the parent/child relationship there is an interdependence, built not on mutuality, but on the need to exert and relinquish control and responsibility).

Women's priesthood is a window of opportunity, both for women and for the Church. The ordination of women did change the face of priesthood and offered the potential to shape new sacerdotal models of ministry which are egalitarian, committed to individual growth, and collaborative in their approach. The spiritualities of lay and ordained are interwoven, co-dependent parts of the same body in which each fulfils their individual and corporate potential in God, and through the Church. The possibility for change is still with us but it cannot happen in isolation. Women by their mere presence will not sufficiently alter the power structures of the Church, indeed the reverse could happen and women priests lose sight of their time, on the edges of the Church, in the wilderness. Change will come as women and men recognise ingrained patriarchy as anti-Christian, consciously choose to adopt alternative models of being and doing priesthood, and support each other in a revolution of mutuality where power is not accumulated, but shared. Women need a coherent framework, an alternative, anti-patriarchal worldview to enable them to foster change in the Church, and feminism can offer that framework.

WOMEN PRIESTS AND FEMINISM

Feminism offers a praxis to the Church which is essentially congruent with Christianity. It is an antidote to the hierarchical oppression of patriarchy which distorts human relationships. Feminism emphasises shared support, a collective, anti-competitive network of relationships which enables members to develop and grow - a theme which is echoed in the body-Church of Corinthians. In feminism each person's story is a vehicle for individual and corporate learning which resonates with the conversion journeys and testimonies of faith in Christianity. Finally, feminism calls for solidarity as a means of achieving social transformation, a concept which reverberates in Christianity[11] - from the manifesto for a new world order in the sermon on the mount (Luke 6:20-38) to the liberating baptismal statement in Galations 3:28 "There is neither Jew nor Greek, there is neither slave nor free man, there is neither male nor female; for you are all one in Christ Jesus." Despite this potential for harmonious co-existence, Christianity, as it is expressed in the Church, and feminism have, in the main, been in conflict. A dualistic worldview has pervaded religious and feminist thought through their rigid dichotomisation of spirit and mind/flesh; both have ignored the potential for growth and development in a holistic integration of mind and spirit, reflection and action.

We are living in a supposedly post-Christian, post-feminist age, in which feminism and Christianity are now perceived as outdated and dispensable. However, if feminism is redundant because women have achieved equality, why are women five times more likely to be in part-time work than men? Why do women still earn 50-60 % of what men earn if they are in full-time work?[12] Does the popular rise of the "lad" and the "laddette" in modern culture mean that equality is determined by women's ability to ape sexually stereotypically male behaviour? Oakley and Mitchell, in their book *Whose Afraid of Feminism?* (1997), identify a public backlash against feminism which, masking the existence of inequality through a veneer of equal rights, demonstrates that society is resorting to cultural misogyny. Feminism is not dead or redundant, it is just unpopular. The Church, never a devoted follower of feminism, has been quick to contribute to the backlash, and conservative elements have blamed declining moral standards, ranging from teenage pregnancy to the breakdown of the family, on women's emancipation.

The women's movement in the Church, despite working for women's equality, has had an ambivalent attitude towards feminist principles. Heeney (1988) identified two types of Church feminism in the late nineteenth and early twentieth centuries: the *challengers* and the *persuaders* of authority. *Challengers* campaigned for change, they advocated women's suffrage and broke the law in order to demonstrate and fulfil their ministry in the Church.[13] *Persuaders*, on the other hand, attempted to garner support for their cause by gently proving their worth, thus earning the right to minister.[14] They worked within the Church, using established Church structures and machinery to achieve change. The divergence between *challenging* and *persuading* in Church feminism has remained and was a source of tension in MOW's campaign for women's ordination.[15] Is ambivalence to feminism still a factor for this first group of women clergy, or have they drawn on the principles of support, solidarity and shared stories to gain strength through their initiation to the priesthood? It is not just the attitudes to feminism articulated in the quantitative data which is of interest here, it is also women's use of, and attitude to, feminist language which is significant. Women priests cannot afford to reject feminism or feminist methodology if they are to challenge patriarchy and be part of the Church's transformation.

FIGURE 8f   Distribution of Scores on a Scale for Feminism

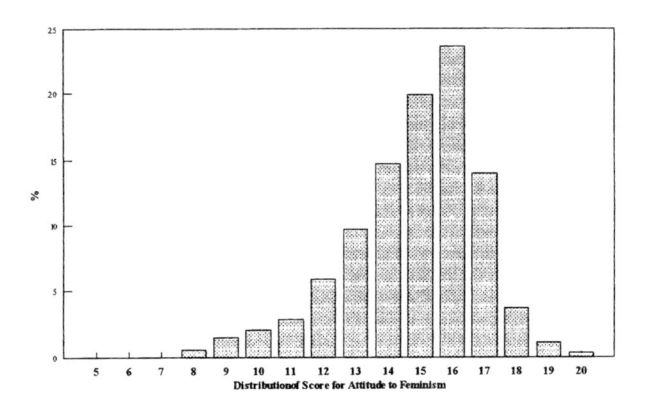

Women Priests: Campaigning and Support

A summated scale was created which combined women's attitudes to support and campaigning with their self-reported involvement in women's groups.[16] The results, in Figure 8f, show women priests do not have a strong affinity with feminism. The distribution of the scores is skewed, showing that the majority of women priests (75%) are antipathetic towards feminism.[17] Once again theological orientation impacts women's attitudes and approach to ministry: women from a liberal and catholic tradition are more likely to evidence a positive approach to feminism than evangelical women, as Table 8g shows:

TABLE 8G   Attitudes to Feminism by Theological Orientation (%)

		Attitudes to Feminism	
		Broadly Positive	Broadly Negative
Theological Orientation	Catholic	25.7	74.3
	Liberal	34.8	65.2
	Evangelical	15.7	84.3

$p \leq 0.000$ n=1065

25.7 % of catholic women and 34.8% of liberal women are feminist, compared to 15.7% of evangelical women. Evangelicalism and fundamentalism are not interchangeable theological positions: nevertheless, elements of a conservative approach to family life are echoed in evangelical traditions and therein lies the antipathy to feminism. Stratton Hawley, in his book *Fundamentalism and Gender* (1994), links the rise of fundamentalism with a conservative desire to re-emphasise the role of women as pivotal to the family. In echoes of Victorian theology, women's spirituality is perceived to be best expressed in the domestic sphere - as wives and mothers. Fundamentalist theories have arisen in response to disaffection with the rational, modernist worldview which, it is argued, has resulted in the fragmentation of society and the disintegration of the family, and therefore the social, unit (McCarthy Brown 1994, Tomlinson 1995). Feminism, which seeks to liberate women from patriarchal family structures, is perceived as anti-family and therefore anti-society, and ultimately, as anti-Christian. Women from evangelical traditions, whilst they are unlikely to concur with the extremes of the fundamentalist position, are nevertheless more antagonistic towards feminism, a position which arises from their theological understanding of the role of women in society.

The quantitative data gives no in-depth indication of whether Heeney's nineteenth century *challengers* and *persuaders* still figure in the women's movement in the late twentieth century Church. Evidence from the qualitative data, however, does elucidate women's different approaches to campaigning and shows how their perspective on the need for further change is conflicting. Indeed, there are two clear responses to campaigning in the data, the first is essentially opposed to organised action, believing that women priests will only gain acceptance if they prove they can do the job. The *persuaders* shun association with militancy and deny the need for further campaigning, convinced that their efficacy, capability and spirituality are sufficient testimony to women's ministry:

> Women working well and doing a good job enhance women's ministry and help others to see it's all right. If we can mix with the community and be seen to be unthreatening and "normal", people will go on responding to our calling.

> It all just feels very normal now, women are where they always should have been - like coming home. There is a deep sense of completeness but I do feel strongly that we now have to just get on with doing the job God has called us to do well.

In both these extracts the respondents are structuring their success (see chapter 7), demonstrating that women's priesthood is right, not just for the women themselves, but also for the Church. Any further altercation or campaign could jeopardise women's sense of relief at their success; reluctant to return to conflict, women signal their desire to get on, quietly, with the job in hand. One woman expressed surprise at questions in the survey relating to support, campaigning and women's groups, all aspects of pre-ordination days which she now deems unnecessary. Reluctance to engage in active campaigning does signal a degree of complacency which is a cause for concern. Certainly women will earn respect and credence for their ministry by getting on with the job, but they will fail to challenge the androcentric structures of the Church if they are not committed to the feminist tenets of support and campaigning.

The second attitude to campaigning in the data is based on the recognition that women's struggle for equality in the Church did not end at ordination. The *challengers* believe that there is still much to be done to unravel inherently sexist thought and practice in the Church. This group of women are committed to conscious, organised opposition to patriarchy and are prepared to challenge its dominance over women:

> I think the role of women in the Church of England is standing still at the moment. We have perhaps all been too complacent after the joy of the positive vote five years ago. The priesting of women has probably disabled lay women's role to a degree.

Some feel weary with the sense of struggle and are tired of having to continue to fight for equality:

> I think those of us in this early group of ordained women have paid some very heavy costs, both emotionally and in the knock on, physical consequences. Some of these are still on-going. I, for one, have little energy and strength for the continued struggle that is so clearly needed institutionally.

Some women express the feeling that women's radical edge has been lost now that they are part of the institution of the Church and others feel pressurised to stop campaigning:

> There is an underlying sense that women should now become silent Church mice and be content with our lot.

The *challengers* have, I believe, a more realistic assessment of the situation women priests currently find themselves in. They are conscious of the internal, emotional costs of counteracting patriarchy, yet remain committed to an ongoing campaign for change. Many identify the goal of ordaining women to the episcopate as the next milestone for women in the

Church. Whilst I acknowledge the validity of their goal, I am concerned, not just that women reach positions of power, but that they avoid using the currency of power as a means of securing women's place in the Church.

In the qualitative data some women priests characterise feminism in negative terms. Their use of language suggests that women are not value-free or neutral in their attitude to feminism.[18] In their narratives, some women chose to disassociate themselves, in vehement terms, from what they describe as "militant" or "aggressive" feminist behaviour. The campaign for women's emancipation is characterised as belligerent agitation, and in these accounts some women priests pander to the very worst kind of feminist stereotypes which Austin and Oakley (1997) attribute to the cultural backlash against feminism:

> I have an understanding, sympathetic nature, I am no way a pushy or bullying person. I have never been a militant woman minister. I have never experienced agro or the woes of women priests - often because they are too domineering (feeling threatened?), too bossy, often aggressive to male colleagues (feeling inferior?) - too competitive with colleagues. I had to resign from one post because I could not stand a woman colleague who was all of those things. Finally I have had the good fortune to work with male clergy who have been good to work with.

In this quotation the respondent describes women priests who are involved in active campaigning as "militant", "bossy", "aggressive" and "competitive". She uses vocabulary which is usually connected with traditionally male stereotypes inferring that any problems women experience are due to their own intransigence. In this extract the respondent clearly estranges herself from dissident women.

It is painful to hear women disassociating themselves from the feminist struggle and aligning themselves with patriarchy in a scathing parody of "women's lib". It is also harrowing to hear women oppress women, to see them define themselves, and their success, in patriarchal terms, and watch as they turn their backs on feminism - their opportunity for freedom. Patriarchy is effective because it maintains a hierarchy in which the oppressed help to maintain the structures which dominate them. "Internalised oppression" is where the oppressed define themselves and their achievements by the enfeebled expectations of their oppressors.[19] To live thus is to deny oneself full personhood, by failing to comprehensively explore one's humanity and spirituality (Chittister 1998). Women priests who, having internalised patriarchal oppression, fail to engage with feminism, are colluding with the structures that have, and will continue to, dominate them. As such, they remain victims of patriarchy and are in danger of perpetuating that victim status for women who follow them in ministry. Women priests cannot afford to shun feminism; in doing so they not only stunt their own self-realisation, but also hamper other women's journey to wholeness.

Heeney's typology of Church feminism has been present throughout the campaign for women's ordination and now shapes the reality of women priests. Some women seek to adopt a more feminist approach to change in the Church through challenging its structures; others believe in the art of gentle persuasion. In general, women priests are ambivalent, if not antagonistic, towards feminism, something which seriously compromises women's capacity to be the catalysts for long-lasting change in the Church. Is this attitude to feminism replicated in women priest's approach to inclusive language in worship? Or are they demonstrating a desire to engage with new liturgical forms which affirm, rather than deny, women's experiences?

Women Priests and Language

In Western culture language is highly prized; words are our predominant means of external communication. Despite the power of symbol, image or gesture, verbal and written communication remain the primary vehicle for self-expression and serve the furtherance of our joint identity. Society and culture are shaped by language, but similarly the shape of society is expressed through language. It is the means by which we name our experience and, as such, is integral to our sense of self and our sense of community. Language reflects the patriarchal core of society, in which culture is defined in male, not female, terms. It is only when women's experiences are named, when corporate identity is female and male, and when female imagery is an integral part of our core symbolism that the male will cease to be normative. In this secular age, God still remains an indispensable part of our shared metaphor, a central "male" icon, in our universal understanding. When God is she, when language about God reflects female history, then perhaps we can know some freedom from patriarchy. Women priests have changed the face of religious symbolism to an extent, their presence modelling the fact that God is female too. Is their use of language, however, changing the way the Church expresses its spirituality?

A summated scale which measured women's use of, and attitude to, inclusive language was created.[20] The results in Figure 8h show that the majority of women priests are committed to the use of emancipatory language in worship. 64.9% of respondents score highly on the scale, indicating a positive response to inclusive liturgical language. Attitude to language is affected, however, both by age and by theological orientation. Younger women are more likely to use generic language which is inclusive and which reflects God's female nature, indicating that feminist thought has impacted the younger generation in an enduring way. Despite the popular backlash against feminism (often expressed in antagonism to "politically correct" language), younger women remain immutably committed to expressing and naming women's experience, particularly in relationship to worship.

FIGURE 8h
Distribution of Scores on the Scale for Attitudes to Inclusive Language

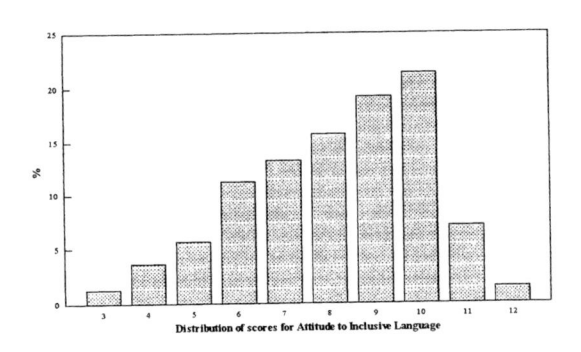

Distribution of scores for Attitude to Inclusive Language

Theological orientation also affects women's attitude to inclusive language, with women from evangelical traditions more antagonistic towards the use of female God-language. Table 8i illustrates how the relationship between age and language alters when a third variable, theological orientation, is introduced.

TABLE 8i Attitude to Inclusive Language by Age Group and Theological Orientation (%)

	Catholic		Liberal		Evangelical	
	Attitude to the use of Inclusive Language					
	Positive	Negative	Positive	Negative	Positive	Negative
Younger	84.7	15.3	87.5	12.5	74.1	25.9
Middle-aged	73.9	26.1	82	18	52	48
Older	56.9	43.1	51.7	48.3	33.6	66.4
	$p \leq 0.000$	n = 538	$p \leq 0.000$	n = 148	$p \leq 0.000$	n = 450

Two thirds of older women from an evangelical tradition have a negative attitude to inclusive language, compared to less than half of the same age group from liberal or catholic traditions. The inverse relationship between age and attitude to language is stronger in women from an evangelical background, which further emphasises the findings in the previous section of a clash between feminism and evangelicalism. The association of women's spirituality with the domestic sphere and the identification of women with stereotypically feminine qualities mitigates against their participation and visibility in the public sphere. Similarly, evangelical theology is based on biblical authority, and this can lead to an unquestioning acceptance of generically male language and imagery in relationship to God. To alter any aspect of the Bible (even though it may have suffered at the hands of androcentric male translators) by using female pronouns for instance, can be viewed as tampering with the word of God. Therefore, women from evangelical traditions are more cautious in the use of inclusive language, particularly in worship.

Overall, the picture is one where women priests do recognise the importance of language and seek to use it appropriately. This commitment to inclusive language is generational, evidence of the enduring impact of feminist thought. Attempts to trivialise the use of inclusive language have not succeeded, women are aware of the importance of being named. Women priests are seeking to give voice to women's experience in worship and in God-language. They are attempting to ensure that human spirituality is not presented in a definitively male way.

One of the most profound findings from this section of my research is the impact, on attitudes and behaviour, of theological orientation. A factor which demonstrates that our internal cultural maps, in this case theology, are endemic to the way we participate in our social worlds. Gender is one force which shapes the world as we see and experience it, but it is not the only one. This is a salutary thought for those who expect women to change the Church solely because of their inherently different gendered approach to ministry. Women priests are not a uni-dimensional, homogeneous group, they are diverse and varied in both attitude and approaches to ministry. They will not redeem the Church from patriarchy, or change its hierarchical structures, simply because they are women.

Women are demonstrating a collaborative approach to ministry which, coupled with a desire to work non-hierarchically, has the potential for transformation in the Church. However, evidence of women's clerical socialisation and equivocal approach to empowerment and egalitarianism compromise their capacity to change the Church. Feminism offers a coherent framework which could enable women to gain support and cope with the painfully bitter experiences outlined in Chapter 7, but their ambivalence, and in some cases antagonism, to it is detrimental to their capacity for development. Despite this, the first group of women priests are conscious of the need for religious language which includes women and reflects their experience. This is a seminal moment in Church history because women's ordination signalled the potential for a new dawn, an age of co-operation and interdependence resulting in new models of lay and ordained ministry. History is in the balance and women must together choose to be counter-cultural in their approach to ministry. Women in the Church must view Christianity through the lenses of feminism and feminism through the lenses of Christianity. The result could be a Christian feminist approach which has the potential to change the Church and perhaps, in a dynamic synergy, could also have a profound impact on society.

CHAPTER 9

WOMEN PRIESTS - THEIR STORIES

Women's voices need to be heard and their experiences made visible in a feminist research approach. In this study I have consistently grounded my work in both the experiences of women priests, and the voices of women theologians and feminist theorists. However, as a researcher I do not simply absorb and reflect back uncritically the material I receive, but it is processed through the filter of my analysis and the framework of my own thoughts and belief systems.[1] As Reissman says "We cannot give voice, but we do hear voices that we record and interpret." (1995:8). Thus there are three voices in this study: those of women priests, of feminist writers, and my own. They are not always harmonious or in unison, but in both their unanimity and their disparity understanding is developed. In the previous chapters I focused on my own analytical concern: drawn from the literature, from interviews with women priests, and from my own research interests. Yet there were other themes and nuances arising from the research which originated solely in women priests' accounts. These concepts occur repeatedly in the qualitative data and represent an important, significant part of women's priesthood narratives not covered earlier.

There are four main themes not reflected in the previous analysis, which occur in the qualitative data. The first two are experiential: the impact that the Act of Synod has on the lives of women priests, and their sense of historical significance as a group. The remaining themes are attitudinal: women's use of gender discourse in their stories about priesthood, and their perception of the need for, and the possibility of change in the Church. On the surface these themes appear relatively unrelated; they are disparate, left-over elements from the analysis. A closer examination, however, reveals a seam running through, threading together each part. Gender is the link between these four themes. Here is a group of people who are identified, not solely by status (i.e. as priest), but also by their sex. Male clergy are known simply as priests, their female colleagues are inexorably labelled "women priests". This is connected to a number of factors. In the first place, women's sense of historical significance as a group is associated with their sex; they are the first group of women priests. Secondly, the Act of Synod - legislation which institutionalises gender as a source of conflict - originates in a fundamentally opposing view of sex differences in the Church. Thirdly, women use gender as a core element of their priestly narratives to enhance their position as priests. Finally, women's potential to change the Church is intrinsically linked to the concept that they have a contrasting approach to ministry from men because of their different gender.

On the one hand, the fact that women in professions are identified by their sex and not just their job (women priests, women doctors, women judges etc.) signals the level of inequality which still exists. Once again, in patriarchal structures, the male is the norm, the female is "other" and is, therefore, distinguished separately. On the other hand, whilst as women we are still identified by our sex, it is a reminder of our commonality. Gender, which may have caused conflict and oppression, is also a source of solidarity, support and unity. Women from different races, classes and cultures, although they have very different experiences of life, can be united in a shared consciousness of patriarchy and its effects.[2] This common understanding has the capacity to bring greater emancipation for women and for other marginalised groups in society. Thus we have the choice as women of whether gender is a mark of our oppression, or a symbol of our unity and our transforming potential in society and in the Church.

A SENSE OF HISTORICAL SIGNIFICANCE

Women have been priests or ministers in other denominations and in different parts of the Anglican Communion for many years. The participants in this study are not the first group of women priests; nevertheless they are an historical, unique and important group. The sense of history in the making which surrounds them is neither overplayed nor hollow, for in the first instance, the Church of England is one of the largest, and most influential Churches to ordain women. Secondly, it is traditionally seen as the mother Church of the Anglican Communion and, as such, has a degree of influence in the ecumenical movement, particularly in relation to the Orthodox and Catholic Churches. When women were ordained as priests in the Church of England, it was as if some taboo had been broken, a line had been crossed from where there was no going back. In England women had entered one of the last bastions of male exclusivity, so their ordination had social as well as theological ramifications. This sense of historical significance is an important part of women's priesthood narratives in both their interview and written data.[3] They contain poignant accounts of occasions connected with women's priesthood, moments of meaning that help to make sense of the pain, conflict and waiting they have experienced.

In their accounts, women priests indicate their sense of historical significance by referring to three main occasions that have personal and spiritual meaning: the vote in Synod,[4] ordination and their first eucharist. These occurrences are imbued with significance, they are markers in women's lives that are akin to other rites of passage (baptism, marriage). After the turmoil of the debate about women's ordination, the euphoria of the vote was quickly dampened by the wave of mourning that appeared to sweep the Church.[5] The first ordinations in Bristol, on March 12th 1994, seemed to break the sense of self-doubt that had pervaded the Church, and the ensuing ceremonies throughout the country rekindled the nation-wide support and affirmation for women's priesthood. Finally, the eucharist, for many the ultimate symbol of priesthood, was also a moment of great meaning and significance for women. In their accounts women demonstrate that, through these events, they are taking a special, unequalled place in history - something which is beyond the experience of most women.

When the occasions that signify women's historical significance are marked in the priesthood narratives they are described in spiritual, not functional terms. There is a sense of transcendence that somehow, through their ordination, women are connected, beyond time, with God. The mundaneness or difficulties of life post-ordination are illuminated by the memories of these experiences. They justify women's individual calling and the corporate rightness of their priesthood:

> When the vote happened, I expected it to happen, I was there throughout the day. It sounds arrogant doesn't it, but I knew it would be OK. I knew it would go through and I knew it was all right. I knew I didn't need anyone outside of me to affirm me as a priest, I knew I was a priest.

In this quotation the vote in Synod (at which this respondent was not actually present) is described as a deeply spiritual experience, signified by the repetition of the phrase "I knew".

Here the respondent is not referring to factual knowledge, but a deep inner sense of premonition or prophecy, a "gnosis". The vote brought healing and affirmation for women who had suffered years of alienation and rejection. At ordination, women were fulfilling both their own individual destiny, and the destiny of the Church. It was, for many, a momentous event:

> And then we walked in and the cathedral was so full and it was incredible. It was very, very special and I remember thinking about half way through the service, that this is what I've been struggling for, for 16 years. I'm actually here at this moment and I didn't want it to end.

The occasions of the vote, ordination and first eucharist have a symbolic use in women's narratives. They are the means by which women convey the significance of their priesthood. One woman described how the doors of St. Paul's cathedral opened to admit them on their procession journey to ordination. The huge, normally locked doors were metaphors for the patriarchal exclusion of women in the Church. Their opening intimates the significance of women walking through into an arena of life previously denied them. Similarly, in the quotation below the respondent uses the moment in the eucharistic service where the priest stands behind the altar, to symbolise the opening of sacred space to women:

> I actually stood right behind the centre of the altar, instead of what I had done for many years which was to prepare the table and then stand aside. And not standing aside, but standing in that place that I'd never stood before, did feel very moving and calm. And maybe using that image of claiming the space seemed important in some way.

Women have been excluded from the space behind the altar for centuries because of their gender and sexuality. Menstruation and pregnancy, biological determinants of being female, have in the past rendered women unclean and therefore unable to participate sacramentally in full. Through standing behind the altar this respondent indicates that she is not only reclaiming male space, but she is reversing centuries of women's oppression by affirming female sexuality.

Women's accounts of the vote, ordination and eucharist are often deeply moving. They deserve greater acknowledgement than I can give in the limited space of this thesis. They signal women's sense of their historical significance and indeed their uniqueness. Their stories are poignant because they are the result of struggle, they light up and make sense of the pain women experienced as they waited for ordination. Suffering enables us to feel joy more acutely and the celebration in these accounts is heightened by the pain which encapsulates them. This is something which male priests, and the ensuing generations of women priests, will not necessarily experience.

Women priests also communicate their sense of historical significance by conceptualising themselves as pioneers, a role which is hard, but rewarding. Many acknowledge that, in spite of the pain it has caused them, they are glad and grateful to have lived to see women's ordination. To have been part of this pioneering group is, for many, a privilege. However, by defining themselves as the first, as ground-breakers, they are distancing themselves from second generation women priests. There was evidence from the qualitative and quantitative data that an unhelpful differentiation exists between the first and second group of women priests.[6] The former consider the second generation to be unaware and oblivious of the struggles that women priests face:

> Many of the first women to be ordained priest were fighters, visionaries, pioneers. Today, many women candidates for ordination that I meet do not have this dimension...They seem to wish to continue the ministry of the Church in the same well-worn ways in which they were brought up.

In contrast, of the few second generation women who were part of my sample,[7] several felt excluded from, and unsupported by, the first group of women priests:

> I feel that many women who were deacons/deaconesses for a long time do not think that we really "suffered enough" and treat us with what borders on hostility.

Women cannot afford this degree of distinctive separatism. It is only through their unity that they can hope to find strength and courage for facing the opposition which is still threatening them. Clare Herbert (1994) recognises that this loss of cohesion is caused by women no longer being viewed as the outsiders or the "opposition" in the Church. Now that they have been accepted into the Church hierarchy, women find themselves in competition for jobs and in conflict about whether or not there is a need for continued campaigning. First and second generation priests need to rediscover a sense of unity amongst themselves and with lay women, if they are to fulfil their potential to shape history.

The great historical significance of the first women priests in the Church of England is in no doubt. No-one can rob them of their place in history, but the events in the Church after the vote in Synod have seriously tarnished the radience of women's achievement. The Act of Synod has overshadowed women's entry into the priesthood and, six years on, it is hampering and diminishing the effectiveness of women's ministry. So what are the implications for the Church and for women, now that the Church has not only further institutionalised, but also positively legislated for sexism?

THE ACT OF SYNOD

When the Act of Synod was passed in 1993, few realised its theological and practical ramifications, both for women's ministry and for the Church. Grateful that the vote to ordain women had been cast in their favour, proponents of women's ministry were anxious, and indeed were pressurised, to comply with the Act and ensure its smooth passage through Church legislative procedures. A few voices sounded warning,[8] but they were ignored. It is only six years on that the full implications of the Act are now being discovered. There is growing disquiet that what had been intended to be a tool to develop consensus is, in fact, prising the unity of the Church further apart. The Church is affected at the highest levels with rumours circulating that priests have declined communion from the Archbishop of Canterbury because he has ordained women. Certainly the impact of alternative episcopal oversight is felt at a diocesan level,[9] where bishops have experienced the development of virtual no-go areas in their diocese and, as a result, their own ministry is curtailed. There are even calls for a non-geographical third province which would be a theological haven for those who dispute the Church's right to ordain women.[10]

The growing publicity concerning the Act, and the calls for it to be rescinded, may have affected women's responses to this study, but nevertheless it was a recurring theme in the qualitative data. In their accounts, where they refer to the Act of Synod, women priests do so in an overwhelmingly negative way. It is assessed in two main ways: the impact it has on the Church and the impact it has on women themselves. In the first instance, which is most prevalent, the Act is viewed as being harmful to the Church, institutionalising schism, polarising and disintegrating ecclesiastical structures. Secondly, and less common, the Act is seen to violate and harm women because it undermines their identity, self-understanding, worth and work. It legitimates sexism and misogyny and, some women feel, gives credence to the malicious and malevolent behaviour they have experienced in the Church:

> I feel we have been disempowered by the Act of Synod and its divisive consequences. My personal ministry has been affirmed in a variety of ways, but nevertheless there is an insidious feeling of having been fundamentally undermined by the very institution which voted strongly for women's fulfilment as priests in the Church of God.

One women describes the Act as a form of spiritual apartheid, and it is this view that the Act is fundamentally undermining of women which highlights why it is harmful and offensive. The system for alternative episcopal oversight does have the potential to be schismatic in the Church since it cuts across the diocesan structure and ultimately weakens the authority and power of the House of Bishops. However, it is the underpinning anti-women philosophy behind the idea of "two integrities" which is most alarming. In essence, the Act of Synod invalidates the ministry of a male priest because he has ordained a woman. No other issue, apart from gross indecency or financial mismanagement, has the capacity to challenge holy orders in this way. What does this say about the Church's attitude to women? To some people the ministry of women is so offensive and unacceptable that a separate Church structure is required which enables them to remain "untainted" by women. This view diminishes women and men, it stunts our understanding of humanity and warps our view of a God who could sanction such a degree of inequality. The Act of Synod hurts the Church because it hurts women. That, surely, is grounds enough for rescinding it.

The pressure on supporters of women's ministry to disengage from conflict was one reason why the Act of Synod was passed almost unquestioningly. The second contributory circumstance was the fact that MOW, considering its job completed, wound down its organisation and disbanded in 1994. It was November 1996 before a national campaign organisation (WATCH) was re-established and during the intervening years opponents of women's ministry had not been inactive:

> The role of "Forward in Faith" in proselytising and sowing seeds of dissension has not been given enough attention and condemnation. The Synod of the Church voted to ordain women and yet this group is allowed freely to encourage others to flout what has been through all the democratic processes.

A second theme in the qualitative data relating to the Act of Synod and "Forward in Faith", is the concept that opponents of women's ordination have been re-grouping after the vote and are stepping up their subversion of women's ministry. There is a perception, demonstrated in the quotation above, that members of "Forward in Faith" are actively recruiting new ordinands. Where groups of parishes come under the jurisdiction of one priest and, if one parish has chosen alternative episcopal oversight, it is impossible for a woman to be in charge.[11] It is also difficult for a clergyman, sympathetic to women's priesthood, not to compromise himself in this situation where his own ministry may be unwelcome. There is a feeling of anger among several women that more attention appears to be given, in the Church, to those who oppose women than to the women priests themselves.

It is easy, with the benefit of hindsight, to identify the intermediate period between MOW and WATCH as lost years. Nevertheless I believe this to be true. Fuelled by unrealistic expectations of the ease with which women's ministry would be accepted, and tired after a long and burdensome campaign,[12] MOW disbanded, leaving a political vacuum and the Church with no national voice for women. I can understand why MOW dispersed, but I regret it, for with it went the particular brand of lay/clerical support and co-working which was unique and which women in the Church need again.[13] The vibrant local groups of MOW have largely failed to be rekindled in WATCH and the gap before its formation meant that the Act of Synod could take root in the Church relatively unchallenged. It was a mistake to think that women's ordination would put an end to the opposition and animosity towards their ministry, a mistake for which the Church in general, and women in particular, are paying now.

There is a third response in the qualitative data to the Act of Synod, and that is one of denial. Here women either refuse to acknowledge the problems or, whist recognising the difficulties, indicate that forgiveness and love are the only way to deal with opposition:

> It is my opinion that those who are still opposed to women priests cannot be pushed into changing their views. They must see something in us that touches their hearts (Christ-like qualities). I have worked alongside male colleagues and lay people who cannot accept my priestly ministry, but like and value my pastoral ministry.

In these instances respondents appear to be aligning themselves with a Christian ideal-type which negates, or overlooks, the shadowy, negative side of human interaction and fails to understand the structural flaws in the organisational systems of the Church as an institution. Indeed, love and forgiveness should be hallmarks of a Christian response to personal enmity, however, they are states of being that are reached by facing, not disregarding, the conflict and contradiction in human relationships. Anger, too, can be a "Christ-like quality" and is, I believe, an essential component in the journey towards resolution, which begins with the acknowledgement of wrong-doing. Until women admit the reality of on-going opposition and antipathy towards their ministry, as expressed in the Act of Synod, they perpetuate the status quo. In patriarchy, internalised oppression means that women can affirm rather than challenge oppression, colluding with the structures that ensnare them. The Act of Synod is one such structure which requires confronting. As women and men cultivate an anti-patriarchal consciousness, there develops the capacity to tackle the institutionalised sexism represented in the Act.

The Act of Synod is patriarchy unmasked. It represents the totally unacceptable concept that women are objects of taint and abnormality. In which other organisation would this insidious premise be overtly expressed, let alone made part of policy or legislation? Where the Act is discussed in women's priesthood narratives, emphasis is given to its potential to polarise and cause further dissension in the Church. However, it is the pervading sexist implications of the Act which are most harmful. The "two integrities" affirm, and therefore condone, those who find women's ministry abhorrent. Alternative episcopal oversight provides a structure which enables these opponents to sideline anyone who holds an alternative integrity, thus invalidating the holy orders of those "tainted" by women's ministry.[14] Surely this concept is inadmissible on any level - social or theological. Not only does it contradict all moves towards a more equal, fairer society, but it belies a core value of Christianity which enshrines human dignity and equality. It is abhorrent, from a religious and cultural perspective, to presume that a person is ineligible for ministry because of their biological sex. The Church should stop attempting to hold together increasingly disparate strands; it must stay true to the emancipatory roots of Christianity which promise freedom and inclusivity for all, in Christ. For it is hard to understand why the unity of the Church is more important than the dignity of women and the wholeness of humanity.

GENDER DISCOURSE IN WOMEN'S ACCOUNTS

Gender, as a conceptual way of identifying and explaining women's oppression, was developed by feminists in the 1970s. By separating the biological distinction between women and men from the cultural definitions of "masculine" and "feminine", much feminist writing in this period characterised the way in which the social world had constructed female difference and inferiority (Oakely 1972, Greer 1970). Over the last two decades the term gender has been constantly revised and challenged, both by feminist and non-feminist writers, until the present day when it has become an intrinsic part of vocabulary and, in many cases, is interchangeable with the concept of biological sex.[15] In its original form gender was used to describe how cultural and social expectation created differences between women and men, assigning them contrasting social roles and attributing discrete characteristics to each sex. However, an alternative and not necessarily complementary concept of gender differences has also re-emerged in this intervening period. A body of feminist writing which celebrates women's different, and superior, characteristics became prominent:

> Women are celebrated for their distinctive approach to knowledge, emotion, moral choice, parental thinking and diverse forms of nuturance and altruism.
> (Oakley, 1997:43)

The reinterpretations of the "equal but different" argument by feminists (albeit into "equal but superior") reverted to the idea of natural differences between women and men. This is a philosophy which has been so problematic for women in the past that feminists had good reason to be initially suspicious and critical of it. The concept of gender difference has been well used as a tool for women's exclusion, and nowhere more effectively than in the Church. Opponents of women's ordination concurred heartily with the concept of innate male and female difference, women were equal, they said, but their gifts were just not suited to ministry.[16] In contrast, supporters of women's ministry appropriated the new-found feminist celebration of difference, arguing that women, because of their distinctive gifts, would enrich the ordained ministry of the Church by complementing men. I remain suspicious of the "natural identity" argument because there is a lack of internal consistency within it. In a quest for a women-centred alternative to patriarchy, women dismiss some characteristics, such as gentleness, sensitivity and caring, as socially constructed stereotypes, whilst at the same time appropriating more acceptable attributes, such as collaboration, egalitarianism and empowerment which can become more acceptable feminist stereotypes.[17] As a result women are left with no coherent, consistent framework with which to understand female inequality and consequently they inherit a confusion of messages concerning their relationships with men.

Research has shown that women in religious traditions who are involved in formal ministry perceive that there are differences in the way in which women and men approach ministry.[18] Whilst I am interested in whether or not my research concurs with these previous studies, I am concerned to move beyond women's perception of gender differences, to understand how they use gender discourses in their priesthood narratives. In the first instance, where gender is used in women's accounts, the premise is that women and men are different and, therefore, bring complementary gifts to ministry. Where the concept of gender is discredited, women are not dismissing any inherent differences between the sexes, rather they are implying that gender is not a source of conflict in their ministry:

> I have had few difficulties with gender, probably because of my age and upbringing. I have no inclination towards feminism, and find charm works better than confrontation but I have two old friends who won't receive communion consecrated by me (we remain friends).

This quotation illustrates the contradictions in women's accounts. The respondent begins by disassociating herself from any problems associated with gender, but she then gives a conflicting statement which reveals that people refuse her sacramental ministry, and gender is clearly an issue in her case. The denial that women's sex is problematic, like the negation of the Act of Synod's impact, is, I believe, evidence of internalised oppression. No matter how positive individual experience of priesthood is, the ministry of women is still a source of conflict in the Church, and antagonism towards women is evidenced widely, both here and in other parts of the Anglican Communion.[19]

The primary use of gender discourse in women's priestly narratives is to emphasise the importance and justify the authentic nature of women's ordination. Women's priesthood, it is suggested, has brought a wholeness and completeness to ordained ministry in the Church. Leadership in the Church is expressed as a partnership between women and men in which both are able to manifest their separate giftings. Implicit in this notion are several underlying concepts. First, women can only make complete that which was incomplete and, therefore, an exclusively male priesthood lacked certain qualities and characteristics that women are now able to bring. Secondly, difference between the sexes is conceptualised in the idea of gender complementarity. Here female and male are seen as two distinct parts of one whole, and by ordaining women the Church has created a holistic and representative priesthood. Women priests emphasise gender difference and complementarity in their narratives in order to justify women's priesthood and to demonstrate their success and the benefits they have brought to the Church. As a narrative device, discourse on gender difference asserts women's positive contribution to the priesthood by highlighting how women supplement the ministry of their male colleagues and therefore enrich the Church. It allows women to demonstrate their ascendancy without being seen to boast about individual achievement.

Certainly women bring completeness to Church ministry, not necessarily because of any inherently different attributes, but because of the uniqueness of each individual. By excluding half the human race the Church denied itself a rich resource of female experience which it can now access. If, however, women emphasise gender difference in order to communicate their success, they are in danger of giving credence to the counter argument that sex differences are a reason for excluding women from priesthood. Secondly, the concept that by including women in ministry, the priesthood is fully representative of all people, is unfounded. There are very few priests from working class or ethnic minority backgrounds; by stressing gender exclusively as a source of wholeness in the Church, women deny other economic, social and cultural factors which would ensure the priesthood identified with people at all levels of society.

There is, however, an apparently contradictory stream of thought that is also present in women's gender discourse. On the one hand difference between the sexes is emphasised in order to illustrate the effectiveness of women's ministry, demonstrating how women's ordination has had an ameliorative impact on the Church. On the other hand, women seek in their accounts to minimise the difference between female and male priests in order to normalise their status. They are keen to drop the gender prefix to the word priest which constantly identifies sex as an issue in ministry and is used only when referring to women. The male priest is normative and is simply alluded to as a priest. We are reminded of the unusualness of women's priestly status, and their abnormality is underlined by repeatedly specifying their gender:

> I hate being described as a woman priest - I am a priest who happens to be a woman.

> I think women's priesthood now being possible in the Church has brought a completeness and richness to the Church. In my own parish women play an important part in the leadership. At almost every service men and women both lead, gender is secondary to people's gifts of leadership.

In the second quotation, the respondent demonstrates the mixed messages in women priests' gender discourse. She begins by establishing the success of women's ordination, articulating the benefits they have brought to the ministry. This emphasises the difference between male and female approaches to priesthood. Having accentuated gender difference as a source of strength and opportunity for the Church, she then delivers the apparently contradictory statement that "gender is secondary", implying it is unimportant. In their priesthood narratives women use the concept of difference between the sexes to sure up their position and contribution to the Church, whilst at the same time discounting the effect gender has on women's status and acceptance in sacerdotal ministry. Women see gender difference as an acceptable vehicle for demonstrating their success, but distance themselves from over-identification with the concept of difference when it threatens their approval and credibility in the Church.

The variance and conflicting messages in women's use of gender discourse in their narratives is a reflection of their concern for Church acceptance, but also of their ambivalence towards feminism. When the difference between the sexes is minimised, it is often done in order to distance the respondent from feminism which, some feel, perpetuate women's victim status and portray women as marginalised by the Church. Women priests want to be integrated into the Church, feminism is perceived to accentuate women's non-acceptance which, in turn, challenges their self-reported success:

> I believe in complementarity in ministry, much to my joy we (women priests) work well collaboratively - often better than men, and should learn to enjoy each others styles of leadership, not emulate them. I prefer not to belong to "women's groups" and have not felt the need for this. We should be appraised for who we are and how we carry out our work - not on the grounds of our gender.

Here the respondent begins by articulating women's achievements in ministry, she establishes the importance of gender difference (and in some cases women's superior gifts) before proceeding to negate them by surmising that sex is immaterial to the priesthood. In doing so, the respondent distances herself both from feminism and from other women, claiming that gender is inconsequential. She does not want to be singled out, nor the differences between women and men's status to be emphasised. She wants to communicate the "normality" of women priests; by highlighting women's precarious position in the Church, feminism is a threat to their perceived recognition.

Gender difference is an important element of women's priestly narratives which is used to demonstrate the benefits of women's ministry, but then discredited in order to emphasise women's acceptance in the Church. The results of the qualitative analysis confirm the lack of a consistent and coherent gender framework, with women priests alternatively emphasising and then discounting differences between the sexes.

Gender is a term which describes the differences between women and men resulting from generations of patriarchal socialisation. The social construction of identity is not limited to an individual's lifetime, it is inherited, passed on from generation to generation until it appears endemic. However in-built they may be, psychological and character differences between the sexes are not necessarily part of our genetic code. Men are not immutably rational, analytic and competitive, neither are women intrinsically collaborative, empowering or egalitarian, but a process of generational socialisation has enabled us to appropriate these attributes more easily.

Women have the potential to enrich the Church through their experiences of oppression and marginalisation, not because of their inherently different approach to ministry. In order to fully effect change, women need to develop a conscious alternative way of doing and being priests which is the antithesis of patriarchy. They must then choose to walk in these new ways, gaining support from other like-minded people. My empirical research shows women are collaborative, but not overly egalitarian or empowering in their approach to ministry. If this is to change and women are to model an essentially different priesthood to men, then they must choose to be different and not rely on the assumption of inherently superior sensibilities.

ATTITUDES TO CHANGE IN THE CHURCH

The debate about women in the priesthood linked women's ordination to the possibility of change in the Church. Through their different and complementary gifts women would, it was argued, enrich and enhance the all-male ministry in the Church.[20] Inherent in this premise is the concept that the Church will benefit from the change and indeed is in need of the transforming potential in women's ordained ministry. Feminism in general, and feminist theology in particular, concurs with the need for liberation in ecclesiastical structures. The

Church is identified as a patriarchal institution and therefore it requires rehabilitation. Women have the potential to begin the process of transforming the hierarchical, male-dominated authority of the establishment.

The ordination debate and feminist theology are twin voices calling for change in the Church, although they have differing ideas about how change can be achieved. The former believes that admitting women into the heart of Church structures, in itself, will organically metamorphose sacrality. The latter calls for a more radical appraisal of the organisational ethos of the Church and it challenges the very structures to which women have, at last, gained entry. So what do women themselves think about change in the Church? Is there a concern to do things differently? Are women conscious of a need to develop new models of priesthood that will change the Church? If not, it is unlikely that they will intentionally work for internal transformation or develop new ways of working.

There is, however, a form of double-speak inherent in the arguments concerning the merits, for the Church, of ordaining women. Women will be both instruments of improvement and also protectors of the status quo. To the conservative majority, many of whom do not acknowledge the Church as a patriarchal institution nor share a concern for its radical reshaping, it is not women's capacity to change things which is of foremost importance, but it is their commitment to maintain the structures and practices of the Church which is significant (Hiatt 1996). Thus women are walking a fine line, they must show how their presence will benefit the Church without being seen to cause too much disruption. Whilst their sacramental presence must be portrayed as beneficial, women are also concerned to reassure critics that it will not cause radical change. That is a hard and narrow place to be.

Identifying the Need for Change

The need for women to be agents of change is a theme in some women's priesthood narratives; it is present in the data, but not universally so. Where the concern for transformation is strongly articulated, it is accompanied by evidence of feminist consciousness:

> As a feminist working in four very conservative parishes I feel constantly torn....I believe this is an important time for women priests to discover who they are as priests and as women and use these insights to free lay women to reflect on their ministry too...I will stay with it as long as I can retain my sanity and as long as these kind of changes continue. Ultimately I am driven by the belief that Christ did not abandon Israel but transformed it - and so my contribution is to stay within the Church and try and do the same.

In this extract the respondent draws both on feminist tenets and Christian symbolism to inform and support her desire to be different. It is a conscious choice, born out of a concern for equality and empowerment, but it is also clearly a lonely road to walk. To live counter-culturally within the structures that dominate and oppress women, not only threatens sanity, but strikes at the very heart of a core identity. To be a voice for change from the outside, or on the margins of an organisation, is very different to working from within the culture, translating principles into action, and revolutionising paternalistic structures. It is isolating, it requires that one be in an almost constant state of conflict, and ultimately the sheer "normality" of patriarchy is engulfing. It is no wonder that few women strongly identify with the need for ecclesiastical reformation in their narratives. After years on the edge, to be accepted and enfolded into Church structures is comforting and affirming. Ministry is more than a means of employment, it integrates personal and spiritual identity so that occupation and calling become one. For the majority of women, having at last experienced a holistic priesthood, to sacrifice this in order to work for further change is too much.

Once again feminism offers women the intellectual framework and emotional support to enable them to effect change. Christianity provides the spiritual context and motivation to work for the deconstruction of patriarchy, whilst feminism is a bridge to practical action. If harnessed together, there is the potential for real and far-reaching change. Whilst women priests remain ambivalent towards feminism and ignore the liberating potential in their faith, there is unlikely to be an unequivocal movement for change in the Church. Although not loud, there are voices which challenge the androcentric structures of the Church. They are sometimes despairing, but they also contain whispers of optimism, of hope spawned by the subtle shifts and changes in the way priesthood is being expressed by women. Time will tell if these murmurs will gain strength and become shouts of liberation, or whether they will be silenced by the raucous, cacophonous sounds of patriarchy.

Obstacles to Change

The number of women expressing a conscious desire for change in the Church is relatively small. However, by stipulating the obstacles facing women who are attempting to work differently, a further group is implying that transformation does need to take place. The pressures that women face are external (to conform and stay silent), and internal (to prove their success as priest), and both mitigate against women's capacity to be different. This is compounded by what some women regard, and indeed evidence, as their innate desire to convince rather than challenge or confront, for women are well schooled in the art of self-sacrifice. Finally, some women, looking around at their female colleagues, fear that there is evidence that women are conforming to male norms and ways of being and, in so doing, fail to fulfil their potential for transformation in the Church.

In the interviews and qualitative data several women identified that they felt pressurised to conform and stay silent now that they were priests:

> One of my concerns at the moment is that we seem to be "muzzled" and fear to speak out because we do not want to rock the boat.

Yet the statistical evidence did not overwhelmingly conform to the qualitative analysis. 19.1% of women said they felt speaking out about women's issues might affect their job opportunities, and 30.7% said they felt pressurised to stay silent. Although not conclusive, it is still alarming to think that nearly a fifth of women clergy feel intimidated and fear for their jobs if they try to change the Church, and a third feel they must suppress any further reforming action. However, a greater cause for concern is the fact that younger women felt more intimidated than women from the bridge or older generations. Women who are at the outset of their careers in the Church feel pressurised to conform to the existing models of priesthood because they feel they must prove themselves as priests. They feel that by challenging the establishment they are risking their future in the Church. If this trend continues for women coming into the ministry now, then the radical reforming voices will die out and this window of opportunity will be lost to the Church. If ever women, both lay and ordained, needed support from each other, it is now. They cannot afford to neglect or discard the concept of sisterhood. By prematurely rejecting it (or indeed failing to recognise its importance in the first place) women seriously jeopardise, not only their capacity to bring change, but also their own well-being and internal health.

Now that they are priests, a number of women articulated a concern that they felt pressurised to prove themselves in ministry and to be successful. The empirical research also revealed that 57.6% of women were burdened by the need to acquit themselves well, the responsibility of other people's expectations sits heavily upon their shoulders:

> I do carry the concern that if I am a "bad vicar", they (the congregation) may say later "we tried a woman and it didn't work", so I am probably over-anxious to succeed.

As the first, many women feel the spotlight of attention is upon them. They are concerned that women's ministry will succeed or fail on the basis of their performance. This is an understandable perception and, one suspects in many cases, a realistic one. Whilst male incompetence is attributed to a particular individual's non-performance, female failure is often blamed on her sex. Therefore, a "bad" woman priest is considered evidence that women are not suited to sacramental ministry, whereas a "bad" male priest is simply inept. Women are concerned that their conduct could jeopardise the future of women's ministry in the Church; they are therefore cautious about appearing unduly zealous in changing the way things are done. So, in a pragmatic concern for the continuation and acceptance of women's priesthood, the first group of women priests are circumspect about being agents of radical change in the Church. It is an understandable, but lamentable situation. Women are in a unique position to bring something new into established Church structures, but they are held back by a fear, not only for their own future, but for the future of women following them into ministry.

The third obstacle to women's transmuting potential is their reluctance to engage with confrontation or challenge. Many mistake the fruits of the spirit (love, joy, peace, kindness, goodness, gentleness, faithfulness and self control, Galations 5:22-23) as a prescription for placid acceptance of injustice. The compounding forces of a false Christian ideal-type and the traditional expectations of "feminine" virtues are a potent mix which disables women, forcing them to internalise their anger and their sense of being wronged:

> Perhaps all of us who are priests are a bit conformist, and often my conformist bit makes me long for approval and safety from the hierarchy.

This perceptive self-analysis reveals an underlying desire for orthodoxy which, I believe, fuels women's reluctance to engage with overt confrontation or challenge to the system.[21] History has shown the benefit of active campaigning or direct action. Women's right to vote and the fall of apartheid were both the result of high profile public, and often international, campaigning and conflict. Society does not change naturally, it is resistant and requires a degree of activism to engender a paradigm shift. The organisational culture of the Church will not be altered by women simply and quietly getting on with their jobs. A radical evaluation and campaign to change Church structures is the only way to ensure new models of priesthood.

The final theme relating to women's attitude to change is a fear that women, now that they are part of the Church hierarchy, are simply continuing to approach priesthood in the same way as men. The concept that women would bring new and complementary gifts to the ministry was integral to the sense of hope that invaded the Church with the new dawn of women's priesthood. It was an often repeated hymn to change which inspired confidence and expectation in those who supported the ministry of women. Five years on from the first ordinations, the reality of life on the inside has to some degree tarnished that sense of hope. Some women are disenchanted with the Church, some are disillusioned with each other: [22]

> Since 1994 those women who used to meet regularly no longer do so - are we so busy, lacking in trust, or are we in quiet competition with each other?

> I have watched the development of ordained women and am disappointed to find that some of those who I knew as trainees and who are still ministering have become very similar to their male counterparts, and the younger women have a competitiveness which makes it difficult to see how they can give the rounded wholeness to the Church which I had hoped women could have brought.

Women are disappointed because they had unreal expectations about the job they are now doing, and their capacity to change, in isolation, structures and practices which have developed over centuries. They underestimated the force of opposition to their ministry and disregarded too easily the support and campaign structures which could have helped them as they embarked on their journey into the patriarchal core of the Church. For many women ordination was the prize, the goal to which they aspired and which they attained; perhaps too little thought was given to life after the laying on of hands.

In reality women's priesthood is just a step on a long and painful journey to work for emancipatory Church structures which foster equality. Women's presence in those structures in greater numbers is a start, but in itself, will not bring about the far-reaching change that is required. This is something that women priests are now beginning to understand. There are "voices of protest" (King 1989) that ring out in women's priesthood narratives but, after years of campaigning, isolation and marginalisation, they are weary. They need new blood, new shoulders to share the burden, fresh voices to call for change and creative networks of support to cradle the challengers:

> I will go on in my priestly role, I can do no other. I will continue to hurt, I will continue to believe in and work for an inclusive community built on mutuality. I will continue to stand alongside the broken and the suffering and the sick. I will continue to stand against inequality however it manifests itself. I will continue to enable women's stories to be heard. I do have a "passion to make and make again, where all unmaking rules". But for now I am tired.

Feminism calls for the patriarchal structures of the Church to be deconstructed. Christianity calls for models of leadership which serve and empower, rather than control and manipulate. Women priests need to hear and respond to these twin summons and listen again to the hope that fuelled their entry to the priesthood. The stirrings for change are there, but they need wider acknowledgement and greater sustenance. The energy and commitment of lay women, which has been largely disregarded, must be harnessed again to form a cooperative of transformation among women. This is not the time for women in the Church to turn their backs on feminism. History has shown that feminism has been a catalyst for social change, transforming the attitudes, beliefs and the shape of culture today. History has also shown that feminists declare victory too soon:

> We fight to enter patriarchal institutions and are so overcome with gratitude on our admittance that we fail to continue to work to change and humanise those institutions.... We Christian women who have fought for women's ordination are in danger of quitting too soon in this round of feminist reformation. Our retreat would be welcome relief to those who still hold power in the Churches and who fear and distrust meaningful change. We must be vigilant not to allow what is presented as strategic retreat to develop into hasty and unwise accommodation to sexist patterns.
> (Hiatt, 1996:223)

Women priests in the Church of England are in very real danger of "quitting too soon" and I would underline Hiatt's sense of urgency at an opportunity being lost, for this first group are in a unique position to work for change in the Church. Their novelty, something which they wish to disregard, is their passport to new territory, their licence to do things differently.

Gender, the theme which links all these elements of analysis, is still the cause of conflict in the Church as the Act of Synod reveals, but it is also a source of opportunity. The first women priests in the Church of England are a unique group of women who are conscious of their place in history. The danger is that the opportunity they represent for the Church can be lost as women yearn for acceptability, and in struggling to achieve it, they conform to a patriarchal priesthood. Women offered the Church a chance to change, not because they are inherently different from men, but because they bring a fresh perspective. They have viewed Church life from the margins, they have experienced what it is to live on the edge; if they can translate that experience into action then there is hope for the future. Through their entry into the priesthood women unsettled the male-dominated structures of the Church, opening the way for new possibilities in ministry. Women's full entry into ordained ministry will only generate a paradigm shift if they continue to campaign collectively for change and development in the Church.

CHAPTER 10

FACING THE FUTURE: OPTIONS FOR CHANGE

The first women priests in the Church of England embodied the hope for a new dawn. They represented the dream of a fresh start and provided a powerful, inspiring new vision for the Church. Supporters of women's priesthood drew on the idea of inherent gender differences to point to exclusive, special contributions women would make to enhance the ordained ministry.[1] Women's capacity to enrich the priesthood, it was suggested, is augmented by their essentially distinct and unique gifts. Women's ministry was expected to complement men's, enhancing and making the priesthood whole. However, enhancement implies change, and change is not a concept which is universally welcomed by the Church. So women find themselves resolutely stuck in an impasse, facing an almost impossible task - they must prove that their ordination has benefited the Church and, at the same time, demonstrate that their presence has not fostered radical change.

The vision for women's ministry was one of increased collaboration, empowering styles of leadership, and egalitarian ecclesiastical structures. Women priests, it was hoped, would be less concerned with clerical status and more committed to democracy, and to promoting the role of the laity in the Church. However, the reality of women's ministry proves to be less conclusive, as the results of this study show. They reveal that women do work collaboratively and favour an empowering style of leadership, but they are not overly egalitarian their approach, nor do they necessarily disregard their clerical status in favour of the laity. At the same time my research revealed that some women have experienced unacceptably high levels of discriminatory treatment which originates, in the main, from the internal structures of the Church. If the Church is ambivalent about change, then this degree of antagonism to women alone highlights and emphasises why the Church cannot afford to stay the same.

There are other equally powerful arguments for change from feminist and Christian sources. Feminist theology offers the lens through which to view the essentially patriarchal, hierarchical nature of the Church which creates a propensity to dominance and privilege.[2] In doing so, feminist thought reveals structures and practices in the Church which are contradictory to the core message of Christianity. At the heart of the Christian religion is a concern for equality, where all humanity, created in the image of God, is of equal value and importance. It is a movement of liberation which aspires to spiritual, emotional and social wholeness for all people, regardless of race, class or gender. The Church is the physical representation of Christianity, it is the body of Christ, it is a community to transform communities. If the Church of England is to make this vision of inclusivity more than just a utopian dream, then it must change. So, what needs to happen if women are to change the Church and what are the responsibilities for change in the Church itself? How might women's ordination affect the Church's capacity to fulfil its destiny, to be a community of faith and equality which is a source of transformation and renewal in the spiritual and earthly realms?

HOW WOMEN CAN CHANGE THE CHURCH

My research has clearly shown that women are unlikely to be agents of transformation in the Church through their presence alone. The claims from romantic, and also, to some extent radical, feminists that women are inherently different and superior to men do not appear to be borne out by this study.[3] Even if the proportion of women priests in the Church of England increases to make their numbers comparable with men, there is no guarantee, or indication, that their presence will radically reshape the ordained ministry in the Church of England.

This initial group of women priests do, however, bring with them a unique set of experiences that enable them to identify with life on the margins. They have first hand knowledge of alienation in society, something every woman faces, which is compounded by their experiences of rejection and isolation in the Church. Women priests have the potential to draw on their experiences of being on the edge and use them to identify with other marginalised groups, working together for a more inclusive and empowering Church. However, deep-rooted change will only come as women choose to be different. That choice will be an uncomfortable one; it will ensure that women will continue to be misunderstood, their actions misrepresented and even ridiculed.

The journey to priesthood has been a long and arduous one for this first group of women priests, many of whom felt at their ordination a sense of "coming home". To truly bring transformation, women must experience again the place of exile, but this time from within the walls of priesthood itself. Feminism offers us as women a praxis for change which we disregard at our peril. Through shared experience and consciousness-raising, mutual support and non-violent campaigning, lay and ordained women in the Church can gain strength to make a difference; they need to stay angry, stay connected, and stay involved.

Staying Angry

Anger is an emotion which women in general, and Christian women in particular, do not express easily. Years of conditioning in society, and in the Church, have taught women to internalise their frustration.[4] The process of gender socialisation which identifies women's anger as "unfeminine" and "aggressive", teaches women to use manipulation rather than confrontation to achieve their aims. This attitude is reflected in some women's accounts:

> I feel that women have been their own worst enemies by being too forceful and "belligerent" - dignity, sensitivity and understanding have been much more effective in my experience.

Unresolved anger is, of course, a destructive force, but anger against injustice and oppression can be a motivating catalyst for change. Feminism has enabled women to perceive their own oppression and to be angry about it, thus fuelling their desire to challenge the status quo. Women in the Church need to first acknowledge and understand the debilitating effects of patriarchy, then they must feel their anger, whether for the first time or once again, and use it to provoke change.

Patriarchy is a system of control and institutionalised sexism which allows one sex to dominate the other.[5] It is sexual apartheid, confining women and men to separate spheres of unequal influence: women traditionally control the domestic sphere, whilst men have domain over the public arenas of work, politics, religion and finance. Power is synonymous with male identity. Even the sexual act has the potential to be an act of male domination as cases of rape and sexual abuse indicate. The Genesis creation story[6] in the Old Testament includes the prophecy that, as a result of sin, men would dominate women. In the New Testament the redemptive death of Christ overturned the old world order and created the possibility of a new worldview, based on a manifesto of love and equality[7] exemplified in the "table-sharing community" of the early Church (Schüssler Fiorenza, 1983). By the fourth century, however, the Church had adopted structures and practices of governance which reflected the hierarchical ordering of society from which women were excluded. Leadership in the Church evolved from the *diakonos* model of servanthood and mutuality, to the separatist, hierarchical, power-based model embodied in the privileged stratified systems of society. The Church was no longer a place of liberation for women, it became a place which mirrored the patriarchal norms of society where women's voices were unheard, their experiences ignored, and their contributions unrecognised.

Though much has changed, not least women's admission to the ranks of ordained priesthood, men still dominate ecclesiastical power bases, whilst the Act of Synod perpetuates sexism and institutionalises misogyny in the Church. Yet women and men have lived so long with their gendered roles and expectations that they are blind to the insidious effects of patriarchy which present a truncated, mutated view of humanity. Both sexes are prevented from fulfilling their full potential by the constraints and self-limitation of their separate, dichotomous spheres and identities. Theologically, if to be human is a reflection of the Divine, then patriarchy presents a warped, one-dimensional God whose redemptive powers are severely curtailed by overly masculine identification. It is no wonder that women need to be angry. It is time to enter the temple courts and overturn the tables of intolerance, of dominance and of oppression. It is time to be angry.

Once they have identified patriarchy in the Church and felt their anger, how can women then use their knowledge and understanding as a catalyst for change? Firstly, through education, by passing on wisdom and life-experience to those who follow. By sharing personal stories, women priests impart their corporate history to the next generation. This is no cascading of purely cerebral knowledge, but it is the generous gift of experience which can be used to enrich and inform other women, helping them to make sense of their world. It is of concern, therefore, that my research showed a gap in understanding and acceptance between the first and second generations of women priests. The former consider that women entering the priesthood now are unaware of the struggles and barriers faced by the first female priests. The latter group feel excluded and unsupported by those who have pioneered women's ordained ministry in the Church. There is no room in the Church today for a gulf between the first and second generation of women priests, nor is there scope for separatism between lay and ordained women. We need to listen and learn from each other.

Consciousness-raising, one component of education, is a concept which was adopted by feminists but, because of its pejorative overtones,[8] it has to a certain extent fallen out of favour. However, the principle of consciousness-raising is an important one; it describes the slow dawning of understanding, the development of a new way of seeing, which women undergo as they begin to realise their own oppression.[9] The gender hierarchy of society is so intrinsic that it is often simply perceived as "normal". Women are so used to being excluded from the public arena, that it is their presence, rather than their absence, in places of power and influence which incites comment. The process of consciousness-raising is the journey of self-discovery through which women see their position of exclusion as "abnormal" and unjust. Lay and ordained women in the Church have discarded or ignored feminism, and the quest for feminist consciousness, too easily. Through listening to the voices of feminist theologians, and by reflecting on our own experiences of powerlessness and dominance, women can discover a new consciousness. This consciousness challenges the taken-for-granted ways of knowing in society[10] and develops a new spiritual understanding. Feminist consciousness in the Church will provide a different worldview which will enable women and men to discover new depths to their own spirituality. It will uncover roots of liberation in the Christian faith which are not just transforming for individuals, but have the potential to be a force for change in society as a whole.

Finally, in order to be catalysts for change, women need to name their experience.[11] Women's accounts of their priesthood journeys were bitter-sweet. Experiences of sexism and discrimination were contextualised by stories of success and affirmation, difficulties and abuse were mostly recounted within the context of individual success. Women want to prove that their presence has benefited the Church; continued wrangling and disunity over women's ordination is perceived as harmful, and so women priests are keen to demonstrate their effectiveness and acceptability. However, women need to name the reality of their experience, they need to name their oppression. Unity will not be won in the Church by ignoring difficulties or burying pain. History has taught us the importance of naming experience as a critical step on the journey to forgiveness and reconciliation.[12] Unequal, distorted power relationships appear to damage most profoundly those who are oppressed, yet in reality both parties are impaired. Oppression is a destructive force, emotionally and spiritually, for its perpetrators and its victims. If the Church is to be a place of wholeness, a healing community in a broken society, then it must face and repent from its own "internal demons". Women, by naming their experiences, can help the Church to face its demons of sexism, misogyny and dominance.

Recognising patriarchy in the Church, and feeling anger at the unequal distribution of power between women and men, is the first step on the path of change. As women recognise the injustice of their position, name their experiences of oppression and share their understanding, they can lead the Church into a place of greater wholeness. This is not a journey that can be undertaken by lone individuals, it is a corporate journey. Women priests need to find strength from other lay and ordained women if they are to counteract the effects of patriarchy. They need to stay connected.

Staying Connected

Feminism quickly recognised the importance of women connecting and acting together. Feminists saw that, if women were to deconstruct sexism in society, they needed support and encouragement from each other. Women's strength lies not in the competitive manoeuvrings of the professional world, but in their ability to create networks of support. Webs of relationships have the potential to hold women and sustain them in their increasing conflict with the male dominated structures of society. Feminist theologians echoed the importance of women together, recognising that, if women are to find freedom in religious and spiritual expression, there needs to be a women-centred alternative to the all pervasive masculinity of institutionalised religion (Maitland 1983, King 1989). Women's groups were an important source of support and vision in the struggle for women's ordination. They are still needed to give women clarity of purpose, confidence in their ability and support in the on-going campaign for greater equality in the Church.

Women need to connect with each other, either in close personal relationships,[13] or in groups, in order to maintain a sense of perspective on our position in society and in the Church. Stanley and Wise (1983) describe this perspective as a "valid paranoia" which affirms women's alternative way of viewing the world, even though it is totally opposite from how the world sees itself. Women need to support each other in order to maintain this "other" vision of society, to be reminded that their alternative way of seeing is authentic. Even though women have achieved a degree of cultural equality, enough to suggest to some women that there is no further need for feminism, we have not fully overcome the process of gender socialisation which leaves women with poor self-esteem and reticent to participate in mixed-sex groups. As a result women still need space away from men in order to reverse the process of gender education and to find our own voices, our own sense of power.

Women in the Church need a safe space, apart from men, where they can be connected with each other and find support to engage with the process of change and transformation. Change can, however, be a source of painful, schismatic conflict and it is hard for women to be the cause of pain and disunity. Isolated, women will be unable to shoulder the projected guilt and antagonism arising from the division over their ordination. Women priests need to stay connected with each other in order to gain strength and find the courage to be different. Women priests must also remain connected with lay women, allowing themselves to be challenged and provoked about their ministry. By remaining in close contact with lay women, women clergy can develop their role and function as priests within a feminist community of faith. Through reflexive group processes women can gain strength and vision for change in the Church. They can find the support to be different, and the encouragement to choose new ways of working. Women together can be advocates for collaborative, egalitarian and empowering models of ministry.

Finally, women in the Church must invest, once again, in a national campaigning support structure. MOW provided a model which unified women from various backgrounds - feminist and non-feminist, old and young, catholic, evangelical or liberal - in a localised and national framework for action and support. After a fallow two years a campaign group was rekindled. WATCH is now actively campaigning for women bishops and for the rescinding of the Act of Synod. The need for such an organisation is not universally recognised, but it is of utmost importance. It has the potential to reunite lay and ordained women in a search for a more inclusive, less hierarchical ministry. WATCH maintains a careful balance in its leadership structures between lay and ordained people, and it can therefore provide a forum for debate and challenge about women's role in the Church.

Feminism recognised the importance of women together. It understood that the careful weaving of relationships provides a powerful means of support and a strong protective force for women as they discover, and seek to break free from, their individual and universal oppression. Woman-church is a theological concept which enshrines the connectedness and shared support needed for women's engagement with patriarchal social structures. It is not, Elisabeth Schüssler Fiorenza states, a separatist, exclusively female strategy, but "it means simply to make women visible as active participants and leaders in the Church, to underline women's contributions and suffering through Church history, and to safeguard women's autonomy and freedom from spiritual-theological patriarchal controls" (1996:10). For together women can find the strength to be different, the support for dealing with conflict, the encouragement to discover new models of priesthood, and affirmation for women's alternative, authentic way of seeing and naming the world. Together women can discover the resources they need to stay involved and engaged in the struggle for greater equality in the Church.

Staying Involved

Change can only take place in the Church if women choose to engage in active campaigning. However, my research demonstrated a lack of cohesiveness in women's attitudes to campaigning. Whilst some clearly recognised the importance and effectiveness of direct action, others were more concerned to prove themselves able to do the job, and thus believed this might be the way to change opponents' anti-women attitudes. This ambivalence to campaigning is, I believe, stronger in women from Church backgrounds than it is in women from the wider society. The Greco-Roman, dualistic worldview which pervades western society is compounded for women in the Church by a theological inheritance which favours personal spirituality over political or social action. Feminism can provide a praxis for change, but women priests also need a theological context in which to locate their action. Liberation theology, which originally evolved out of a specific South American context but has been widely used elsewhere (for example in South Africa and India), has provided for some feminist theologians a basis for their own manifesto for change.[14]

In their accounts, women priests emphasised the spiritual elements of their journey to priesthood: in particular their sense of call, the vote in General Synod, their ordination and first eucharist. Women's entry into priesthood was not, in the main, motivated by a desire for justice, but in response to a call from God. In their narratives, women emphasised their own personal spirituality in preference to the concept of political action. In doing so, they are reflecting the philosophical and theological influences which dominate western Christian thought. In the first instance, dualism has created a paradigm of separation, where the physical and the spiritual are two disconnected states of being. These two realms became associated with natural sexual dichotomies in a hierarchy of importance: the inferior physical realm was linked to women, whilst the superior spiritual realm was connected to men. This legacy of binary thought still pervades the western worldview, and partially explains women's desire to present their priesthood journeys in spiritual, rather than socio-political terms.

The second influence on western Christian thought is neo-Platonic philosophy which emphasises the contemplative in preference to political or social action (Lobkowicz 1967).[15] The story of Martha and Mary (Luke 10:38-42) was interpreted by early Church writers[16] to admonish the active Martha and to praise Mary for her concern for higher, spiritual matters.[17] Personal spirituality continued to gain preference as a means of salvation, over and above any concern for political or social change, until practical Christian action became confined to the concept of acts of kindness or charity. This emphasis on contemplative has also fuelled women's reluctance to identify their priesthood journeys with a concern for justice and a desire for political change in the Church, and in society at large. However, women need to develop a philosophical and theological framework which not only legitimates their campaign for equality, but makes it an intrinsic part of women's calling.[18] Feminism provides the praxis, a feminist liberation theology can provide the theological context for women's continued involvement in campaigning.

Feminist liberation theology draws on the basic tenets of Latin American theology, but enlarges them to address the global oppression of women. Liberation theology implies a number of intrinsic approaches which are of value as women seek emancipation in the Church. First, liberation theology questions the role of the Church in perpetuating social oppression and is critical of developmentalism. It stresses the importance of education as a means of individual self-determination. Finally, liberation theology emphasises the liberating, integrating power of the Gospel on three connected levels: socio-political, utopian, and spiritual (Fiorenza 1975, Ruether 1972). A feminist liberation theology is not just a theoretical worldview but a liberation movement for social and ecclesiastical change in which the quest for women's dignity is synonymous with a quest for God. It strives for "wholeness", for the overcoming of theological dualisms which separate body and soul, female and male, spiritual and earthly, but at the same time, it recognises that this cannot be achieved without the dismantling of hierarchical dominance in theology and in the Church (Schüssler Fiorenza 1996).

A feminist liberation theology enables women to rediscover the radical, unequivocal social message of the Gospel [19] exemplified in Mary's exultant, prophetic words of the Magnificat (Luke 1:46-55), and Christ's "mission statement" at the outset of his ministry: [20]

> The spirit of the Lord is on me, because he anointed me to preach good news to the poor. He has sent me to proclaim freedom for the prisoners, and recovery of sight to the blind, to release the oppressed, to proclaim the year of the Lord's favour. (Luke 4:18-21)

This passage, and others like it, are often interpreted metaphorically as referring to the spiritual realm, but from a liberationist perspective, they speak of socio-political transformation too. How can Christianity be good news for the poor unless it intrinsically advocates the alleviation of poverty? How can Christianity mean freedom for the oppressed unless it can contribute to social transformation and the creation of a more egalitarian society? Therefore, women, as the poorest and most oppressed members of society, must benefit from the promise of a new world order inherent in the Christian message.

Feminist liberation theology critically appraises the Church's role in the maintenance of gender imbalance and the unequal power distribution in ecclesiastical structures. It challenges the developmentalist approach, apparently adopted by most women in the Church, who seek to quietly reform existing structures. A feminist approach requires an extensive evaluation of practices in the Church and a more radical restructuring, in order to facilitate greater opportunity for women. Women's self-determination is dependent on a process of consiousness-raising; as with liberation theology, education is the key to the establishment of greater equality. Through education individuals are empowered to fulfil their full potential within the Church and beyond. A feminist liberationist theological framework conceptualises the Gospel as a holistic transforming force, which operates within a socio-political dimension where women and men have equal access to public and private arenas. It offers the vision of a new world order in which patriarchal social structures are transformed. On a spiritual level, the Gospel is seen as a means of liberation from sin and the re-establishment of communion with God - it is the process by which social transformation is made possible. A feminist liberation theology offers a theological framework which justifies and validates women's involvement in campaigning. It advocates a critical assessment of the Church's attitudes to women and thus legitimates continued action for change.

Finally, my research brought out clearly the fact that women's theological orientation impacted their attitude and approach to ministry in the Church. Catholic, evangelical and liberal traditions are powerful paradigms that influence women's response to the priesthood. There has been much debate about whether or not each element of Christian tradition contains a theologically coherent argument for women's priesthood.[21] Yet there is little dialogue about the interaction between theological orientation and feminist approaches to priesthood. Women need, therefore, to move beyond the concept of ordination to discover a feminist model of sacrality within their individual theological positions. Women must determine how they can maintain their theological integrity whilst appropriating feminist tenets. How, for instance, do women from a catholic background preserve the sacramental symbolism of priesthood without developing hierarchical, exclusive rituals? Similarly, how do women from an evangelical position ensure that faithfulness to biblical sources does not result in a conservative view of women's role in Church and in society? Women from both traditions need to ask how their understanding of priesthood can embrace and enhance the ministry of all people in the Church.

The first group of women priests in the Church of England have the potential to be prophetic voices for change if they draw on their experiences of marginalisation as a source of inspiration. They can be instigators of transformation, helping the Church to fulfil its destiny as a community of faith, liberation, equality and inclusivity. However, whether women choose to do so is not a foregone conclusion. It is a free-will decision, a choice which faces each individual priest. Feminism and Christianity are an unlikely partnership in the face of their historical, mutual hostility, but where combined, they offer women the theoretical framework and practical means to transform social and ministerial interaction in the Church and in society.

Together they create a vision for communities of shared support and equality. As they recognise the effects of patriarchy, remain connected with each other and stay engaged in practical movements for change, women in the Church, both lay and ordained, can work towards a new future.

HOW THE CHURCH CAN CHANGE

The responsibility for transformation in the Church does not lie with women alone, a corporate, organisational response is also required to the issues raised by my research. Change occurs at the interface between the powerful and the powerless. When grassroots action co-incides with an attitudinal shift in the hearts of the power brokers, the combination results in social and political change.[22] Campaigning and direct action are motivating, transforming forces, but they only cause real, non-violent change when they are accompanied by evolutionary conversion in the hearts of the policy makers. The same is true for the Church and, therefore, women can only change the Church to the extent that the Church is prepared to let itself be changed. My research has identified potential structural and attitudinal shifts which need to take place in the Church in order to fully embrace the ministry of women.

Attitudinal Changes

Women's ordination has, I believe, highlighted the need for a radical re-evaluation of ordained ministry and an appraisal of the priest's role and function. This exercise is necessary, not solely to increase women's involvement in the Church, but also to develop a model of ministry which is relevant to the culture in which it is located. The secularisation of society in the post-war period is largely blamed for the decline in Church attendance [23] although, in reality, it is interest in institutionalised religion which is diminishing, and not fascination with spirituality. The

Church is in danger of becoming an island in the community, a marginalised and increasingly irrelevant force in society, because its main focus is the maintenance of its own internal structures in which the priest is a central figure. The Church sees itself as the centre of spirituality for the community, it is the focus of the Christian "family", where the priest has a parental, nurturing role. It is this idea of priest as parent which is problematic, not least because it has mitigated against women as they entered the priesthood.

When the priesthood was confined to men, father-identification was sustainable because of gendered parental roles in society. In gendered family relationships, the role of the father has clearer boundaries than that of the mother. He is not expected to be with his children all the time and, because of his involvement in the public sphere, is only available to the family at certain times of the day. On a practical level, a male priest may also have a wife to maintain his home context, so that his role as spiritual father to his congregation does not overly conflict with his paternal role within his family. In contrast, the gendered role of the mother-priest is inherently dysfunctional and almost impossible for women to fulfil. Where the father's role has boundaries, the mother's role is boundaryless. She is expected to be constantly available to, and responsible for, her children - her ideal-type is to be an all-nurturing, ever-present and self-sacrificing figure. For a woman priest, to be totally available to family and parish, to nurture children and congregation, is both practically problematic and damaging at an emotional and spiritual level.

The parental identification of the priest is harmful to women because it places them in an almost impossible ministerial situation, but it is also damaging to the Church since it can infantalise laity spiritually. Spiritual dependence on the priest means that lay members of the Church can fail to develop their own spiritual maturity, and this curtails their effectiveness in the community. Thus, the Church's sphere of influence in society is largely dependent on its ordained ministers. The functional role of the priest evolved from a position of social superiority where "gentleman and parson were very closely allied, the profession and status were scarcely separable" (Heeney 1988:78). The priest was an influential and often powerful force in local communities. As a key figure in society the priest also represented a bridge between the sacred and the secular: he was a visible symbol of the sacramental in every day life. The decline in Church attendance has coincided with the diminishing social status of the priesthood and so, if the Church is to remain a symbol of Christian sacrality in society, new models of ministry are required. The focus in the Church needs to shift away from the centrality of the hierarchical ordained ministry, to a theological understanding which embraces fully the concept of "the priesthood of all believers".[24]

The image of the body-Church represented in 1 Corinthians:12 is a powerful picture of an interdependent community of believers, where each person has a role, and where no one role has a superior status to another. It is a Church which is focused on people rather than buildings, on relationships rather than structures. It is a Church which symbolises human connection and inter-relatedness. It is a Church where each member, through their involvement in the work place, school, home or neighbourhood, is a sacramental presence in their community. God in the everyday-ness of life is represented by the body-Church in the community. Here, the role of the priest is as a facilitator of faith, one who empowers members of the congregation to find their own strength, sense of self, and purpose in God. The priest is not mother or father, but sister, brother, friend.

The priesthood reflects symbolically, through a sacramental presence in the Church, the sacred role each individual has in his or her community. One element of the eucharistic symbolism involves the priest sharing in the brokeness of Christ, and in doing so acknowledging the individual pain of the congregation and the corporate suffering of their community. Yet it is this brokeness which brings wholeness and unity, a symbol to the world of this body-Church called to share the love of God and to work for justice in its communities. This interpretation of Church is more congruent with feminist principles. It stresses the importance of individual self-development and awareness, and it emphasises the connectedness and shared support of a network of relationships. Finally, the body-Church is a community of liberation which empowers each individual member to engage with social and political change. Is this a utopian feminist dream, or is it a vision of a potential new future in the Church? How can the Church respond to the voices of the women it has ordained?

The second attitudinal change that is required for the process of transformation is one of repentance and turning away from the sin of sexism. Rosemary Radford Ruether (1983) describes conversion journeys that individual women and men need to undertake in their disassociation from patriarchy. Women's conversion is centred, partly, around their discovery of anger, self-worth, and pride - a developing understanding of women's oppression and alienation. Women's growing confidence in their own personhood is one part of the journey from sexism, but true transformation requires a parallel male journey. Ruether identifies two stages in the male response to feminist consciousness. The first is to trivialise and ridicule women's critical appraisal of sexism in society. The second stage Ruether describes as co-option, where men become aware of the huge polarisation of the sexes and realise the loss they have suffered in being denied access to the "feminine" side of their nature. These approaches, she says, are ways of resisting true conversion, for "real conversion from sexism begins to happen only when a man is able to enter into real solidarity with women in the struggle for liberation" (1983:191). Conversion demands a willingness from men to take risks and sacrifice, often at the expense of their economic status and privilege.

Ruether rightly advocates individual conversion experiences in the process of liberation from sexism. However, I believe that an organisational response is also required from the Church. The personal conversion journeys need to be reflected corporately and gathered together in a public acknowledgement of the Church's treatment of women - a process which demands that women's stories of alienation and oppression in the Church are heard and responded to. Repentance is the outward sign of an inward change of heart. It is a literal turning away from the sin of sexism. Patriarchy is institutionalised sexism, and therefore the Church needs to redeem itself from the sin of sexism at an institutional level. Only when individual transformation is reflected in a corporate change of heart is there the potential for healing, reconciliation, and restoration of gender relationships in the Church.

Structural Changes

Attitudinal transformation, unless it results in a structural, practical response, is insufficient. Noble words and thoughts are meaningless unless they cause action. Nevertheless the *metanoia* experience is the origin of lasting change, it is a prerequisite foundation for policy and organisational development. There are several key operational and legislative concerns, identified in my study, which affect women's acceptance by, and experiences of, the Church.

These areas of policy, practice and legislation, if addressed, could provide a significantly improved working environment for women priests.

The main item for immediate action is the Act of Synod. WATCH believes that the Act is "so theologically and doctrinally unsound, divisive and ecumenically objectionable" that it should be rescinded (Mayland 1998a). My research has revealed that it is also deeply harmful to women on a practical, emotional and spiritual level.[25] The Act of Synod, and the provision of alternative episcopal oversight, are offensive to women because they legitimise women's exclusion and create a form of sexual apartheid by creating areas in the Church where women's ministry is unacceptable. Emotionally, women are damaged by the constant sense of rejection, unworthiness and the abusive behaviour that the Act can generate. Spiritually, the Act fosters a theology of "taint" whereby a man's ministry is made void though his association with a woman priest. In a binary, dualistic view of sexual difference, the Act legitimises male spirituality, whilst it denies women's acceptability before God and denigrates their ministry.[26] The Act of Synod encourages unjust and discriminatory practice and it fosters intolerance against women. The Church cannot maintain its theological integrity, nor can it be a credible voice in society if it fails to rid itself of this divisive legislation. Therefore, the Church cannot develop inclusive models of priesthood which enhance women's ministry, unless the Act of Synod is rescinded.

The second legislative change required is a measure to allow women to be bishops. The original legislation, passed by General Synod, allowed women to be ordained priest, but stopped short of admitting them to the episcopate. The "stained glass ceiling", as one women priest described her experiences in the Church, is not just an invisible attitude barrier to women's advancement, it is a tangible obstacle to their preferment. Internationally, there are already a number of women bishops in the Anglican Communion. However, because of the Act of Synod, there are far-reaching implications if women in England are ordained to the episcopate. For instance, whilst the diocesan bishop is male he has access, at least theoretically, to every parish under his jurisdiction. A woman bishop could be legitimately excluded from a parish in her own diocese, since the legislation allows for congregations to choose not to receive the ministry of a woman priest.

Since women were only ordained priests in 1994, there is a presumption that it is too soon to justify their promotion to the episcopate. However, my research has shown that the majority of the first women priests have served the Church for many years in a variety of roles. They have a depth of experience gained at all levels of parish and sector ministry, and many are suitably placed for senior Church appointments. The time has come to recognise women's contribution to the Church by opening up senior positions to them, including the episcopate.

Both the Act of Synod and the inaccessability of the episcopate to women highlight the fact that the Church of England is exempt from employment law and is not compelled to conform to the Sex Discrimination Act. In most other organisations it is illegal to be biased against women in recruitment processes, let alone positively discriminate against them in organisational policy. It seems an anathema that ecclesiastical law, which is actually passed by Parliament, so fundamentally contradicts employment law. As a result clergy are alternatively left in either a vulnerable position with no employment rights or, if they are in a tenured postion, with near immunity from dismissal, whatever their misdemeanors. However, it is women who are most disadvantaged by the Church's exclusion from current employment legislation. There is no formal monitoring of the deployment of women,[27] nor is there access to redress if women feel they have been discriminated against. Finally, if women or men are harrassed or abused at work, there is no guarantee that the perpetrator will be dealt with appropriately by the Church. Women (and men) in the Church need the protection of employment law, in particular the Sex Discrimination Act. The Church needs to develop good employment practice on a national, not just diocesan, scale and should regulate its performance through thorough equal opportunities monitoring.

There are clear indications throughout the study that women who are married to clergy, or who have young children, are particularly disadvantaged in the Church. In fact, women who are married to clergy and have very young children find it almost impossible to fulfil any priestly role. The problems that face women in these situations, are complex and relate to the accepted working practices of priests, and the policy of the Church regarding more senior appointments.[28] First, the unpredictable and unsociable working patterns of priests mitigate against finding good, affordable childcare. This concern is further compounded for clergy couples, where financial and time considerations mean it is nearly impossible to combine joint parish and family responsibilities.[29] The Church must address how it can provide a working environment for priests which is more conducive to family life.

There are a range of developments which would benefit the family: the provision of childcare allowances, recommendations about acceptable and unacceptable working hours, a system of on-call clergy so that people could protect their time off, the rescheduling of activities and offices so that they do not conflict with family times. Above all there needs to be a degree of understanding and consideration for family relationships which does not, at the moment, appear to be present in the Church. Women feel guilty at what they perceive to be extra pressure placed on their colleagues because of women's childcare responsibilities. In reality, it is the nature of the all-demanding priestly role which is constraining and requires re-evaluating.

The second area of concern relates to women who are married to priests.[30] Each diocese has a different response to clergy couples: some pay according to the post, others pay a part stipend to one of the couple (even though they do a full-time job), whilst some couples have only been offered one stipend for two posts. Women have also been unable to gain promotion at a parish level if their husband is an incumbent. The lack of foresight and inconsistency about the way clergy couples are treated has led to inequalities in the Church which need to be addressed. The Church must deal with this problem at a national level, with the development of Church-wide guidelines on the deployment of clergy couples. Joint clergy marriages are here to stay and their numbers will increase as more women come through into the priesthood. The Church cannot afford to continue ignoring the difficulties couples face when both partners are priests. Nor can it disregard the problems experienced by women with young children. Unless it chooses to respond to the issues raised here, it could loose a large proportion of the high calibre women who have been called to serve the Church.

Finally, I began this section by acknowledging that whilst heart change is a pre-requisite for practical action regarding women's ministry in the Church, real attitudinal shifts must result in tangible outcomes for women. One of the clearest indicators of a change in heart is a change in language. Inclusive language is not about political point scoring, it is the evidence of a paradigm shift. Where patriarchy is unmasked, and women and men realise the structures of domination and segregation that have governed them, "other" language is no longer acceptable. New, alternative means of expression are created which include and reflect the experiences of women. Language no longer imprisons women in the invisible straight jacket of male identity and experience. Nor, in worship and prayer, does it represent a male-identified God. If the Church is serious about fully including women, so that their role and contribution is embedded in the sinews of Church life, then life-giving, women-affirming liturgy is required. Ultimately, inclusive language is not about legislation, although the official liturgical committees in the Church would benefit from engaging with the work of St. Hilda's Community and WATCH, but when the female can be fully acknowledged in religious expression, then there will be a more inclusive Church.

It was erroneous to assume that the ordination of women is synonymous with women's equality in the Church. This is not the case, for the process of women's liberation is a journey. Emancipation and fulfilment does not come in a one-off act, it is developmental and evolutionary. In her book *A Map of the New Country* (1983), Sara Maitland raised several concerns about the campaign for women's ordination. She was fearful that, once co-opted into male clerical circles, women would be absorbed in to the patriarchal structures of the Church which would "in the long term, serve to increase the dichotomy between lay and ordained, rather than eliminate it" (1983:36). Citing the American experience,[31] Maitland warned that equal access to ordained ministry did not necessarily equate with equal employment opportunities or salary levels. Finally, she intimated that the ordination of women would obfuscate and detract from the real problem of "in-built sexism and dualism in the Church" (1983:104). The results of my study suggest that Maitland's sense of foreboding was justified and that her prophetic words are, to a considerable extent, proving to be true.

Is it too late then for change? Is the window of opportunity for transformation in the Church closing? Women can, I believe, still be catalysts for change. Through coalitions of support and justice seeking, women can help the Church to discover an alternative worldview, one in which women are not alienated, or their experiences ignored. If women priests remain in touch with their anger, connected to their sisters (lay and ordained), and engaged in campaigning, perhaps then they can help dismantle the sexist, hierarchical structures that dominate the Church and imprison both women and men.

CONCLUSION

> All this was a long time ago, I remember,
> And I would do it again, but set down
> This set down
> This: were we led all that way for
> Birth or Death? There was a Birth, certainly,
> We had evidence and no doubt. I had seen birth and death,
> But had thought they were different; this Birth was
> Hard and bitter agony for us, like Death, our death.
> (T.S. Eliot, *The Journey of the Magi*)

It is nearly seven years since the General Synod of the Church of England voted to ordain women to the priesthood. It is five years since the first joyful ordinations took place in Bristol Cathedral. Already women priests are an acceptable feature of our cultural landscape; they are a regular presence in popular media,[1] and there are indications that their ministry has been warmly accepted by the majority of people associated with the Church.[2] Women's priesthood birthed the hope of a new beginning - for women and for the Church. Women's ordination regenerated interest and re-focused attention on the Church. It also gave hope to women, when the Church as one of the last bastions of male exclusivity gave way to the dawning of more inclusive practice.

There is no doubt that women's priesthood was a sign of birth, of new opportunities, of hope for the future. Yet it was also a sign of death. Women's journey to the priesthood had been long and hard, many women have been lost on the way, both to the institutionalised Church and to the Christian religion. The pain and sense of alienation which accompanied women's journeys did not cease at ordination but has continued, for many, after priesting. In many ways women's priesthood has also signalled the demise of the unique bond between lay and ordained women which was forged as they stood together and worked for the recognition of women's ministry in the Church. Women could justifiably ask, therefore, "were we led all that way for Birth or Death?" For indeed women's priesthood is both a sign of birth and of death in the Church and elsewhere in society.

The first group of women priests in the Church of England are historically unique and significant, both to the Church and to society. Their ordination ended centuries of an all male priesthood and, in doing so, one of the last strongholds of male separatism crumbled. Unlike in many other professions, women have entered the ordained ministry in significant numbers not slowly, but at once, and their presence has the potential to provide a critical mass for change. So how will history remember this first group of women priests in the Church of England? Is the hope of a new beginning, which heralded their ordination, being fulfilled?

This is an in-depth study of the backgrounds, experiences and attitudes of women priests. The overwhelming participation of women in this research has resulted in a far-reaching, representative study which provides a base-line evaluation of women's ordained ministry in the Church of England. This initial cohort of women priests are unique; they are women of experience, patience and endurance. No other group of women will experience again what these first female priests have been through. Even now, just five years on from the first ordinations, women's perspectives of ministry will be very different. This research is a bench mark from which to assess the integration of women's future ministry in the Church and to evaluate women's impact on ecclesiastical structures and practices.

The first group of women priests in the Church of England are not a monochrome, homogeneous group, they are diverse and multi-faceted with contrasting attitudes and conflicting experiences. They share a predominately middle to upper class background and are, in the main, well educated, but they represent a variety of marital and family states, they identify with a range of theological positions, and span several generations. Each journey represented in this study is individual and multifarious, each a testimony of faith, endurance and call. As a researcher I have identified patterns in women's priesthood narratives, not discrete, concrete truths.

The women who participated in this study bring an enormous and extensive wealth of experience to their ministry in the Church which is reflected in their age profile.[3] The length and range of their service in the Church is complemented, for many, by professional and educational backgrounds (teaching, nursing, and professions allied to medicine) which supplement and enhance their ministry. This contribution and depth of experience is not yet reflected in women's status in the Church. There are a disproportionate number of women in chaplaincy, sector or non-stipendiary ministry[4] and there are still relatively few women in senior positions. The Act of Synod and resolutions A, B, and C, which enable individuals and parishes to refuse the ministry of women, mitigates against women's advancement and legislates for their exclusion and marginalisation.

The results from this study show emerging patterns of conflict for women between the demands of priesthood and the effects of their marital status and family responsibilities. Women in clergy couples struggle to maintain their career progression in parish ministry, whilst women with young families find it almost impossible to sustain active involvement in priestly ministry. Women's experiences of priesthood severely challenge paternalistic sacerdotal models which demand near total availability, and which fail to foster spiritual growth and individual empowerment in Church members. Women (and men) need new representations of ministry which enable them to combine family and ecclesiastical life in a way which is complementary and not conflicting, and which creates relationships between lay and ordained which are interdependent, not dependent.

The first group of women priests have a strong sense of call and vocation; they also possess a clear identity with the Anglican Church which has sustained them, and kept them faithful to the Church, throughout their years of exile.[5] Women priests are intensely aware of their historical significance as a group and, as a result, they imbue the great highs and lows of their priesthood journeys with profound spiritual significance. The euphoria of the vote in General Synod, the joyful ordinations and first eucharists will never again be experienced so poignantly by women or men. These women have experienced considerable success in their ministry which has brought them great personal fulfilment and a sense of completeness. They felt more acutely the warm acceptance, affirmation and fulfilment of their priesthood because of their wilderness years. Yet these are also women who have experienced great darkness; some have known, and some still experience the pain of rejection, abuse and bullying. Their stories are bitter-sweet and weave together strands of light and shadow in ways which enable the tellers to demonstrate and affirm the success of their ministry, whilst speaking out about their unjust and painful treatment in the Church.

How far, then, are the first group of women priests contributing to the development of new, alternative models of priesthood? Feminist theological thought identifies the Church as an essentially patriarchal institution which reflects the sexist norms of society (Ruether 1983, Maitland 1983, Chittister 1998). Liberation from sexism will be achieved if women challenge the patriarchal structures of the Church and choose to transform it by engaging with its hierarchical structures of dominance (Maitland 1983, Carr 1988). In the ordination debate, proponents of women's priesthood argued that women would change and improve ordained ministry in the Church through their inherent, gender-specific gifts and abilities. (Hoad 1984, Perbedy 1985, Furlong 1994). This study investigated women's approach to ministry and explored the extent to which they were demonstrating an essentially empowering, non-hierarchical style of leadership.

The first group of women priests show a strong predilection to working in a collaborative manner, both with fellow clergy and laity. Although there was no conclusive evidence that women priests identified with an overly empowering model of ministry, they did demonstrate a tendency towards a facilitative style of priesthood. The evidence suggests, therefore, that women's team approach will challenge the traditional model of "one man" ministry and reinforce the developing commitment to team ministry which is currently emerging in the Church. Women priests are in a position to make significant contributions to collaborative, team-based ministry which involves partnerships between its lay and ordained Church members, by strengthening their own co-operative approach and affirming collaboration in others.

In contrast, the first group of women priests in the Church of England are not particularly egalitarian in their attitude to Church affairs, nor are they concerned to de-emphasise their clerical status. It was clear that women priests are far from united in their understanding of the need for change in the Church, nor did they necessarily enter the Church with a specific agenda for transformation.[6] These factors, coupled with an ambivalence towards feminism, seriously limit women's capacity to be radical agents for the Church's transformation. If women priests do not make a conscious decision to work towards an alternative, anti-patriarchal model of priesthood, and if they continue to disengage or distance themselves from feminist tenets, then it is unlikely that women's priesthood will fundamentally affect the attitudes, practices and organisational structures of the Church.

My research has shown that women bring a different, fresh approach to, and perspective of, ordained ministry in the Church. Their experiences have opened the way for women and men to question inherited, out-dated models of priesthood; women have affirmed new emerging, embryonic patterns of Church ministry. Women's priesthood narratives have illuminated issues which male priests may well have faced but felt unable to address: the conflicting pressures of parish and family life, the bullying and oppression which can exist in hierarchical structures, and the desire to work in collaborative, empowering ways. Women's stories are a catalyst for debate and dialogue in the Church which will ultimately benefit women and men. However, unless women and men develop an anti-patriarchal consciousness which overtly challenges systems of domination through the feminist tenets of consciousness-raising, support and campaigning, they will fail to radically alter the ethos and expression of Church life. Until this happens women, whilst they enhance and benefit the ordained priesthood, will not fundamentally change it.

The findings from this study are of considerable theological and ecclesiastical interest; however, the methodology adopted in this research is also significant. I set out to develop an integrated methodology which combined quantitative and qualitative research elements in partnership. Unhappy with the usual dichotomised approaches to research, originating from positivist and interpretative sociological paradigms, and cautious of the feminist methodological presumptions which preferred qualitative to quantitative methods, I advocated a synthesis of the two. I identified key tenets of a feminist methodological approach and integrated them into my research design: I paid particular attention to my role as a researcher through self-reflection; I ensured that women's experience of priesthood was central to my analytical interests, and I am actively seeking to ensure my study can contribute to political and practical change in the Church.[7] How far, then, have I achieved my aims to produce an integrated research framework which is firmly embedded in a feminist methodological approach?

First, I have attempted to understand how my own personal spiritual journey is somehow interwoven, both with the stories and experiences of women priests, and with the process of research outlined in this study. I am not a neutral, value-free researcher who simply records and analyses the factual realities of the women represented here. I am a participant in the research, something which I have attempted to make myself aware of through the use of a research diary. I must own the profound way in which this study has shaped me - in my spiritual journey and, perhaps more acutely, in the development of my feminist consciousness. My own understanding of leadership and ministry has developed through my engagement with feminist theology and with women priests themselves. I have sought to integrate this understanding into my personal Church life.[8] I have also learnt much about myself during this study: for instance my capacity to be focused and tenacious, and my ability to be self-motivated. I have recognised and, I hope, faced my innate reluctance to sit with chaos. My desire to create order out of the formless resulted in a tendency to find patterns and categories in the research too quickly. I had to learn to wait in the disorder, to plumb the depth and richness of the data and there I found a metaphor for other areas in my life.

My research journal was an important tool for self-reflection, but with the pressures of such large scale data collection I did not utilise it as thoroughly as I had intended, as a third data source. It clearly helped me to understand my role as a researcher during the main data collection, but, towards the end of the study, the pressures to analyse and write up took precedence. The integrated methodology enabled me to remain in contact with participants of the research for far greater periods than a segregated approach would allow. However, as I moved firmly into the writing phase, I felt less association with the women priests and more affiliation to the role of objective researcher than I would have liked. I needed to maintain a critical perspective without developing a critical voice - a factor which raised for me the tension between recording women's experiences and analysing them.

Feminist discourse is indefatigably concerned with the importance and validity of women's experience. Therefore, the task of a feminist researcher is to make visible women's often invisible experiences of their social world. Is the role of the feminist researcher then, simply to record, and give voice to the women she studies? Or is she also concerned with the interpretation and the meaning of her study? An essential and distinguishing element of research is the process of analysis. In my study I needed to combine the emphasis on experience with a concern for interpretation and analysis in a healthy, but sometimes uncomfortable, tension and dialogue.

I ensured that women's experience was central to my study by using the qualitative data as a source for the quantitative survey. By constantly returning to the qualitative information I was able to engage with the issues, interests and difficulties faced by women priests. The focus on personal experience in a feminist research methodology demands more than just collecting and restating women's stories. My circular research design enabled me to remain connected to women's experiences of priesthood, and at the same time be engaged in the process of analysis. In this way my analysis was rooted in women's priesthood experiences, but was also shaped by my own interests and the voices of feminist theologians. In this study I have faithfully reflected the issues and concerns raised by participants in the study, but I have not done so uncritically.

The synergy between qualitative and quantitative methods created an effective, holistic, rigorous source of knowledge development. The partnership between the two approaches, with each alternatively leading the other, provided rich, in-depth and generalisable data. At times the contrasting methods were harmonious and congenial, then conflicting and discordant - both states were a source of understanding and insight. The qualitative data counteracted the reductionist tendencies of quantitative approaches[9] and was more nuanced, revealing the themes and issues of particular relevance to women priests. In contrast, the quantitative element of the study enabled me to assess the big picture and make generalisable statements based on results from the questionnaire which was carefully compiled, administered and analysed. Although a study of this scale and depth is impractical for anything other than large research projects or postgraduate studies, nevertheless this synthesis of methods can be adapted and used effectively in smaller research settings.[10] The binary delineation between quantitative and qualitative methods, which forces a researcher to choose one above the other, is an unhelpful dichotomisation which hinders, rather than helps, the process of social research.

Research raises as many, if not more, questions than it answers, and my work has highlighted different aspects of women's ministry which require further study. The ideas for future projects, which are summarised here, represent a lifetime of research and, even then, this list is not definitive. In Britain, whilst we have an ever-growing body of feminist theological and spiritual insight, we lack a strong tradition in the social exploration of the impact of gender on religion, as experienced by both women and men.[11] In the United States of America, for instance, more has been done to assess the repercussions of women's ordination in different denominational settings. The Church in Britain would also benefit from conducting large-scale, national studies on the position, experiences, and effect of women in religious institutions.[12]

The most obvious question that my study raises is the extent to which the backgrounds, attitudes and experiences of women priests are comparable with those of their male colleagues. What proportion of my findings are phenomena which arise from gender differences and which ones can be attributed to other sources, for instance ecclesiastical and theological tradition? My research is exclusively concerned with women's experiences of priesthood, but it would be of great interest to adopt a comparable methodology and administer the same questionnaire to a representative sample of male clergy.[13] To repeat my study five or ten years on would also be crucial in understanding the position of women priests in the Church. How have women's experiences of priesthood changed? Are women developing significantly different approaches to ministry? Has the Church responded to the employment issues relating to women's marital and familial status?

The second major theme not covered by my research is the attitude of lay people to women priests.[14] How real are women's perceptions that the laity have embraced and accepted their ordained ministry? Are the "conversion stories", where an individual is converted to the ministry of women through contact with a woman priest, which are articulated in my study, as widespread as they appear? Ed Lehman's study *Women Clergy in England* (1987) investigated the attitudes to women clergy of lay people in Baptist, Methodist, URC and Anglican Churches. He concluded that Church members in these denominations shared positive attitudes towards women in ministry. They perceived clergywomen in flexible and accessible terms, were satisfied with women undertaking most clergy roles and would be happy with a suitably qualified woman as their minister. Over a decade later, a comparative study would be beneficial, with particular attention paid to those who oppose, or used to oppose, women's ordination.

Finally, an international comparative study could be undertaken which contrasts the experiences of women priests in different areas of the Anglican Communion. Such a study would contribute significantly to a global perspective on women's ministry. It would also draw on different cultural and racial perspectives in a way which could develop great insight into the divide between the northern and southern hemispheres. By focusing on women from the Anglican Communion it would be possible to develop a relatively common understanding of the concepts being researched. However, with sufficient time and resources, an interdenominational study, which compared the backgrounds, attitudes and experiences of women ministers from a variety of traditions (for instance Anglican, Methodist, Baptist, Presbyterian and Pentecostal,) would be of the greatest interest.

The vision of Church encapsulated in my study is as a community of faith where women and men, lay and ordained are linked together in a relationship of interdependence and equality, and where all members reflect the incarnational presence of Christ in their neighbourhoods, homes, schools or work-places. This is a body-Church where each person's worth is recognised and where every member has a role. It is a place of spiritual growth, a source of individual self-actualisation, and a movement for corporate action - working for Christian principles of justice and liberation. It is all-inclusive and all-affirming. A Church where the priest is a facilitator of faith, a partner in empowerment, and a symbol, serving as a reminder, through the eucharist, of the suffering God who walks with humanity in our brokenness, offering hope and resurrection.

Women's ordination to the priesthood was, and still is, authenticated or denied through theological dialogue. Yet, the real argument for women's priesthood centres on justice; the Church risked losing integrity and its right to speak out to the nation if it failed to ordain women. However, the priesthood of women was not the end of a journey, it was a beginning. The first group of women priests are uniquely placed to help fulfil the vision of Church summarised above; they were ordained in sufficient numbers so that their presence could make a difference, and they can also draw on their first-hand experiences of marginalisation, oppression and rejection to inform their leadership approach. Women priests can, therefore, stand alongside others to create faith communities which are empowering for all members, and which are built on principles of egalitarianism and collaboration.

There are signs of hope: women are clearly collaborative and tend to favour an empowering approach in their priestly ministry, but ultimately this will not be enough to counteract the debilitating effects of patriarchy in the Church. A coherent, consistent framework is required to help women and men dismantle the hierarchical structures of dominance present in the Church, as evidenced in some women's experiences of ministry, and reflected in society. Such a framework can be found in the relationship between theology and praxis which is embodied in the unlikely partnership between Christianity and feminism. Feminist liberation theology, with its critical appraisal of the Church's role in the maintenance of gender imbalance and its support for political and social transformation, provides a theological framework, whilst feminism, with its emphasis on shared experience, consciousness-raising, support and socio-political change, provides a praxis for change.

The ordination of women to the priesthood provided a paradigm shift in the Church which created a sympathetic climate for change and fostered the sense of a new start. The responsibility for change does not lie solely with women priests, but this first group are uniquely placed to herald a new approach to ministry in the Church. They could ask, as Eliot did, "Were we led all that way for birth or death?", for experiences of birth and death have accompanied women's journey to priesthood. My hope is that women can be catalysts for birth and death: the birth of new and inclusive practice, and the death of sexist attitudes and androcentric structures in the Church and in wider society.

Women's ordination was a significant "moment" in the Church's journey towards gender equality. It was a defining historic moment *of* change, achieving greater emancipation for women, and *for* change, signalling the need for new, authentic models for our faith communities. Let us journey on towards this vision of an inclusive, anti-patriarchal, non-hierarchical Church which is actively engaged in justice-seeking and liberation.

NOTES

INTRODUCTION

1. For a moving account of the vote in Synod see Chapter 11 in Margaret Webster's book *A New Strength, A New Song* (1994).

2. It is not possible to be absolutely specific about numbers because no central registers were kept. My figures are taken from a list, compiled by the Reverend Ian Shield from the ordinations lists published in the Church Times.

3. Other Churches, and different parts of the Anglican Communion, had ordained women prior to this. For instance, the first woman was ordained in England in the United Reformed Church in 1917, whilst the first Methodist woman minister was ordained in 1974.

4. See for instance Furlong 1991, Webster 1994, Dowell and Williams 1994.

5. In the area of theology and religious studies feminist academics such as Elisabeth Schüssler Fiorenza, Phyllis Trible and Kari Elizabeth Børresen have applied a critical gender perspective to historical sources in order to reconstitute an understanding of history in a way which includes, rather than excludes, women's experience. Schüssler Fiorenza advocates a hermeneutics of suspicion when analysing historical, biblical sources, showing their androcentrism.

6. In 1987 the General Synod voted to close the Order of Deaconesses to new recruits and open the way for women to be ordained to the diaconate. Traditionally the diaconate was seen as a preparatory year before full Holy Orders were undertaken; however women deacons were ordained to the diaconate indefinitely. A deacon can do all that a priest does except preside at eucharist, and give absolution or a blessing.

7. When an organisation institutionally favours one group above another, the perceived wisdom is to increase the numbers of the marginalised group in order to facilitate reform. For example, the findings of the commission which investigated the murder of black teenager Stephen Lawrence indicated that some areas of the police force were institutionally racist. One of the recommendations to counter this was to increase the number of police officers from black and ethnic minority groups.

8. For instance Rosemary Radford Ruether, Joan Chittister, Sara Maitland.

9. For instance Mary Daly and Daphne Hampson.

10. The title Community Church denotes a Protestant Free Church which is part of the movement known popularly as "The House Church Movement".

11. The dissertation for my MSc. was an empirical study of gender differences in Church leadership in the Pioneer Network of Churches, of which my Church is a member. See Helen Thorne, *My Pastor Says Some of His Best Men are Women: A Study of Gender Difference in Church Leadership* (1996), Unpublished MSc. Thesis, University of Surrey.

12. The process of analysis is multi-layered and I always begin my analysis with a basic description of my research findings. I refer to this in the text or in the notes section where applicable. I have also included, in Appendix V, a basic summary of the descriptive statistics from the questionnaire.

CHAPTER TWO

1. The Christian movement itself brought about profound social change when it first began. As Christianity spread through missionary endeavour, it changed the way society was structured in different nations. Constantine's conversion changed the face of the Roman Empire. In 312 Constantine legalised Christianity; as a result the Church and state were merged. The Church began to take on the trappings of civil power and the state began to adopt Christian principles in government.

2. Women like Josephine Butler, Florence Nightingale and Elizabeth Fry were actively engaged in prison reform and social justice. Other forms of social work were also undertaken ranging from the Church Mission to the Fallen, which sought to provide reform and refuge for prostitutes, to the British Women's Temperance Association, which attempted curb alcohol abuse and address social problems arising from it (Gill 1994, Webster 1994).

3. The sharing of economic labour, nevertheless, has not precipitated the sharing of domestic labour. Women still largely take the main responsibility for family maintenance. This raises the question whether greater involvement in the workplace has actually brought more freedom for women or just added more pressure.

4. The role of the Sunday school teacher was clearly linked to women's sphere of influence in the home and family. However, out of this role came the first theological training opportunities for women. As attendance at Sunday schools increased, the need for properly trained teachers grew, resulting in a college being set up in Blackheath to provide training (Heeney 1988).

5. Rosemary Radford Ruether (1990) shows how, in Church traditions where ministry is associated with preaching of the word, women have been ordained more easily than in those traditions where ministry is seen in sacramental terms. The Church of England lives constantly with a broad theological spectrum and thus moved more slowly towards women's ordination.

6. Women were prevented from preaching and teaching in consecrated buildings as this was seen as being too close to the priestly role. The life of Maude Royden was pivotal in unlocking the ministry of preaching and teaching to women. She was a gifted preacher and challenged the authority of the Church to deny women's ministry in this area. On Good Friday she preached in St Botolphs against the wishes of the Bishop of London and eventually became Assistant Preacher at the City Temple. See Sheila Fletcher (1989), *Maude Royden: A Life*.

7. See Armstrong (1993 chapter 7) "Suffragettes, Church Feminism and the End of Silence" for a discussion on the links between the suffragette movement and the Church.

8. Lambeth Conference 1930.

9. There is some dispute about whether or not the Archbishop actually penned the letter of reprimand to Bishop Hall. The letter was not signed by William Temple but by Geoffrey Fisher, Bishop of London, who became increasingly involved in the controversy as the Archbishop's health deteriorated. It is suggested that Fisher wrote the official reprimand, since Bishop Hall received a separate hand-written note from the Archbishop which affirmed his personal affection for the Bishop (Webster 1994:69).

10. Florence Li Tim Oi continued to minister in the Chinese Christian Church until the communists came to power. As a pastor she experienced hardship and suffering under the revolutionary government until the end of the cultural revolution when she was able to take part in the re-building of the Chinese Church. In 1971 she resumed her priestly orders when the Bishop of Hong Kong, Gilbert Baker, ordained two other women to the priesthood. She visited England in 1984 to celebrate the 40th anniversary of her ordination. See Li & Harrison (1985), *Much Beloved Daughter,* for an account of Reverend Li's life.

11. The Church of Sweden had, after bitter controversy, ordained the first woman priest in 1960. The Church of Scotland had ordained women in 1968 and the United Free Church of Scotland since 1929. In 1972 the Synod of the Church of Burma accepted the principle of women's ordination as did the Church of New Zealand (although it refused to implement it). In 1974 the Episcopal Church in America remained unsure about ordaining women and so 12 women were illegally ordained. These ordinations were subsequently legalised.

12. MOW did also contain a number of women who worked for the Church and hoped, one day, to be priests.

13. See *Celebrating Women,* edited by Ward, Wild and Morley (1995) for examples of liturgy, prayers, poems and worship material which reflects women's experiences and explores the female nature of God using inclusive language. The first edition of this anthology was brought out in 1986 by Women in Theology and the Movement for the Ordination of Women; it has since been republished by SPCK.

14. Although it was illegal for women ordained overseas to preside at the eucharist in England (ecclesiastical law is also the law of the land), on specific occasions individuals chose to break that law and invited women to celebrate illegally. In 1977 Alison Palmer presided at the eucharist in St. Thomas's, Newcastle. In 1986, MOW was censured for inviting Reverend Joyce Bennett to celebrate at their AGM in Church House. Bishop Hugh Montefiore established that it was, in fact, legal to invite a woman to celebrate in his private chapel.

15. From an interview with a woman priest.

16. Resolutions A and B enabled parishes to refuse, by vote, to have a woman incumbent or a woman presiding at the Eucharist. Parochial Church Councils (PCCs) in a united benefice can prevent a woman ministering in other parishes in the benefice, even if those other parishes have not passed Resolutions A and B. Resolution C, a result of the Act of Synod, enables parishes to opt for alternative episcopal oversight.

17. 440 priests left the Church over women's ordination, 11%, 50, have since returned (*Statistics of Licensed Ministers* 1987). Each stipendiary minister was given £30,000 compensation, costing the Church over 10.5 million pounds. Initially, it was predicted that

between 1,000 and 3,000 priests would leave the Church, thus giving the Church a staggering compensation bill. Given the fact that the Church Commissioners had lost large amounts of money in the stock market crash of 1987, the threat of a ruinous compensation bill partly contributed to the desire to placate opponents in the months after the vote. Incidentally, those who have since returned into stipendiary ministry are not required to repay the money they received (Furlong 1998).

18. From an interview with a woman priest.

19. The Act of Synod described itself as recognising "the integrity of differing beliefs and positions concerning the ordination of women". This quickly became known as the "two integrities", which effectively sanctioned the opposing view to General Synod's measure to ordain women. It was therefore acceptable to oppose women's ordination and still remain within the Church. See Judith Maltby, "One Lord, One Faith, One Baptism, but Two Integrities?" in Furlong, M. (ed.), *Act of Synod - Act of Folly?* (1998, pp 42-58)

20. For a detailed look at the Act and its theological and practical implications see *Act of Synod - Act of Folly?* edited by Monica Furlong (1998). In July 1998 the House of Bishops set up a group under the chairmanship of the Bishop of Blackburn to review the "pastoral and practical implications of the Act". This group will not, however, be examining the theological implications of the Act.

CHAPTER 3

1 See Kenneth Leech (1992) *The Eye of the Storm*, for discussion of the essential unity and integrated nature of Christian spirituality and Christian social and political commitment.

2. Lehman (1987) summarises the links between the secular feminist movement and women's involvement in the Protestant church. The suffrage movement in the early 1900s achieved the right to vote for women around the same time as the Baptist and Congregational Churches allowed women to minister formally. Prior to this, Methodists and Anglicans initiated the Order of Deaconesses to create a formal outlet for women's ministry. The next major feminist resurgence occurred in the 1960s in response to the Civil Rights Movement which was mirrored by further developments in women's ministry. In the 1970s the first woman was ordained in the Methodist Church and the Church of England consented that there were no theological objections to women as priests.

3. The media backlash against feminism originates in a one-sided, stereotypical presentation of the feminist movement which scapegoats radical feminists "so as to avoid the challenge of having to take the real issues of feminism seriously and give full consideration to the alternative proposed by women" (King 1989:12).

4. For instance the story in Genesis 19 where Lot, rather than allow the men of Sodom to abuse his male guests, offers his virgin daughters in their place. Trible (1990) argues that one approach to feminist biblical exegesis is to address such Bible stories of abused women as horror stories. She suggests that, by retelling these stories with sympathy for the victims and with attention to their suffering, feminist theologians can challenge the patriarchal recording of scripture.

5. The influence of the dualistic worldview can be evidenced in the writings of the early Church fathers; Tertullian wrote that women were gateways to the flesh and devil, that they were like temples built over sewers. This theme presented itself as late as the twentieth century in the debate about the ordination of women, when the Bishop of London, Graham Leonard, infamously said in a radio broadcast that he feared that the ordination of women would be inappropriate because it would bring sexuality to the altar: "My instinct when faced with her (a woman at the altar) would be to take her in my arms...Sexuality is built into human life and you cannot get rid of it", quoted in Furlong, M., *A Dangerous Delight* (1991:121). In the twelfth century Thomas Aquinas developed a theology based on Aristotle's idea that women were biologically inferior to men; he argued that women were, in fact, mis-formed male embryos and were inherently inferior to men and, as such, should be subservient to men (Armstrong 1993).

6. Also see Lang 1989, Edwards 1989, Clark 1983, Evans 1983, Williams 1984, Storkey 1985 and Armstrong 1993 for a description of women's involvement in the ministry of Jesus and the early Church. Jesus confounded the order of the day by including women in his ministry in a revolutionary way. He had intimate conversations with, and touched, ritually unclean women in public, he challenged the traditional domestic role of women and affirmed them as disciples in their own right, and he consistently revealed deep spiritual truths to women. Women were the main witnesses of his death and, more importantly, his resurrection and were present when the Holy Spirit descended. Similarly, despite the later writings of Paul there are clear indications from the epistles (Acts 16:12-15,30, Romans 16, Acts 18: 18, 26) that women held positions of power in the early Church and were actively involved in its public ministry through prayer and prophecy.

7. "To be a Pilgrim", after J. Bunyan (1628-1688), Percy Deamer (1837-1936). *Hymns for Today's Church*, (1982) Hodder and Stoughton, London. The second verse makes the point about male language and imagery more poignantly:

> Who so beset him round with dismal stories
> Do but themselves confound - his strength the more is:
> No foes shall stay his might, though he with giants fight;
> he will make good his right to be a pilgrim.

I believe there is a more modern adaptation of the hymn, however this was reproduced in a book from 1982, so it is probably still in general usage.

8. Mary Daly moved from the notion of using the word God as a static noun into a verb of "Be-ing". However, as she moved away from the Christian religion, she changed her position. Deciding that the word God was hopelessly male-identified, she moved on to use the term Goddess.

9. See also *The Power to Speak, Feminist Language and God* (1992), where Rebecca Chopp states:

> Women will be forever strangers unless their words and their voices revise the social and symbolic rules of language, transforming the law of ordered hierarchy in language, in subjectivity, and in politics into a grace of rich plenitude for human flourishing. (Chopp 1992:2)

10. In a recent rail crash the one fatality was a woman. Newspaper headlines described her as "the mother of one son". No mention was made of the fact that she was also a senior medical journalist returning home from work. Had she been a man, no doubt the reverse would have been true. The use of language in this case reflects the values and norms of society: namely that, however senior a woman is in her profession, she is largely identified by her family status.

11. See also *The Power of Naming: A Concilium Reader in Feminist Liberation Theology* (1996) edited by Elisabeth Schüssler Fiorenza.

12. Sara Maitland (1983) traces the origins of women's groups in the Church to the Mothers' Union and missionary groups in the late nineteenth and early twentieth centuries. The Movement for the Ordination of Women (MOW) was a later example of women's groups in the Christian feminist movement. It was a national campaigning organisation which was based on small local groups offering mutual support and encouragement.

13. See for example Valerie Saiving (1979) "The Human Situation: A Feminine View" in which she shows how the notion of sin and grace have been defined in relation to men's experience.

14. This often-held perception that feminism is quintessentially middle-class and white is, in fact, unrepresentative of the feminist movement. There is a growing body of feminist literature and feminist theology from the developing world. See for instance *Feminist Theology From the Third World. A Reader,* edited by Ursula King (1994)

15. Arguments from both sides of the debate are well documented in the MOW archives which are held at the Fawcett Library, London Guildhall University. See for instance pamphlets by Howard 1949, Wijngaards 1977, Moore 1973, Hewitt & Hiatt 1973, Howe 1982, Hopko 1983, Powell 1978.

16. As stated in a document of the Sacred Congregation for Doctrine of the Faith, "Inter Insigniores" October 1976.

17. Just as the Pauline passages give instructions for women's place in the Church, they also describe how slaves should behave (Ephesians 6:5-6). If one takes the literalist argument, then slavery is morally defensible because Paul gives instructions on how to manage it (indeed this argument was used by anti-abolitionists).

18. For a detailed discussion about the way in which the Bible has been used and abused in the debate about women's ministry, see Mary Hayter's book *The New Eve in Christ* (1987).

19. Some believe this statement in Galatians was a baptismal formula, quoted by Paul, which marked the rite of entry of the believer to the Christian Church (Schüssler Fiorenza 1983).

20. Tertullian initiated the idea of ordination as a rite which separated the chosen few from the rank and file of the Church. Then when Constantine legalised Christianity and the Church became mainstream, it began to adopt the secular organisational structures in which the more

senior leaders (bishops) took on the trappings of power associated with their secular counterparts (Armstrong 1993).

21. Ruth Wintle (1996) summarises the modern role of the priest in the following way: to hand down the Christian faith within the Church and witness to it in the wider community, to discern God's will and understand God's word, to worship and enable others to worship. Although Wintle acknowledges that the role of the priest is to enable the laity to fulfil their individual Christian ministry, she appears to have no problem with the separatist, hierarchical nature of priesthood. Her argument that the priestly order is valid because it is part of the tradition of the Church is dangerously close to the one used to keep women out of the priesthood - namely the priesthood should be exclusively male because it is part of Church tradition.

22. I have used this definition of patriarchy for the purposes of this study. However, there is a wider definition which acknowledges patriarchy as a "social-cultural-political system of graded subjugations and dominations. Sexism, racism and militaristic colonialism are the roots and pillars of patriarchy" (Schüssler Fiorenza 1996).

23. This point was brought home to me during my research when I attended a eucharistic service where a woman was preaching and presiding at communion. My reflections on this experience were recorded in my research diary:
> I was struck by the way in which the liturgy, worship and symbolism celebrated the "feminine" and appeared to minimise the distance between lay and ordained until it came to the ministry of the word and sacrament. As I watched the ordained woman climb the stairs to the pulpit to tower above us in her full liturgical vestments, and as I offered my hands and lips in supplication for a morsel of bread and a sip of wine, I felt that there are more ways to exclude than just language.

24. Harriet Baber (1999) makes an important distinction between "across-the-board" differences which she says are the distinguishable, absolute characteristics which define male and female, and the "on-the average" differences which describe psychological gender differences. There are, she says, far fewer proven "on-the-average" differences than folk wisdom suggests.

25. Liberal and Marxist feminists argue that the inequalities between women and men are largely structural and bear no relation to inherent differences in the attributes and abilities of each sex. In contrast, romantic, and to some extent radical, feminists argue that women are inherently different from, and superior to men. However, women will only have equal status when the male-centred, patriarchal structures of society, which alienate and discriminate against women, are replaced by those constructed by women, based on their strengths and orientations. It is also important to point out that there is a third, less widely discussed, theory about gender differences. The androgynous approach acknowledges that there is a dichotomy in human personality traits which have been broadly labelled "feminine" and "masculine", but that the ownership of these psychic capacities is not dependent on sex. The fact that both these traits have been associated with each sex is largely due to social stereotyping rather than at the actual differences between women and men (Ruether 1983).

26.   For a discussion about the different feminist interpretations of "women's special nature", see Carr & Schüssler Fiorenza (1991) (eds.) *The Special Nature of Women*, Concilium Vol. 6. This collection of essays highlights the diversity in feminist theory and shows how the question of women's difference has informed feminist theological thought.

27.   For examples of the arguments against women's ordination see Bruce 1972, Saward 1978, Powell 1978, Oddie 1984.

27.   However, I do not think the Eysenck scale should be used uncritically. The scale and the validity of the pejorative descriptions of the categories it uses are, I believe, problematic. The extrovert scale, which is largely attributed to the male population, is described positively (social, lively and assertive). The neurotic scale, which is identified with the female population is described using negative vocabulary (anxious, depressed, tense). First, this polarisation of male and female with positive and negative categories is androcentric. Secondly, it cannot be presumed that tests designed and applied by men, can be equally applied to women. Although Francis finds the Eysenck trends reversed in his research, he fails to question the assumptions behind the categories which present women as more "tough-minded" than men. His conclusion that this difference is caused by women's experiences of conflict in the Church is not based on evidence from the women themselves.

29.   Simon, Scanlon and Nadall (1993) compared the backgrounds, motivations and experiences of female rabbis and female clergy from Protestant denominations in America. Their results showed that both groups felt that they approached their role in a different way from men. This theme was further developed by Simon and Nadall (1995) in a study which looked at whether male clergy agreed with the female self-perception of a more egalitarian and approachable form of ministry. Their findings suggest that male clergy did not agree with many of the differences between the sexes that were asserted by the women.

30.   It is important to point out, however, that the need for change in the Church is not universally accepted, either by men or women. Suzanne Radley Hiatt (1996) suggests that advocates of women's ministry have consistently reassured opponents, who fear and mistrust change, that the ordination of women would not change the ministry and therefore the Church.
  Harriet Baber (1999) states that the most effective argument for women's ordination is precisely the fact that women do not threaten to change the Church.

CHAPTER 4

1.   Durkheim, Lazarsfeld and Popper are key theorists who contributed to the development of the positivist approach to social research which for many years was the only way of investigating social life. Although few people would adhere to a purely positivist stance in current research practice, nevertheless methods associated with this approach remain popular, widely-used and much quoted in the public arena.

2.   The Chicago School of social research, which originated in the 1920s, pioneered ethnography and participant observation - two key methods in qualitative social research. Philosophical forerunners to interpretative sociology included Mead and Weber.

3. Glaser and Strauss (1968) contributed significantly to qualitative approaches to social research by developing the concept of grounded theory. In the grounded theory approach researchers use data, which have been systematically obtained and analysed, to develop theory rather than measure it.

4. Whilst feminism has challenged core tenets of social research, the debate has remained largely within the feminist community. "Mainstream" social science has, in the main, failed to engage with the feminist discourse on research. This is exemplified in Martin Hammersley's book *Social Research, Philosophy, Politics and Practice*. Published in 1993, this book contains three chapters which are written from a feminist perspective, however all three were written in the early 1980's. In reality the debate within the feminist community has moved on from the positions outlined in the book.

5. For instance, social class, a major variable in social analysis continued, until quite recently, to be determined by the occupation of the male "head of the household". See Delphy 1981, Llewellyn 1981, for discussion about the validity of this approach. Stanley (1974) analyses the content of three major British sociology journals and discovered the majority of the research focused on men and boys.

6. See for instance Stanley and Wise 1983, Harding 1987, Mies 1993, Maynard 1994.

7. The women's movement, which influenced the feminist approaches to social research, rejects abstract modernist thought because the male view point is conceptualised as neutral and objective. Secondly, feminist politics are rooted in a concern for the oppressed and marginalised. Finally, feminism emphasises the equation between the personal and the political (Leech 1992). These three tenets are inherent to the feminist approach to research.

8. The association of "hard" quantitative data with a masculine paradigm and "soft" qualitative data with a feminist paradigm is problematic for some feminists, not least because of the sexual connotations in the word association, but also because the former is seen as more valid than the latter (Roberts 1978, Bernard 1973, Morgan 1981).

9. See Janet Finch (1993) for a detailed discussion on the ethics of engendering rapport in interviews through one's status and position as a woman.

10. At a seminar on the developing world (Greenbelt 1998), Christine Sine used information from the World Bank Database (global statistical information concerning the economic and social status of individual countries) to demonstrate the fact that female education significantly improves infant mortality rates. She illustrated how this information could be used to benefit women on a world-wide basis by justifying the need for women's education.

11. See for instance Tobias 1978.

12. See for instance Millman & Moss Kanter 1975, Stanley & Wise 1990, Jayaratine & Stewart 1991, Fonow & Cook 1991, Mies 1991, Maynard & Purvis 1994.

13. This also refers to the politics of academy, where feminist researchers are concerned to develop collaborative ways of working which move beyond the traditional division of labour

and status in research teams (data gathering and processing elements of research are often consigned to female administrators and research assistants, whilst the theorising, analysis and writing remains the domain of the, largely male, academic). Much of the writing on feminist research is co-authored and the result of collaborative processes which are alien to much mainstream social research. See Kelly, Burton & Regan 1994, and Ward & Grant 1991.

14. A small number of in-depth interviews may be used to prepare a large scale survey, or basic statistics compiled to provide additional information for qualitative studies.

15. This is distinct from Cook & Reichardt's suggestion that the research method is chosen according to the requirements of the research question rather than the paradigmatic stance of the researcher (1979). Cook & Reichardt's approach still presumes that the researcher will chose either qualitative or quantitative methods.

16. One of the ways in which feminist writing has contributed to the understanding of research is by drawing attention to the realities of doing research. See for instance Maynard & Purvis 1994 and Stanley 1990 for reflection on the anomalies between the theory and the practice of researching social life.

17. In the grounded theory method, Glaser and Strauss (1968) suggest the development of "mini-theories" in the course of the data collection, which are built on or discarded as more data are gathered.

18. Developing an action-oriented approach to research has time and funding implications which require considerable commitment on the part of the researcher and her sponsoring body. In my case, having already raised funds to carry out the research, more income is needed to fulfil the dissemination aims I have outlined. Significant effort will be required after the completion of the PhD to ensure that this happens, and I am grateful to Professor Ursula King, the Department of Theology and Religious Studies at the University of Bristol, and, in particular, the Centre for Comparative Studies in Religion and Gender (CCRSG), for their on-going support in the dissemination of this study.

19. From an interview with a woman priest.

20. From an interview with a woman priest.

21. Two questions were asked about call in the questionnaire: the first was based on an individual sense of call - "God spoke clearly and directly to me about working for the Church", and the second represented a more developmental sense of vocation - "My sense of vocation developed gradually".

CHAPTER 5

1. See Kim Knott's chapter "Women Researching, Women Researched: Gender as an Issue in the Empirical Study of Religion" in King, U., (ed.) *Religion and Gender* (1995, pp 199-218), for an insightful exploration of the research journey as a source of personal growth for the researcher.

2. The time period 1994-1995 ensured that I included all women in my sample who had waited for ordination and had seen their hopes and dreams actualised. From the lists I was given, it was not possible to separate women in that period who were part of the "second generation" of women priests. However, the inclusion of some members of this group provided interesting insights into potential conflict between the first and second group of women priests.

3. Reverend Shield used this information to track the deployment of ordained women which he has collected in three papers: "Opening Season", "Marking Out a Baseline" and "On Court", which are available from Revd Shield.

4. It is impossible to have a completely definitive list of priests in the Church of England, since there are no centrally held registers. *Crockfords Clerical Directory* is the most accurate source of information, but it admits that the entries are not exhaustive.

5. The Advisory Group consisted of Professor Ursula King (Research Supervisor, Department of Theology and Religious Studies, University of Bristol), Reverend Dr Judith Maltby (Chaplain at Corpus Christi College, Oxford), Canon June Osborne (Residentiary Canon at Salisbury Cathedral), Professor Phyllida Parsloe (Professor Emerita, University of Bristol), Christina Rees (Chair of WATCH), Bishop Barry Rogerson (Bishop of Bristol), and Jane Williams (author and lecturer at Trinity College, Bristol).

6. For discussion about the different forms of interview see Hughes 1976, May 1993, Fielding 1993, Silverman 1993. The standardised or structured interview is covered in full by Moser and Kalton 1971, whilst Silverman 1993 is a helpful guide when undertaking qualitative, semi-structured, or non-standardised interviews.

7. See for instance Oakley 1981, Mies 1993, Stanley & Wise 1983, Fonow & Cook 1991. See also the preceding chapter where section 4.3.2 describes how I addressed feminist concerns in my research design; it also demonstrates in particular how I used my self-reflection, in the form of a research diary, to evaluate my own participation in the study.

8. Nigel Fielding, in his chapter "Qualitative Interviewing", in Gilbert, N., (1993) *Researching Social Life*, suggests that researchers must make a choice between verbatim and selective transcription, but he recommends that any sample, with less than 20 interviews, should be transcribed fully. Selective transcription requires that the researcher has already identified the key areas for analysis. Since I wanted to remain open to the voices of women priests in the research, I chose not to pre-empt the categories for analysis in the qualitative data, preferring instead to transcribe all my material fully and then look thoroughly at the emerging issues. As Fielding also points out, transcribing one's own data enables the researcher to "start making connections and identifying themes for analysis" (1993:147).

9. In summary these broad themes were: attitude to campaigning, employment difficulties, attitudes and experiences of sector/chaplaincy ministry, view of opponents of women's ministry, attitudes to support, lay views of women's ordination, gender differences and similarities, the impact of marital and family status on priesthood, call and vocation, obstacles (non-institutionalised), obstacles from within the Church structures, problems with doing the job, reflections on the status of NSM priests, success, historical significance of the first group of women priests, emphasis on collaboration, change in the Church, filling in the questionnaire,

feelings about the priesthood, attitude to the priesthood, the struggle and the second generation of women priests, empowerment of the laity, a concern to respond according to Christian values.

10. Reissman also cites Bruner 1990, Gee 1985, Mishler 1986, for reflections on the ways in which narrative forms help individuals to make sense of past events.

11. Vieda Skultans began a medical anthropological study in post-Soviet Latvia, looking at psychiatrists' much used diagnosis of neurasthenia or nervous exhaustion. As she listened to people's stories, which contained accounts of severe trauma and loss, she became aware of common devices used by the respondents to structure their narratives. Through the analysis of these accounts Skultans felt she was given a much clearer understanding of Latvia's painful history. This study is published in the book *The Testimony of Lives: Narrative and Memory in Post-Soviet Latvia* (1998).

12. I have discussed the problems of empirical research from a feminist perspective in chapter 4. See for instance Stanley & Wise 1983, Mies 1991, Jayaratine & Stewart 1991.

13. Whilst I took care to compile and pilot my questionnaire, it clearly did not reflect adequately the experiences of women priests in chaplaincy or sector ministry. I used the follow-up interviews to address this imbalance in my research.

14. Moser & Kalton (1983) *Survey Methods in Social Investigation*, and De Vaus (1990) *Surveys in social Research* are both important source texts for understanding and using surveys appropriately in social research. See also May 1993, Newell 1993.

15. For instance, I measured women's response to inclusive language by asking how regularly they used liturgy which emphasised the feminine side of God, how often they used pronouns in worship which were not gender specific, and whether or not they thought that too much emphasis is placed on politically correct words in worship.

16. A Likert scale asks respondents to indicate their agreement with a question by placing their response on a numerical scale from 1 (strongly agree) to 4 (strongly disagree). There is discussion amongst social researchers about the preference of using a four or five point scale. The five point scale allows respondents to choose a category, neither agree or disagree, whereas the four point scale forces respondents to indicate a preference. I chose the latter because I was concerned that women would choose the "safe" neutral option to some difficult questions. A number of participants found this irritating and commented on the lack of a fifth column on the questionnaire, this may have contributed to a higher missing rate for some variables. However, I feel the information resulting from a four point scale was less ambivalent, and more conclusive than a five point scale. For discussion on Likert scaling see Proctor 1993a:122, May 1993:80.

17. This element of the piloting also enabled me to publicise the survey and I asked all the advisors to inform women in their diocese that the study was taking place. A press release to the diocesan communications officers at the time of the first mailing also raised the public profile of the research, which I hope contributed to the good response rate.

18. The total budget for the survey was £1613.26. This was raised from the Alumni Foundation at the University of Bristol, Bishop of Bristol's fund, Faculty of Arts Research Fund at the University of Bristol, Sarum St Michael Trust, Sir Halley Stewart Trust and WATCH. I am grateful to all these organisations for their support.

19. Unless respondents are particularly motivated to fill in a self-completion questionnaire, response rates of 40% are not uncommon (May 1993). A study into women's experiences of bullying and abusive behaviour by the MSF union only received a 29% response rate.

20. Some women who responded to my questionnaire had obviously been contacted by a number of other researchers, as one commented that the most wearisome factor about ordination was having to fill in numerous questionnaires! Apart from my study, Sue Waldrond-Skinner was conducting research into clergy couples in the Church of England, and Patsy Kettle investigated how women combined marriage with priesthood. There are also a number of smaller, localised undergraduate studies that I have heard of.

21. Ideally I would have liked to interview all the women who responded. However, it was impossible to follow up the 755 people who agreed to be interviewed because of lack of resources: personnel, time and finance.

22. For further discussion about cross-tabulation and elaboration see Moser & Kalton 1971, Hughes 1976, Babbie 1989, De Vaus 1986, Proctor 1993b.

23. See also Michael Proctor "Measuring Attitudes" in Gilbert, N., (ed.) *Researching Social Life* (1993a, pp 116-134).

24. An *eigenvalue* explains the variance in a set of variables, the total number of items represents the total variance (i.e. if there are 15 variables in a set, then the variance is 15).

25. Summated scales can be problematic because they do not necessarily reflect the nuances of individual scoring patterns (someone who agrees strongly with one statement and disagrees strongly with another can have a similar score to someone who generally agrees with both statements). This factor was minimised in my research because I chose not to have a five point scale with a neither agree/nor disagree category, which can lead to more ambiguous scores on summated scales. Since respondents had to indicate the degree to which they agreed or disagreed with a statement, the resulting scores on the summated scales more accurately reflected the underlying patterns in the data.

26. For instance, in the scale which investigated the strength of affiliation to feminist language, the statement "I think too much emphasis is put on politically correct words in worship" is negative. In order to be aligned to other positive variables in the scale, it needed to be recoded inversely (i.e. strongly agree becomes strongly disagree).

CHAPTER 6

1. These statistics are approximate because, whilst the Advisory Board of Ministry of the Church of England regularly produces statistics on the number of priests employed in Church

ministry, this way of accounting does not include those who are retired but still in active ministry. The most accurate picture is found in *Crockfords Clerical Directory*.

2.   These categories are, by necessity, crude. I am not suggesting that all women in the same sector will have the same attitudes but I am giving some framework to proposed generational differences. A similar framework is found in Joanne Gillespies's study "Gender and Generations in Episcopal Women" in Prelinger, C. (ed.) *Episcopal Women: Gender, Spirituality and Commitment in an American Mainline Denomination,* (1992, pp 162 - 222).

3.   The occupation of the main wage earner in a household is now a more generic measure (often combined with the educational level of that person). This acknowledges the fact that women participate more fully in the work force. Some researchers are currently experimenting with the idea that social class is more effectively measured by the educational level of women. This is based on the assumption that women influence the values, aspirations and education of their family through their family maintenance role. Women's education, therefore, is a predictor of a family's values and aspirations and, as such, is an indicator of their social class.

4.   See Goldthorpe, J. & Hope, K. (1974) *The Social Grading of Occupations*, for a more sophisticated analysis of occupation and class. This scale is, however, too complex for the purpose of this study where social class is not the main area for investigation. The Registrar General's classification has also been recently further developed to reflect changing social and employment patterns whereby women can be either the sole head of household, or a major contributor to a family's income.

5.   Nearly all women completed some form of ordination training. The main forms are locally based part-time courses, or full-time residential courses. Some women, because of their family responsibilities, took part in full-time courses but lived outside the college in their family homes. 51.8% of women ordained in 1994-1995 were trained locally, either in a part-time capacity or full-time non-residentially. 46.4% trained in a residential setting. The remainder combined both part-time and residential training or, in a small minority, were ordained because of their experience. When employment status was compared with training, it showed that the type of training received by women did not affect the level they reached in the Church. Diocesan and Chaplaincy posts are more likely to be held by those who trained residentially, but there are no significant differences at parish levels. Those who trained part-time are more likely to be on a part-stipend or non-stipendiary (presumably this is largely accounted for by the fact that some women will have specifically trained for non- stipendiary ministry).

6.   Women's increased social status is reduced when one looks at social class I. 21.9% of the respondents' fathers were in social class I and this figure rises to 28.4% when one adds in the fathers who were clergy (6.8% of women had clergy fathers). This compares with only 6.0% of women in social class I, suggesting that senior jobs are still eluding women. The largest signs of social mobility come in social class II where there are over double the amount of women compared to their fathers. 39.4% of fathers where in social class III or below compared to 16.7% of women priests.

7.   Some single women felt that they were disadvantaged in the Church, particularly in parish ministry. Although there was no evidence that single women were in lower status jobs, some women articulated specific difficulties associated with being a single woman priest in the

qualitative section of the study. This did not develop into a strong analytical theme; however, it is an area which would benefit from further research and investigation.

8.   Of those women with dependent children, 59% have the main responsibility for childcare, 6% say their partner has the main responsibility for childcare, 27% say it is fully shared and only 8% use professional childcare.

9.   This ambivalence is seen in some of the vocabulary used by the Church regarding employment issues; for instance, the word stipendiary is used to denote somebody in receipt of payment for their ministry. This presents an alternative to the idea of the salary structures of secular society. Yet in reality there are clear payment structures (which include housing allowances and expenses) set out for people serving at different levels in the Church.

10.   Wittgenstein's notion of "language games" originates in the idea that in social interaction, in order to understand what is contained in a concept, one has to explore not only what an actual word means but also observe how the word is used. "For a 'language game' is understood not just by what people say, but what they do and how they behave in relation to the use of the particular concept that is being considered." (Robson 1988:108). Each "language game" will have a different set of rules, which are adopted and adhered to unconsciously through a process of communication socialisation.

11.   When employment position is used in the analysis the categories have been condensed to enable easier understanding of the results. The categories are defined thus: curate refers to anyone in a junior position in the Church, including assistant or associate ministers. The term chaplain refers to anyone whose main role is as a chaplain or in some form of sector ministry. Vicar includes those who are vicars, team vicars, bishop's chaplain, incumbent, priest in charge and cathedral chaplain. Rector refers to any women in a rector position or above, for instance team rector, residentiary canon, or archdeacon. Diocesan posts include women who are on bishop's staff, are lecturing, or are in some form of diocesan or national ministry.

12.   This is a traditional problem for clergy, but a male vicar with dependent children usually has a wife to take the family maintenance role and so is, to a greater degree, shielded from this conflict.

13.   See the report on "Ministry and Marriage" by Patsy Kettle (1997). This study from Christian Research surveyed 283 women priests about their experiences as married priests with children. Based on a 55% response rate and further interviews, the report makes several recommendations about how the Church can improve working conditions for women who have children.

14.   Sue Waldrond-Skinner published her study on clergy marriages in *Double Blessing* (1998). She researched the effect of women's ordination on clergy couples, in situations where both partners were clergy and where a woman priest was married to a non-clergy husband.

15.   This does not imply that chaplaincy work is inferior to parish work, although some chaplains clearly felt they were over-looked by the Church. Some women feel forced into chaplaincy roles because of their marital status, but this is by no means true for everybody.

16. A third of the first group of women priests had worked as deaconesses, 15% as parish workers, 8% in missionary work, 10% as lay workers and 3% had been in religious communities. Other unpaid opportunities for ministry, experienced by women prior to their ordination, were Sunday school/youth worker, lay reader, small group leader, Church warden, vicar's wife and diocesan or chaplaincy work. Some women would have held more than one position, and others had held none, therefore the figures do not add up to 100%.

17. The measure to ordain women to the priesthood did not allow women to enter the episcopacy. Further legislation is required before women can become suffragan or diocesan bishops.

18. This table is based in women's self-categorisation and does not show accurately the true retirement figures. This is due to the different way in which women categorised their positions. Those who said they were retired (but with permission to officiate on an ad hoc basis) have been included here as retired. Others, who are technically retired, but have a more official status in a parish as an assistant priest or curate, have been included in the appropriate employment categories.

19. The National Association of Diocesan Advisors in Women's Ministry (NADAWM) published a statistical survey of women in licensed ministry in 1997. The report compiled statistics from each diocese about the deployment of women and NADAWM will continue to take this monitoring role.

20. 5% gave no reasons for being NSM.

21. Responses to the questionnaire revealed that women in chaplaincy positions felt that the survey was slanted to parish ministry and did not accurately reflect their experiences. As a result 5 of the further 12 in-depth interviews were conducted with women chaplains. It should be pointed out that whilst most women expressed real fulfilment in their role, some felt forced into chaplaincy because they could not get a suitable parish job:

> I think there is a tendency to steer women in to chaplaincies rather than offer them senior positions in parishes...To some extent there is the view that people go into chaplaincy work because they can't cope with a parish.

There was also a clear feeling that chaplaincy ministry is overlooked by Church structures and that it is the "poor relation" to parish ministry:

> I am paid by the NHS and the diocese has no comprehension of support requirement - sadly all they manage is the licence to officiate and an annual supper with the bishop.

22. Male priests in chaplaincy ministry may have also developed a new understanding of their priestly role - this is not necessarily a finding which is related to gender. Further research comparing women's and men's approach to ministry would be illuminating.

23. In the initial stages of the research it was suggested in discussions and interviews that women are being placed in the "back water or difficult" parishes. The results show that 52.6% of those who had parish responsibilities are in rural or inner city/urban priority areas. 25% are

in suburban or middle class areas with 8.3% in large towns and 12.8% in smaller towns. This is not conclusive evidence that women are being placed in difficult parishes, but it does indicate that further investigation should be done in order to assess the level of the problem.

24. Some respondents wanted a theological category that could be described as middle of the road Anglican; one suspects that others may have chosen the catholic/liberal category as describing this.

25. For further analysis this variable has been re-coded, so that those who express a leaning to either a catholic or evangelical position have been included in that category. It is my premise that where liberal is used in combination with another category, it denotes a more open, less dogmatic theological position and therefore only those who have identified themselves solely as liberal have been included in that category. When separated in this way 47% identified themselves with a catholic position, 13% saw themselves as liberal, and 40% identified themselves in some way as being evangelical.

CHAPTER 7

1. See also *Narrative Analysis* by Catherine Riessman (1993) for an in-depth look at the theory and practice of narrative analysis.

2. It is only through the use of a combination of qualitative and quantitative approaches that this is possible. Qualitative interpretation of interview data and written comments show the devices that individuals use to construct their personal narratives and identify the extent to which those devices are shared. However, one of the problems with qualitative analysis is that it is too easy to assume hidden patterns. Quantitative analysis gives credence to the patterns identified in the qualitative data.

3. Jewish and Christian tradition contain many examples of call as a direct intervention in an individual's life. In the Old and New Testament there are frequent references to God speaking to an individual in both an audible and visual way. In Genesis 3 Moses hears the voice of God in a burning bush. In 1 Samuel 3, the boy Samuel receives such a clear word from God that he believes that his master Eli is calling him. This theme is continued in the New Testament where Mary receives news of her pregnancy directly from an Angel (Luke 1:26 - 38), and the Apostle Paul is called on the road to Damascus where he had a vision and heard the voice of God (Acts 9: 3-9). In many of the stories of call, the individual concerned feels unworthy for the task they are being commissioned for.

4. See also Chapter 4 on the methodology for my research. Section 4.4 gives a description of how quantitative and qualitative methods combined to elucidate my understanding of women's call and vocation.

5. This scale combined the reasons women gave for entering the priesthood with the attitudinal question about call, in an inverse relationship to the question about vocation. Those people who expressed their reasons for entry into the priesthood in an external way, that is a strong emphasis on a sense of call from God, had a low score on the scale (the lowest score is

3), whilst those who score highly on the scale expressed a preference for internal processes of developing vocation (the highest score is 12).

6. When using calling as a device in their narratives, women priests were not necessarily referring to a calling to priesthood, for some women it was simply to ministry in the Church. As the opportunities for the diaconate and priesthood opened up, so women pursued these and, as they did so, developed a calling to the priesthood:

> I had a very clear call to do something in the Church, quite what that something was came gradually by working through being a Sunday school teacher, diocesan children's advisor, accredited lay worker, deacon and priest.

Where they were unable to be priests, women from different theological orientations experienced largely different callings: women from an evangelical tradition talked about a calling to the mission field, whereas women from a catholic tradition were more likely to experience calling to the religious life.

7. The "Statistics of Licensed Ministers" published in 1997 state that, in total, 440 licensed ministers (stipendiary, non-stipendiary and retired) left the Church of England between 1993-1997 because women were ordained priests.

8. This scale combined questions which asked about the importance of being the first women priests in the Church of England, ability to fulfil calling outside of the Church and the likelihood of their staying in the Church, had the vote in General Synod prevented women from being priests. Once again each respondent was given a score on this denominational loyalty scale. Those who had a low score showed high levels of denominational loyalty and those who had higher scores were less likely to have a strong allegiance to the Church.

9. There is emerging evidence that women in the General Synod were pressurised to vote for the Act of Synod which protected opponents of women's ministry as a "pay-off" for their victory in the ordination debate:

> "Why should I vote for this?" one woman speaker, a newcomer to Synod asked. "If you don't", the Archbishop replied, picking up a nautical image just used by another speaker "you will sink the ship!" (Furlong 1998:10 - 11).

Similarly there is evidence from interviews I conducted that women felt pressurised to atone for the disruption they had caused the Church through wanting to be ordained by voting for the Act of Synod:

> We had to vote on the "two integrities" measure and I feel very proud of myself that I abstained because we were under such pressure at the time to vote. Only 12 people voted against and three of us abstained. Everybody else did what they were told by the Archbishop of York who was pleading with us to keep the unity of the Church.

10. Over the past three years press cuttings relating to women priests are almost exclusively negative and sensationalist in their content. For example "Women priests: five years of

upheaval" (*Daily Telegraph* 21.11.97), "Dog collar bullies, how women priests suffer tide of abuse by clergymen" (*The Express* 21.4.98), "How unwelcoming men are driving women priests from Churches in London " (*Evening Standard* 20.6.97).

11. Barbara Hudspith's study "An Exploration of the Relationships Between Female Rectors in the Anglican Church of Canada and Laywomen in their Congregations in the Diocese of Niagara" (an unpublished dissertation for Master of Religion, Toronto School of Theology) also found contradictory evidence from the women she interviewed. Women priests, on the one hand, described painful, hostile receptions from some lay women whilst at the same time celebrating the convivial spirit which existed between them and their lay colleagues.

12. A report published by the MSF union "Are Women Priests being Bullied or Harassed?" (1998) had a high profile launch when it concluded that over 27% of women priests had experienced some form of harassment or physical abuse. There were serious methodological flaws in the study which make its findings ungeneralisable. However, in my study 24.7% of women said they had experienced sexual harassment, abusive or threatening behaviour whilst they had been working for the Church (not necessarily since they had been priests, but also earlier, before their full ordination).

13. Whilst many women have had negative responses from members of the public, they have also experienced a high degree of positive affirmation; 41.5% have experienced people leaving the Church because there is a woman priest, but 59% have had people visit or attend their Church because there is a woman presiding. 69.6% have experienced members of the public preferring a man for special or sacramental occasions, but in contrast 81.3% said that people had preferred a woman for the same events. 68.6% have experienced people refusing communion from them.

The picture from within the Church is quite disturbing. 47.3% have had male clergy colleagues refuse communion from them and 56.9% have been treated rudely by colleagues, whilst 41.7% have had difficult relationships with fellow or senior clergy. 27.3% have experienced difficulties getting jobs and 11% have had superiors block their job applications. 36.4% have had communion lists published to show that a woman is presiding.

14. In the process of factor analysis (which is explained more fully in chapter 5), SPSS first produces a list of factors with *eigenvalues* over one. The three main factors are described below. A rotated factor matrix is then displayed which shows which variables have large loadings for each factor. Only variables with loadings of more than 0.5 are accepted as part of the factor. The following table shows which variables feature strongly in each factor.

Factor 1 - Institutional Difficulties

Difficulty in getting a job	0.69
Difficulty in relationship with clergy	0.59
Superiors blocking job applications	0.73
Abusive or threatening behaviour or sexual harassment.	0.64

Factor 2 - Local Parish Difficulties

Communion lists published to show a woman presiding	0.50
People refusing communion	0.70
Parishioners leaving the church	0.59
People preferring a man for sacramental occasions	0.67

Factor 3 - Local Parish Affirmation

People attending Church because there is a woman	0.68
People preferring a woman for sacramental occasions	0.63
Women gaining confidence because of women priests	0.67

15. The Act of Synod, it can be argued, has already legislated for discrimination against women. If the Church does not face up to these stories, then these difficulties will become further enshrined in practice.

CHAPTER 8

1. See Lavinia Byrne's book *Women at the Altar (1994)*, in Chapter 6 "The Methodology of Feminism: Storytelling, Sisterhood and Solidarity" she argues that feminist methodology has important implications for the Church. Shared storytelling facilitates greater dialogue with the scriptures, emphasis on relationship reflects a core value of Christianity, as does the accent on social and political (theological) exploration.

2. This scale combined attitudinal questions relating to authority from ordination (which was recoded inversely), identity with marginalised groups, the effect of ordination on the relationship between the laity and clergy, and a concern for equity in work practices. Those that had a low score on the scale exhibited a strong concern for equality in the Church, intimating a desire to diminish the power imbalance in the institutional Church.

3. This scale combined women's self-reported inclusion of the laity in the eucharist, preaching and pastoral work, with attitudinal questions about the importance of a collaborative leadership style and the fact that competition between the clergy is unacceptable. Since 1 was used to indicate strong agreement, low scoring on the scale indicates a strong identification with the concept of collaborative ministry.

4. See for instance "Church, Committees and Gender" by Pal Repstad in Hansson, P., (ed.) *Church Leadership*, (1997, pp 147-161) where women perceive themselves to be concerned for the participation of others in Church meetings. Simon & Nadall (1995) also conclude that women perceive themselves to have a more collaborative style of ministry.

5. This scale combined questions relating to lay involvement in deciding the direction of the Church, whether success as a priest is measured by the way in which the congregation are empowered, whether ordination places too much distance between lay and ordained people, and whether the easiest way to get things done is to tell people what to do (which was recoded in the scale inversely).

6. The use of the word "father" as a form of address for some male priests illustrates this. There is, as yet, no universal female equivalent, although some women priests have been called "mother".

7. See for instance "Leadership in Collaborative Ministry" by Brian Russell in Hansson, P., (ed.) *Church Leadership*, (1997, pp 162-175) for discussion about models of collaborative ministry in the Church of England.

8. 95.8% of women involve the laity in helping to administer communion, 92% in pastoral work, 88.1% in preaching and leading worship, and 82.7% in leading home groups on a regular, or fairly regular basis.

9. This scale combined attitudinal statements about whether clerical title and dress are important, whether ordination is a mark of authority which sets apart the laity and the clergy, and whether the eucharist is an exclusively priestly task.

10. In Protestant denominations which have less of a sacramental emphasis, women are allowed, relatively freely, to take a leading role in holy communion and baptismal services. However, my earlier study *A Study of Gender Differences in Church Leadership* (an unpublished MSc thesis, University of Surrey, 1996) shows that in a non-sacramental denomination, rites of passage (such as weddings and funerals) become almost exclusively the domain of men. In other words, however a denomination defines authority, women usually have difficulty exercising leadership in this area.

11. In his book, *The Rise of Christianity: A Sociologist Reconsiders History* (1996), Rodney Stark attributes the growth of early Christianity to its counter-cultural approach to community and society. For instance, he argues that Christian communities of faith and the mutual aid systems they operated, enabled Christianity to survive and grow in the pressurised urban, Greco-Roman environment.

12. These figures are from Anne Oakley and Juliet Mitchell *Who's Afraid of Feminism? Seeing through the Backlash* (1997:4).

13. For instance Maude Royden, whose life and ministry is described by Sheila Fletcher in her book *Maude Royden: A Life*, (1989).

14. For instance Louise Creighton, the wife of a bishop, who had a central role in Church women's organisations and who worked within the Church establishment for women's emancipation (Heeney 1988, Webster 1994).

15. See Margaret Webster *A New Strength, A New Song* (1994), Chapter 4, for description of the struggles between the radical and conservative approach to campaigning in MOW.

16. Only 26.4% were involved actively in campaigning for women's ordination (18.2% of them with MOW). 33.6% were members of MOW but did not campaign and 38.5% were not members. In terms of support 67.4% receive spiritual direction (although this is something which is not specific to women priests), 43% attend a support group for women clergy but only 12.9% meet regularly with lay women in a group situation. 23.4% had some form of

supervision, although it must be stated that the understanding of supervisions was mixed. 11.7% of respondents attended therapy/counselling sessions.

17. The scale combined attitudinal questions about the effectiveness of active campaigning, the importance of quietly getting on with the job (which was recoded in the scale inversely) and the significance of support from other women, with questions about women's participation in MOW and in lay/ordained women's groups. Those who score highly on the scale have a negative attitude to feminism, whilst those with a lower score identify more positively with feminist tenets.

18. Although a small scale qualitative research project, which means the findings are not generalisable, Pal Repstad's study "Church, Committees and Gender" in Hansson, P., (ed.) *Church Leadership*, (1997, pp 147-161), also concludes that there is considerable ambivalence towards feminism amongst female leaders. Similarly Barbara Hudspith's study "An Exploration of the Relationships Between Female Rectors in the Anglican Church of Canada and the Laywomen in their Congregations in the Diocese of Niagara" (Unpublished Thesis for Master of Religion, Toronto School of Theology, 1998) also found evidence that the women priests she interviewed chose to disassociate themselves from feminism.

19. Chittister refers to Allport's study "The Nature of Prejudice" (1958) which identifies four ways in which oppressed people deal with the effects of prejudice. They become what the dominant class anticipate for them, living within the perimeters of other people's low expectations. Oppressed people seek the approval of those who dominate them and finally they can internalise the anger they feel about being dominated and turn it in on themselves.

20. This scale combined women's use of inclusive language, their use of liturgical worship which emphasises the feminine side of God, with a question about the importance of using politically correct words. People who scored highly on the scale indicate a positive attitude to inclusive language.

CHAPTER 9

1. The sheer wealth of data I have accumulated, 29 interview scripts, over 350 pages of typed comments from the survey plus the statistical data from 1247 questionnaires, means it would be impossible to present all the information. I have had to make choices about what I include and focus on in this study.

2. For example the charity Womankind Worldwide demonstrates a partnership between women in the north and south to support "women in developing countries in their struggle for personal development and collective empowerment, for the benefit of society and the eradication of poverty and want". Womankind, 3 Albion Place, Galena Road, Hammersmith, London, W6 OLT.

3. Women's sense of historical significance and the importance they give to the period of waiting is also backed up by the quantitative data. 67.8% said that the fact they were the first group of women priests was important to them. 78.6% said the diaconate was an important

time for them, and 57.6% said they felt the importance of the diaconate had been lost to the Church now.

4.   For a full description of the vote in General Synod on November 11th 1992, see chapters 10-11 in Margaret Webster's book *A New Strength, A New Song* (1994).

5.   Several women referred, in their interviews, to unfair criticism levelled at them, that there had been a degree of triumphalism at the success of the vote in Synod:

> Until we were actually promulgated in February, there was silence. The diocese didn't write to us after the vote. We had one semi-official letter to tell us not to rejoice and not to be triumphalist because we must remember that other people were experiencing pain.

This backlash appeared to pre-empt the dramatic moves to accommodate dissenters culminating in the Act of Synod. Monica Furlong, "The Guardian of the Grail" in Waldrond-Skinner, S., (ed.) *Crossing the Boundary,* (1994, pp 17-27), describes this post-vote period as the Church experiencing a nervous breakdown.

6.   65% of respondents said that they felt new women coming into the Church are not as aware of the obstacles as they are.

7.   The majority of women ordained 1994-1995 had worked in the Church for a long time. A few had been accepted for ordination training as the vote went through and so are effectively part of the second generation of women priests. Most women were ordained in all-female groups, some, however, were part of the first wave of mixed sex ordinations which began in 1995.

8.   When Philip Crowe, the then Principal of Salisbury and Wells Theological College, openly disagreed with the Act of Synod, he was told that he would never work again in the Church of England. Since the college was subsequently closed, this statement has turned out to be true (Furlong, 1998).

9.   Lesley Bentley points out in her chapter "At the Grassroots: The Act in the Parishes" in Furlong, M., (ed.) *Act of Synod - Act of Folly?* (1998, pp 101-114), that separate dioceses interpret and work out the Act in different ways. The procedures vary according to the number of parishes in each diocese that have opted for alternative episcopal oversight, the attitude of the diocesan bishop and the theological tradition of the parish. Since the Act is based on a sacramental view of priesthood, evangelicals may be prepared to have a woman celebrant, but not a woman minister in charge of a parish; they are therefore less likely to make use of the PEV's.

10.   Geoffrey Kirk, General Secretary of "Forward in Faith", argues that the PEV system provides the basis for the third province in his article in *New Dimensions*, the journal of "Forward in Faith" (Vol 4, February 1998).

11.   There is no formal research evidence about whether or not "Forward in Faith" is systematically encouraging the opposition that some women priests suggest. Further study in

order to analyse the impact of the campaign by opponents of women's ministry would be beneficial.

12. The strain of active campaigning fell on a relatively small number of women seeking ordination (although a large number of lay women were involved). Only 26% of women priests said they campaigned in or outside of MOW.

13. Although there are no official figures, ex-officials of MOW remember that the majority of their members were lay women rather than women deacons or deaconesses who were hoping to be ordained priest. The majority of WATCH's members are now ordained priests.

14. It should be noted that this does not work in reverse. In theory supporters of women's ministry could quite conceivably deem those under the care of PEVs as having invalidated their holy orders, and could therefore refuse their sacramental ministry. However, this has not to my knowledge happened.

15. On a recent application form I was asked to state my gender and not my sex.

16. See for instance William Oddie *What Will Happen to God?* (1984).

17. See Elaine Storkey *What's Right with Feminism* (1985), whilst I do not share her views on patriarchy she does highlight this conflicting message in some forms of radical feminism.

18. See for instance Simon, Scanlon and Nadall (1993), Simon and Nadall (1995), Robbins (1998), and Repstad (1997).

19. A report from the *Church Times* was highlighted in WATCH's journal *Outlook* (Spring 1999, Vol 6). It stated that in the USA, where women have been ordained priests for two decades and there are women bishops, a traditionalist parish, opposed to women's ministry, held a "cleansing" ceremony after Jane Dixon, suffragan Bishop of Washington had celebrated there. After the service, the rector from the Church went into the sacristy and sprinkled holy water on everything Bishop Dixon had touched.

20. In a special edition of the journal *Signs of the Times* (1972) Peter Selby, Bishop of Worcester, suggested that the evidence from other parts of the Anglican Communion is that, where women are ordained, differences are noticed. There are, he argues, already signs of new styles of ministry, new language, and a new concept of authority and service.

21. Only 41.7% of women said they felt active campaigning was the best way to change the Church, whilst 80.9% said that the best way to change things was to get on with the job.

22. 58% said that they feared women were doing things the same way as men in the Church.

CHAPTER 10

1. See for instance, Hoad 1984, Perberdy 1985, Furlong 1991, Kroll 1994, Farrington 1994.

2. See for instance Ruether 1983, Maitland 1983, Carr 1988, Williams 1994.

3. It is important to remember that this study did not compare female and male approaches to ministry, but rather looked at whether or not women exhibited what have been identified as "traditionally feminine" attributes. Ed Lehman Jr's study *Gender and Work: The Case for the Clergy* (1993) is an in-depth study of gender differences in Church leadership and concludes that where sex differences in ministry did occur, they were dependent on other factors such as race and ethnicity rather than on gender.

4. Christianity appears to identify anger as a sin (Colossians 3:8, Ephesians 4:31), which of course compounds women's reluctance to express anger. However, other passages in the Bible suggest anger is an essential part of life, but that it should not be left unresolved (Ephesians 4:26) and that people should be slow to get angry (James 1:19). The story of Jesus overturning the money lenders tables in the Temple (Matthew 21:12-13) clearly illustrates the importance of anger against injustice.

5. See Rosemary Radford Ruether, *Sexism and God-Talk* (1983:165) and Joan Chittister, *Heart of Flesh* (1998:19-29) for further discussion about patriarchy.

6. Genesis, Chapters 1-3.

7. John 15:9-14, Galatians 3:28.

8. The concept of consciousness-raising is problematic in that it implies that some women have a lesser, or false consciousness which is evidenced by a particular lifestyle. Women who choose to be at home and take main responsibility for childcare can feel inferior and excluded. Women became angry at being told what they should and should not want by other women, a factor which has contributed to the feminist backlash. See for instance Patrizia Romito's chapter "Damned if You do and Damned if you Don't: Psychological and Social Constraints on Motherhood in Contemporary Europe" in Oakley, A., Mitchell, J., (eds.) *Whose Afraid of Feminism?* (1997, pp 162-186), for a discussion of conflicting feminist views on motherhood.

9. It is a mistake to think that consiousness-raising is only relevant for women. Men can also undertake such a journey of self-realisation as they discover the inequalities in gender roles and relationships. Rosemary Radford Ruether describes this process as a "conversion journey", and suggests it is an essential element in the development of new communities of faith and inclusivity (1983).

10. See for instance Stanley and Wise (1983).

11. Ursula King states that "the power of naming is one of the most decisive human activities in constituting the world as experienced" (1989:42). By reclaiming the right to name their experiences women's place and importance in society is affirmed.

12. However flawed the end result, the Truth and Justice Commission in South Africa demonstrated how one country has attempted to find a place of justice without further bloodshed or retribution. In Australia a similar project was undertaken with Aboriginal people, leading to the Book of History which contained the stories of suffering and oppression experienced by the indigenous population.

13. Most of the writing on women's support is centred around the idea of women's groups. However, my personal experience is that the value of close female friendships has actually been a more effective vehicle for me in the development of my own feminist consciousness and awareness. This theme is reflected in Mary Hunt's chapter "Friends in Deed", in Hurcombe, L., (ed.) *Sex and God*, (1987, pp 46-54). She writes:

> Women friends are the best antidote to patriarchy. The way in which we provide for one another, make space in our lives to invite others in, and act in unlikely coalitions of justice seeking friends gives me hope and energy for the task of social transformation. As a theologian I am concerned that women's friendships be seen in the light of ultimate meaning and value. I hold them up to the light of theological investigation. They reveal dimensions of spirituality and the divine which help us to explain why women friends are so central to our lives (Hunt 1987:46).

14. Rosemary Radford Ruether's work resonates with liberation theology. For instance, in *Sexism and God-Talk* (1983) Ruether demonstrates the potential for liberation in Mariology. She argues that precisely because the gospel is for the poor, and because it has the potential to create a new order where the last shall be first, that women, as symbols of the poorest and most oppressed in society, have a place of eminence in the Christian faith. See also her *Liberation Theology* (1972) for an analysis of Latin American Liberation Theology. Elisabeth Schüssler Fiorenza, another leading feminist theologian, describes her own theological perspective as: "A critical feminist theology of liberation which is indebted to historical-critical, critical-political, and liberation-theological analyses and is rooted in my experience and engagement as a Catholic Christian woman" (1996:6).

15. Hugh Boulter explores Neo-platonic ideas in Christian thought in his paper "(Ortho) praxis - A Key Concept in Paul Knitter's Theology of Religions" (1999), an unpublished paper from the University of Bristol, Department of Theology and Religious Studies Postgraduate Conference.

16. Lobkowicz (1967) quotes Clement of Alexandria, Origen and Gregory of Nyssa as referring to this incident.

17. Needless to say feminist writers view this story in a different way. Jane Williams (1984) argues that Jesus is challenging gendered roles in society in this story. By praising Mary who situates herself as a disciple (sitting at Jesus' feet) and challenging Martha's assumption of the housekeeping tasks, Jesus is signalling that women's first duty is as disciples and, as such, they are equal with men.

18. Feminist theology from the Developing or Third World provides a critical perspective on sexism, racism and colonialism. As such, it provides a theological context and praxis to

overcome these triple cords of oppression. See for instance King, U., (1994) (ed.) *Feminist Theology from the Third world: A Reader.*

19. See also Matthew 25: 31-46, Luke 6: 20-38.

20. Latin American theology concentrates on the reinterpretation of Christian symbols from a liberationist perspective. A hermeneutic evaluation of the place of socio-political action in the Christian faith is more in line with political theology (Fiorenza 1975).

21. See for instance Martin Soskice 1988, Norris 1984, Hayter 1987 for a justification of women's ordination from a catholic perspective and Carey 1984, Langley 1987, Scott 1991 and Storkey 1985, 1995, for an evangelical view.

22. The Movement for the Ordination of Women was a catalyst which heightened the Church's awareness of the debate concerning women's ministry, but it was only when sufficient numbers of people were convinced to vote in favour at General Synod that practical action was taken.

23. Grace Davie (1994) acknowledges that whatever measure is used for Church attendance, figures from the Church of England, Church of Wales, Episcopal Church of Scotland and the Church of Ireland are decreasing. For instance baptisms have fallen to 27.5% per 1000 live births and figures for confirmations and ordinations are also falling.

24. 1 Peter 2:9 describes the Christian community as:
> A chosen race, a royal priesthood, a holy nation, a people for God's own possession, that you may proclaim the excellencies of Him who has called you out of darkness into His marvellous light.

25. In response to the Bishop of Blackburn's review of the operation of the Episcopal Ministry Act of Synod 1993, WATCH compiled a formal submission. Mr Lyn Ferraby, the co-ordinator for the response, received 70 letters and many phone-calls detailing women's negative experiences, rejection and ill-treatment as a result of the workings of the Act. 10 bishops also contacted WATCH, in confidence, to express their concerns over the provision of provincial episcopal oversight. The submission is a private document and the above information is from a personal letter from Mr Ferraby.

26. See *Act of Synod - Act of Folly?* edited by M. Furlong (1998) for a detailed theoretical and practical appraisal of the Act.

27. The National Association of Diocesan Advisers in Women's Ministry (NADAWM) has compiled a national review of women's deployment. However, their report has no formal jurisdiction in the Church and the findings are not necessarily acted upon.

28. Many of the issues regarding women's family life raised in this study are probably also problems that male clergy face. The fact that women experience them so acutely opens up the possibility of dialogue and debate, and will enable men to disclose their own dissatisfaction at the conflict between family and Church life.

29.   Although the stipend for a priest is relatively low, it is increased in kind through the provision of housing, and the payment of travel and some housing expenses. If two priests share a house, then they only receive one housing allowance. The Church could consider paying the equivalent of a housing allowance to support women who are working and need to pay for childcare.

30.   Sue Walrond-Skinner's study *Double Blessing* (1998) looked at clergy marriages where both partners were priests and where one was a member of the laity. She found high levels of marital satisfaction in the couples she interviewed; however, in concordance with my own findings, she also found joint clergy couples had experienced employment problems in the Church.

31.   See Brereton & Klein "American Women in Ministry" in Radford Ruether, R., and McLaughlin, E., (eds.) *Women of Spirit,* (1979, pp 302-333).

CHAPTER 11

1.   Women priests figure relatively prominently in popular television and radio (The Archers and The Vicar of Dibley are two examples). They are often portrayed sympathetically and are perceived to be approachable, in contrast to representations of male priests in the media. A recent story line in the popular soap opera "Coronation Street" concerned a marriage between a couple, one of whom was transsexual. Whilst several priests declined to perform the blessing, a sympathetic woman curate eventually agreed to officiate at the ceremony.

2.   The Edward King Institute conducted a consultation whereby lay and ordained members of the Church were asked to keep a diary recording their interactions with, and response to, women priests. The findings, although they do not claim to be representative, suggest that women's ministry is being well received. The results are published by the Institute in a report by David Durston (1997), "Consultation on the Church of England's Response to Women's Ordination".

3.   The majority of women ordained in 1994-1995 belonged to middle-aged or older age groups. This reflected the period of waiting that most had experienced. The age profile of women entering the priesthood since that period can be expected to be younger.

4.   I am certainly not making any value judgements about the importance or validity of these ministries, merely reflecting women's perceptions that they are marginalised by the Church.

5.   The word exile refers to those who have been expelled from their native land, and I use it advisedly. Although women have only recently experienced priesthood, their leadership in the early Church, prior to the establishment of formal ordained ministry had far greater recognition, and it was from here that women were exiled. Several feminist theologians, most noticeably Elisabeth Schüssler Fiorenza, have done much to reconstruct the lives and ministries of these early Church leaders.

6. Most women entered Church ministry in response to a sense of call or vocation, not with the aim to change or transform the priesthood.

7. I am committed to working with my Advisory Group to ensure this study is translated into a format which can be used by the Church on the completion of my PhD, by creating a summary report whose findings can be widely disseminated. I will also send a short summary of the findings to all the women who participated in the research.

8. During the study I was elected as a leader in the Church I attend. I have, therefore, had to struggle with the realities of trying to adopt the egalitarian, empowering, collaborative model of leadership that I have advocated in this thesis. It has been a difficult, and sometimes lonely experience, and I have felt misunderstood and misrepresented at times.

9. As I analysed the qualitative section from the questionnaire I looked specifically at the responses to my methodology. Some women found the reductionist quantitative approach restricting and irritating. Others commented that they found the combination of the qualitative and quantitative sections releasing because it enabled them to air their own opinions and focus on issues not covered in the survey:

> I always find questionnaires difficult to complete - reality is far too complex to reduce to ticks and I would not best serve the situation if I make false inappropriate responses for the sake of conforming!

> I have greatly valued this questionnaire as part of my reflection on my identity as a woman priest and pioneer.

10. This approach demands that the researcher, or research team, are equally grounded in both quantitative and qualitative methods. It is also beneficial to have access to advice and expertise in each of the research paradigms.

11. The Centre for Comparative Studies in Religion and Gender (CCSRG) at the University of Bristol, has been set up in order to develop, initiate and support more research in this expanding field.

12. Work is being undertaken in this field. Leslie Francis and Mandy Robbins at St David's University College, Lampeter, are in the process of researching all women ordained in the Church of Wales. However, I am not aware of any other large scale projects, particularly in denominations which have had women ministers for many years, such as the Methodists and Baptists.

13. Ed Lehman Jr.'s study (1993) *Gender and Work* explored the similarities in approach to ministry of female and male clergy from a sample of denominations in the USA. Leslie Francis' study (1991) *The Personality Characteristics of Anglican Ordinands* investigated gender differences in the personality types of a sample of ordinands in the Anglican Church.

14. Barbara Field's study (1992) "A Poststructuralist Analysis of the Discourses of Resistance to the Ordination of Women in the Anglican Church in Australia" (Unpublished PhD thesis, University of New England) sought to understand why some people in the Anglican Church in Australia resist the notion of women priests and why people seemed unable to hear each other as they exchanged views in the debate about ordination.

APPENDIX I

DECISION MAKING STRUCTURE OF THE CHURCH OF ENGLAND

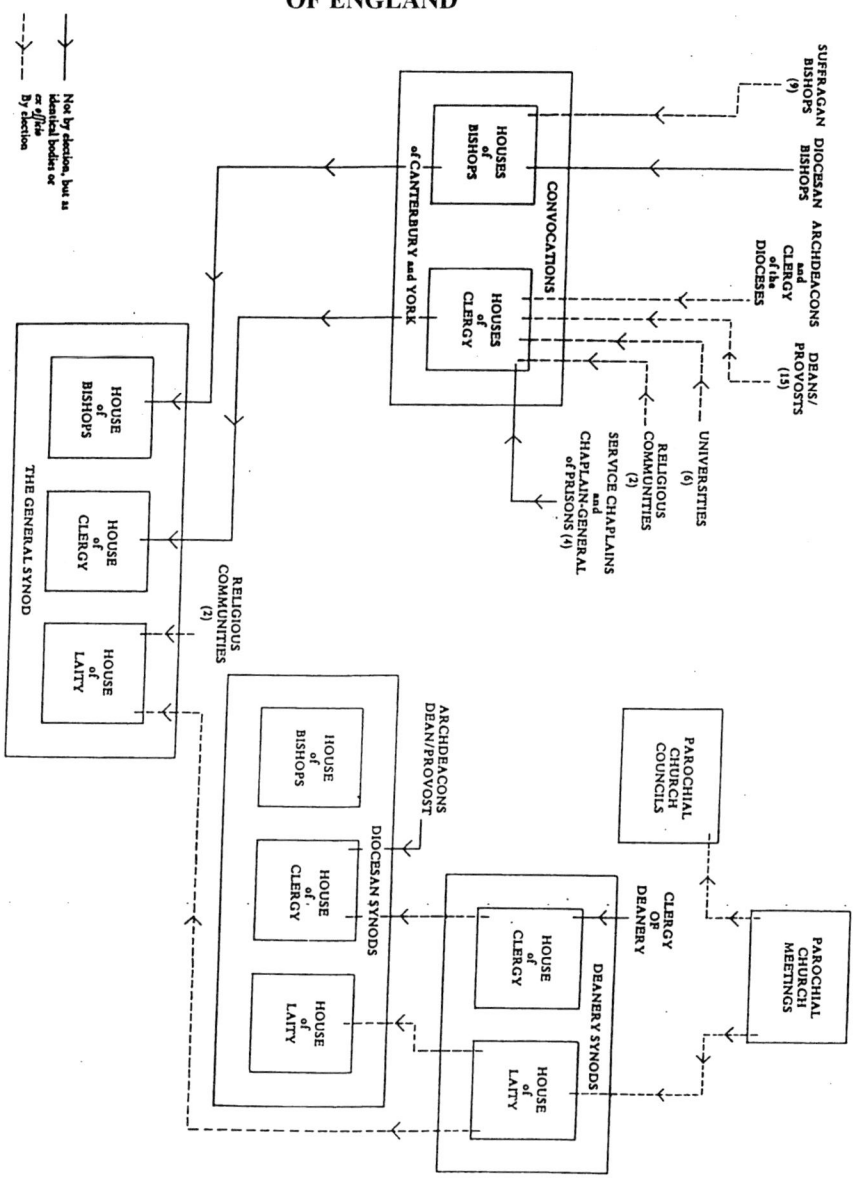

From Wellsby, P., (1985) *How the Church of England Works*, CIO

APPENDIX II

TABLE OF INTERVIEWS

This table includes the basic demographic details of women who took part in the pilot and follow-up interviews

NO.	AGE	MARITAL STATUS	CHURCH BACKGROUND	JOB	EMPLOYMENT STATUS*	DIOCESE	AREA
1	30 - 40	Married	Evangelical	Curate	Part stipend	Bristol	Urban priority area
2	50 - 60	Married	Catholic/liberal	Vicar	Part stipend	Bristol	Rural
3	40 - 50	Married	Evangelical	Vicar	Part stipend	Reading	Urban
4	40 - 50	Widowed	Evangelical/liberal	Vicar	Stipendiary	Reading	Urban
5	30 - 40	Single	Catholic	Chaplain	Stipendiary	Oxford	N/A
6	30 - 40	Married	Catholic/liberal	Rector, Priest in Charge	Stipendiary	Bristol	Rural
7	50 - 60	Married	Not stated	Curate	Stipendiary	Bristol	Urban priority area
8	60-70	Married	Evangelical/liberal	Assistant curate	Non stipendiary (NSM)	Oxford	Rural
9	60-70	Married	Liberal	Sector ministry	Stipendiary	London	N/A
10	40-50	Single	Liberal	Curate/chaplain	Stipendiary	Southwark	Urban priority area
11	50 - 60	Single	Catholic/liberal	Curate/chaplain	Stipendiary	Southwark	Urban priority area
12	30-40	Single	Evangelical	Priest in Charge	Stipendiary	London	Urban priority area
13	30 - 40	Single	Catholic/liberal	Priest in Charge	Stipendiary	Southwark	Urban priority area
14	50-60	Married	Catholic/evangelical	Assistant Curate	NSM	Chichester	Rural

NO.	AGE	MARITAL STATUS	CHURCH BACKGROUND	JOB	EMPLOYMENT STATUS*	DIOCESE	AREA
15	40-50	Married	Catholic/liberal	Curate	NSM	Portsmouth	Rural
16	50-60	Married	Catholic	Curate	NSM	Chichester	Rural
17	40-50	Married	Evangelical/liberal	Curate	Stipndiary	Chichester	Urban
18	30-40	Married	Evangelical/liberal	Not working	N/A	Guildford	N/A
19	30-40	Married	Evangelical/liberal	Not working	N/A	Salisbury	N/A
20	40-50	Divorced	Catholic/liberal	Chaplain	Stipendiary	Gloucester	Urban
21	30-40	Single	Liberal	Priest in Charge/Chaplian	Stipendiary	Bristol	Rural
22	30-40	Divorced	Evangelical/catholic	Vicar	Stipendiary	London	Urban
23	50-60	Married	Catholic/liberal	Area dean	NSM	London	Urban priority area
24	70-80	Married	Evangelical	Retired	Permission to officiate	Leicester	Rural
25	50-60	Married	Liberal	Chaplain	Stipendiary	Southwell	N/A
26	40-50	Married	Catholic/liberal	Chaplain	Stipendiary	Salisbury	N/A
27	40-50	Single	Catholic/liberal	Chaplain	Stipendiary	Salisbury	N/A
28	40-50	Married	Evangelical/charismatic	Curate	Stipendiary	Southwell	Urban
29	50-60	Married	Catholic/liberal	Chaplain	Part stipend	Salisbury	N/A

*   The term stipendiary is used to describe somebody who is paid full time for the job they do in the Church. Those in chaplaincy positions may be paid by the institution they serve and so are technically salaried. However, no distinction is made here between stipend and salary.

APPENDIX III
QUESTIONNAIRE

Section One - Church Life

1. What is/are your **current** post(s)?

   ....

2. Are you? (Please tick **one** box)
   - Full-time ☐
   - Full-time but in two or more posts ☐
   - Part-time ☐
   - Other ....

3. What is your employment status? (Please tick **one** box)
   - Full Stipend ☐
   - Part stipend ☐
   - House for duties ☐
   - Non-stipendiary ☐
   - Other ....

4. If you are an **NSM** what is the **main** reason? (Please tick **one** box)
   - I prefer the freedom ☐
   - It suits my family circumstances ☐
   - I can't move because of my partner's job ☐
   - I am finding it difficult to get a stipendiary post ☐
   - I was stipendiary but it didn't suit me ☐
   - My diocese implied this was the only option for me ☐
   - Not Applicable ☐
   - Other ....

5. Was your training for the ministry? (Please tick **one** box)
   - Part-time ☐
   - Residential ☐
   - Full-time non-residential ☐

6. What is your current diocese?..

7. Have you moved diocese since you were ordained priest?   Yes ☐   No ☐

   (i) If yes, why was this?...

8. Which of the following phrases most describes your **main** theological orientation? (Please tick **one** box)
   - Anglo-Catholic ☐
   - Catholic/Liberal ☐
   - Liberal ☐
   - Evangelical/Liberal ☐
   - Evangelical ☐
   - Evangelical/Charismatic ☐
   - Evangelical/Catholic ☐

9. How old were you when you **first** began to **attend** the Anglican Church **regularly**?....................

10. How old were you when you **first thought** you **might work** in some capacity for the Church?..........

11. What was your **main** reason for entering the Churches ministry?

....

12. How long have you been working for the Church?........................

13. Before you were ordained what positions did you hold in the Church? (Please tick as appropriate)

	Yes	No
Deacon	☐	☐
Deaconess	☐	☐
Parish Worker	☐	☐
Working for a Missionary Society	☐	☐
Accredited lay worker	☐	☐
Member of a Religious Community	☐	☐

Other (please specify)..

14. In how many parishes do you have responsibilities? (Please tick **one** box)
    - 0   ☐   Please go to question 17
    - 1-2 ☐   Please go to question 15
    - 3-4 ☐   Please go to question 15
    - 5 + ☐   Please go to question 15

15. Which of these describes your **main** parish best? (Please tick **one** box)
    - Rural or village   ☐
    - Small town   ☐
    - Large Town   ☐
    - Suburban   ☐
    - City centre   ☐
    - Inner city   ☐
    - Urban Priority Area   ☐

    Other (please specify)..

16. What is the **average size** of your **largest** congregation?..

17. What would you say is your **main** strength in Christian ministry? (Please tick **one** box)
    - Pastoral work   ☐
    - Teaching/preaching   ☐
    - Acting to improve social conditions in your parish   ☐
    - Prayer   ☐
    - Helping others develop their ministry   ☐
    - Administration/organisation   ☐

18. In what area would you say you are **least confident** in your ministry? (Please tick **one** box)
    - Pastoral work ☐
    - Teaching/preaching ☐
    - Acting to improve social conditions in your parish ☐
    - Prayer ☐
    - Helping others develop their ministry ☐
    - Administration/organisation ☐

19. Which posts do you think you might hold in the Church in the future? (Please tick as appropriate)

	Yes	No
Curate/assistant priest	☐	☐
Chaplaincy or sector ministry	☐	☐
Priest in Charge	☐	☐
Incumbent/team rector	☐	☐
Area/Rural Dean	☐	☐
Archdeacon	☐	☐
Residentiary Canon	☐	☐
Cathedral Dean	☐	☐
Bishop	☐	☐

    Other..

20. Have you experienced any of the following whilst working for the Church (Please tick as appropriate)

	Yes	No
Parishioners attending your Church because there is a woman priest	☐	☐
Members of the public refusing to take communion from you	☐	☐
People preferring a woman for sacramental or special occasions	☐	☐
People preferring a man for sacramental or special occasions	☐	☐
Parishioners leaving the Church because there is a woman priest	☐	☐
Fellow clergy refusing to take communion from you	☐	☐
Fellow clergy ignoring you or being rude because you are a priest	☐	☐
Difficulty in gaining suitable posts	☐	☐
Superiors blocking job applications	☐	☐
Other women gaining confidence because there is a woman priest	☐	☐
Difficulties in relationships with senior or fellow clergy	☐	☐
Communion lists published to show a woman is presiding	☐	☐
Any abusive, threatening behaviour or sexual harassment	☐	☐

    Other ....

21. What have you gained personally from being a priest? (Please tick **up to 3** boxes)
    - I have gained confidence ☐
    - I have gained authority ☐
    - I am able to preside at the Eucharist ☐
    - It brings fulfilment/completeness ☐
    - I feel affirmed in my vocation ☐
    - I feel affirmed by the Church/public ☐
    - I am able to hear confession and give absolution ☐
    - I am taken more seriously ☐

    Other (please specify)...

22. How would you describe your involvement in the campaign for women's ordination (MOW)?
    - A member of MOW but not actively campaigning ☐
    - An active member of MOW ☐
    - Not a member of MOW ☐
    - Not a member of MOW but actively campaigning ☐

23. Do you attend any of the following? (Please tick as appropriate)

	Yes	No
A support group for women clergy	☐	☐
A group where lay and ordained women meet together	☐	☐
Supervision	☐	☐
Therapy/counselling	☐	☐
Spiritual Direction	☐	☐

    Other..

24. How far are lay people involved in your ministry in the following areas?

	Never	Rarely	Sometimes	Often
(i) Helping to administer Eucharist	☐	☐	☐	☐
(ii) Visiting parishoners/pastoral work	☐	☐	☐	☐
(iii) Preaching/leading worship	☐	☐	☐	☐
(iv) Leading home groups	☐	☐	☐	☐

25. Do you ever use liturgy in worship which: (Please tick **one** box)
    a) Emphasises the feminine side of God
    - Never ☐
    - Rarely ☐
    - Sometimes ☐
    - Often ☐

    b) Uses pronouns which are not gender specific i.e. 'they' rather than 'he'? (Please tick **one** box)
    - Never ☐
    - Rarely ☐
    - Sometimes ☐
    - Often ☐

Section Two - Background Information

26. **Apart** from your theological training, what is your **highest** academic qualification? (Please tick **one** box)
    - No formal qualifications ☐
    - O'Level/C.S.E./G.C.S.E ☐
    - A' Level ☐
    - Technical Qualification (i.e. HND) ☐
    - Professional Qualification ☐
    - Degree ☐
    - Postgraduate Degree ☐

27. What was your occupation before you entered the Church?..

28. What was your mother's occupation?...

29. What was your father's occupation?..

30. What is your marital status? (Please tick **one** box)

Single	☐	Please go to question 32
Married	☐	Please go to question 31
Divorced	☐	Please go to question 31
Widowed	☐	Please go to question 31
In a committed relationship	☐	Please go to question 31

31. Is/was your partner? (Please tick **one** box)
    Employed ☐
    Retired ☐
    Not employed ☐

    (i) What is/was your partner's job? ....

32. Do you have children? Yes ☐   No ☐

    (i) If yes, who has the **main day to day care** of your children? (Please tick **one** box)
    Me ☐
    My partner ☐
    It's fully shared ☐
    Professional child care ☐
    Not Applicable ☐
    Other ....

33. How old are you? ....

Section Three - Approach to Ministry

The following section includes a list of statements about church leadership. Please say how true each one is **for you**. Please try and be as honest as possible (it's all confidential). Your gut response may be the most accurate!! **Please circle the number which most accurately describes your attitude to the statement.**

	Strongly Agree	Agree	Disagree	Strongly Disagree
God spoke clearly and directly to me about working for the Church.	1	2	3	4
The fact that we were the first group of women to be ordained in the Church of England is very important to me.	1	2	3	4
A bit of competition between fellow clergy is quite healthy.	1	2	3	4
My ministry will be most successful if I can enable my congregation to get along without me.	1	2	3	4
I believe that only ordained clergy should preside at the Eucharist.	1	2	3	4
I feel that I have to prove myself more because I am a woman.	1	2	3	4

	Strongly Agree	Agree	Disagree	Strongly Disagree
My authority as a priest rests primarily on my professional training and ordination.	1	2	3	4
I did not feel able to fulfil my vocation outside the Anglican Church.	1	2	3	4
Now that women are ordained there is a pressure to conform and stay silent.	1	2	3	4
The diaconate was an important time for me.	1	2	3	4
I am afraid that speaking out about women in the Church might affect my opportunities for getting suitable posts.	1	2	3	4
I feel more able to identify with marginalised groups in society because of my experiences as a woman in the Church.	1	2	3	4
I do not feel that active campaigning promotes the cause of women in the Church.	1	2	3	4
I went into the ministry because I had faith that women would eventually be priests.	1	2	3	4
I think ordination places too much distance between the clergy and lay people.	1	2	3	4
A collaborative leadership style works best for me in working with the congregation.	1	2	3	4
I feel the importance of the diaconate has been lost to the Church now.	1	2	3	4
Women who are coming into the ordained ministry now are not as aware of the obstacles as we are.	1	2	3	4
Being with other women is important as it gives me the strength to carry on with the struggle.	1	2	3	4
The easiest way to get things done is to tell people what to do.	1	2	3	4
I prefer to use my professional title and clerical dress when relating to the local community.	1	2	3	4
There is a real danger that we just do things the same way as men have.	1	2	3	4
When I administer the Eucharist I feel that I am doing it on behalf of the Church community.	1	2	3	4
I believe that lay people, not the clergy, should decide the direction in which the Church should go.	1	2	3	4
I think that too much emphasis is put on politically correct words in worship.	1	2	3	4
Too much time is spent in chapter/team meetings on business, we need to spend more time supporting each other.	1	2	3	4
If the General Synod had not voted to ordain women I would have left the Church of England.	1	2	3	4

I firmly believe that the most effective way of changing things is just by getting on with the job.	1	2	3	4
My sense of vocation developed gradually.	1	2	3	4
If women had not been able to be priests I would have been satisfied to stay a deacon.	1	2	3	4
There were times in the struggle when I wanted to give it all up.	1	2	3	4

And finally please use this section to record any of your own thoughts and feelings about the role of women in the Church of England. Please feel free to comment on anything you feel is not covered in the questionnaire or to record any of your own experiences more fully. Please continue overleaf.

....

I am planning to select 20 people for further in-depth interviews. If you would be prepared to take part please fill in your name and address.

Name..

Address..

..............................Post code......................Telephone number............................

Thank you very much for filling in this questionnaire. Please return it in the freepost envelope provided.

APPENDIX IV

RESPONSE RATE BY DIOCESE

1247 women priests replied to the survey, a response rate of 81%. This diagram illustrates the distribution of the responses by diocese.

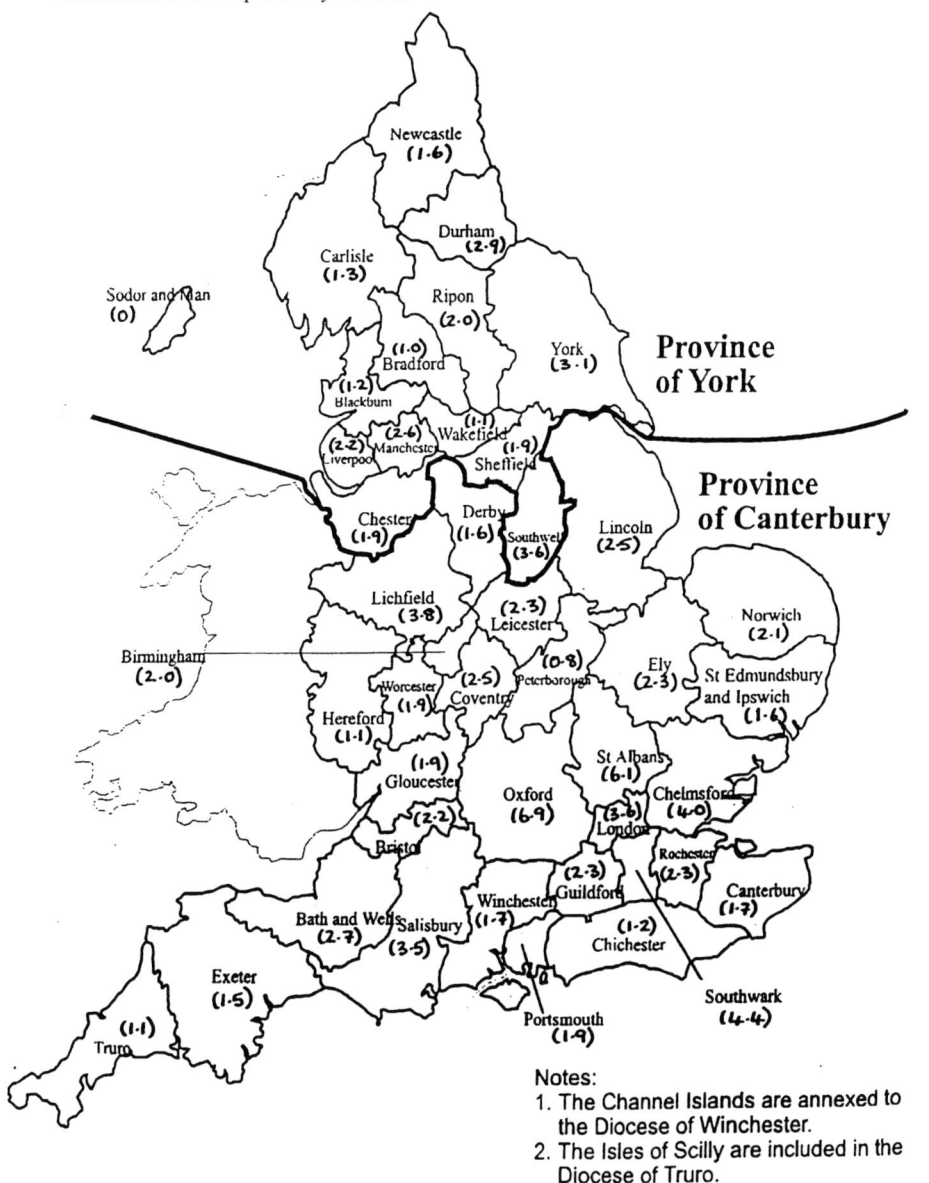

Newcastle (1.6)
Durham (2.9)
Carlisle (1.3)
Ripon (2.0)
Sodor and Man (0)
Bradford (1.0)
Blackburn (1.2)
York (3.1)
Wakefield (1.1)
Manchester (2.6)
Liverpool (2.2)
Sheffield (1.9)
Chester (1.9)
Derby (1.6)
Southwell (3.6)
Lincoln (2.5)
Lichfield (3.8)
Leicester (2.3)
Norwich (2.1)
Birmingham (2.0)
Worcester (2.5)
Peterborough (0.8)
Ely (2.3)
St Edmundsbury and Ipswich (1.6)
Coventry (1.9)
Hereford (1.1)
Gloucester (1.9)
St Albans (6.1)
Oxford (6.9)
London (3.6)
Chelmsford (4.0)
Bristol (2.2)
Rochester (2.3)
Winchester (1.7)
Guildford (2.3)
Canterbury (1.7)
Bath and Wells (2.7)
Salisbury (3.5)
Chichester (1.2)
Exeter (1.5)
Portsmouth (1.9)
Southwark (4.4)
Truro (1.1)

Province of York

Province of Canterbury

Notes:
1. The Channel Islands are annexed to the Diocese of Winchester.
2. The Isles of Scilly are included in the Diocese of Truro.

APPENDIX V

SUMMARY OF BASIC DESCRIPTIVE STATISTICS BASED ON THE QUESTIONNAIRE RESULTS

This is a summary of the descriptive statistics resulting from the questionnaire sent to all women ordained in 1994-1995. The total population was 1547 and 1247 responses were received, an 81% response rate. No attempt has been made here to assess the implications of these results, rather the intention is to give an overview of the basic statistical findings.

(i) Employment status

31.3% of respondents are assistant priests or curates. 10.4% are chaplains or in sector ministry, but this figure rises to 17.4% when those in dual chaplaincy/parish roles are considered. 12.5% of women are in dual roles, either combining parish work with chaplaincy or with diocesan responsibilities. As one might expect, the figures fall as the posts become more senior - 15.1% are in positions of responsibility within a parish (team vicar to incumbent) but only 4% hold the position of rector or area/rural dean. Less than 1% of the first women ordained in 1994-5 have more senior posts than this (residentiary canon, archdeacon etc.). 8.3% class themselves as retired* and 4.3% hold a position on Bishop's staff, a diocesan post or are lecturers. The remainder of respondents are in religious order, not employed, in secular employment or other.

Employment provision in the Church of England is complex and these figures reflect how the women themselves see their employment status. 62.7% of those surveyed work full time and 24% work part time, the remainder are retired, not employed or in secular employment.

34% said they were working for the Church in a non-stipendiary capacity (some were paid for chaplaincy work,** but were also working in a parish as non-stipendiary ministers). 23.35% said they were not NSM by choice, either because the diocese had implied it was the only option for them, they were finding difficulty getting a stipendiary post, or they had tried stipendiary but it had not worked. 17% were non-stipendiary because it suited their family circumstances. 43% were either retired or were too old to hold a stipendiary post (when women were ordained priests, most dioceses introduced a rule that anyone 45 or over could not take up their first stipendiary post). 12% had made a positive choice to be NSM, either because they preferred the freedom, did not need the money, felt called to be an NSM or called to remain in secular work.

(ii) Training for Ministry

51.8% of women ordained in 1994-5 were trained locally, either in a part-time capacity or full-time non-residentially. 46.4% trained in a residential setting. The remainder

---

* Some people categorised themselves as retired and have permission to officiate on an ad hoc basis. Others, however, who are technically retired have a more official status in a parish as a curate. There is a discrepancy, therefore, in the way in which people categorise themselves in the first three variables.
** Chaplaincy work is generally, but not always, paid by the institution, i.e. university, hospital, prison, and not the Church.

combined both part-time and residential training or, in a small minority, were ordained because of their experience.

(iii) Moving Diocese

21.3% of women have moved diocese since their ordination and nearly a quarter of these had moved because they had difficulty getting a job in their old diocese or had had problems in relationships with senior clergy. However, nearly half moved through their own choice, either because they had found a new job or because they felt called to a particular job/diocese. 13% moved because of their partner's job and 8% retired to a new diocese.

(iv) Theological Orientation

42.3% of women described themselves as catholic/liberal and an overwhelming 66.2% clustered themselves around the liberal tag, including 10.5% who said they were evangelical/liberal.

40% of women described themselves as evangelical in some way, in fact evangelical/charismatic was the second largest category with 13.3% classing themselves in this way. Only 4.5% saw themselves as anglo-catholic, but over half described their worship as containing some catholic element (evangelical/catholic and charismatic/catholic).

It should be noted that some people (3.7%) felt this was a difficult question to fill in and that they could not, with integrity, describe their theological orientation in one box. Some wanted a theological category that could be described as middle of the road Anglican - one suspects that others may have chosen the catholic/liberal category as describing this.

(V) Reason For Entering Church Ministry

The overwhelming reason for pursuing ministry within the Church was the sense of an external call or vocation, linked with a desire to serve God. 68.1% of people listed this as important to them. For 10.4% the encouragement of other people was significant. 16.7% cited the fact that it brought fulfilment to them as a person or that it harnessed their skills and abilities. 12.7% felt it was the needs of others, spiritual and physical, which spurred them to work for the Church. Other reasons that people gave were family background (their husband or father was a priest), a gradual deepening of involvement in the Church which progressed naturally to the priesthood, and some joined the Church in order to change it from within. A number tempered their sense of call with the acknowledgement that they had been reluctant to respond to their vocation.

(vii) Positions in the Church

37.6% had been a deaconess, 15.7% a parish worker, 8.6% worked for a missionary organisation, 11.1% were lay workers and 3% were in religious orders. Women had held a number of lay positions in the Church including Sunday school, youth group or small group leaders, 30% of those who indicated a wider involvement in the Church, said that they had been lay readers.

(viii) Parish Responsibilities

Of those with parish responsibilities, 78.6% are in one or two parishes, 14% in three or four, and 7% in five or more. In the discussions and interviews during the initial stages of the research it was suggested that women are being placed in the "back water" or "difficult" parishes. The results show that 52.6% of those who have parish responsibilities are in rural or inner city/urban priority areas. 25% are in suburban or middle class areas with 8.3% in large towns and 12.8% in smaller towns.

(ix) Strengths and Weakness' in Ministry

47.3% of women said that they felt their main strength in ministry was pastoral work, this was followed by teaching/preaching (30.3%) and helping others to develop their ministry (15.2%). In terms of weakness', 53.3% said that they felt least confident acting to improve the social conditions of their parish (although it should be noted that, for some, this could be due to the fact that they do not feel they live in areas which require improvement). Administration and organisation was the second main area of weakness (27.4%).

(x) Ambition in the Church

When one excludes all the people who are/or will soon be retired, 43.7% of women expect to reach the level of incumbent or team rector. 19.8% think they may reach area dean, archdeacon or residentiary canon level (positions which have already been achieved by women), Whereas only 11.4% believe they might go beyond this. More women believe that they might obtain the level of bishop (9%) than believe they will be appointed as a cathedral dean (2%).

(xi) Experiences in the Church

The results of the section which looked at the experiences of women in the Church show a mixed response to women's ordination from fellow clergy and from parishioners. The clearest response came to the question of whether other women in the Church had gained confidence because there was a woman priest. here a resounding 91.2% said this had been true in their experience.

Whilst many women have had negative responses from members of the public, they have also experienced a high degree of positive affirmation: 41.5% have experienced people leaving the Church because there is a woman priest, but 59% have had people visit or attend their Church because there is a woman presiding. 69.6% have experienced members of the public preferring a man for special or sacramental occasions, but in contrast 81.3% said that people had preferred a woman for the same events. 68.6% have experienced people refusing communion from them.

47.3% have had male clergy colleagues refuse communion from them and 56.9% have been treated rudely by colleagues, whilst 41.7% have had difficult relationships with fellow or senior clergy. 27.3% have experienced difficulties getting jobs and 11% have had superiors block their job applications. 36.4% have had communion lists published to show that a woman is presiding. 24.7% of women have experienced abusive or threatening behaviour or sexual harassment.

(xii) Personal Benefits from the Priesthood

It is clear that being ordained priest has had many personal, positive implications for the respondents. 76.4% said being able to preside at the eucharist was an important benefit of their ordination. 63.4% said that they felt that the priesthood brought them fulfilment and completeness. 49.7% said they felt affirmed in their vocation. 40.1% had gained confidence from being ordained priest. 29.4% felt affirmed by the Church/public, and 24.7% felt they had gained authority. 15% appreciated the opportunity to hear confession and give absolution and 10.5% felt they were taken more seriously.

xiii) Support and Campaigning

Only 26.4% were involved actively in campaigning for women's ordination (18.2% of them with MOW). 33.6% were members of MOW but did not campaign and 38.5% were not members. This appears to be confirmed in the attitudinal section of the survey when 54.4% said they did not think active campaigning promoted the cause of women in the Church.

In terms of support 67.4% receive spiritual direction (although this is something which is not specific to women priests), 43% attend a support group for women clergy, but only 12.9% meet regularly with lay women in a group situation. 23.4% had some form of supervision, although it must be stated that the understanding of supervision was mixed. Some saw it as external personal support which enabled them to explore and enhance their working practice. Others felt it was regular oversight of their work by a senior staff member. 11.7% of respondents attended therapy/counselling sessions.

(xiv) Involvement of Lay People

The results show high levels of lay involvement in the ministry of women priests, particularly in helping to administer the eucharist where 87.7% said they often involved laity, 59.9% said lay people were often involved in visiting and pastoral work, 51.9% in home groups and 38.4% in preaching and leading worship.

(xv) Liturgy and Worship

Whilst the majority of women used inclusive language in worship some, or most, of the time the same could not be said about the use of liturgy/worship expressing the 'feminine' nature of God. 62.4% said they rarely or never used liturgy that represented God in a female way.

(xvi) Qualifications and Class

The ordained women showed high levels of academic achievement, especially when one considers that many are from an older age group. 53.2% have a degree or higher degree, and a further 29.3% have a professional qualification (this is excluding any theological qualification associated with training for ordination). This level of qualification is further reflected in the occupations of the respondents prior to ordination. 75.1% were in social class I or II (69% in social class II). Many of the occupations stated were of the professional caring type such as nursing, occupational and physiotherapy; however, the main occupation for women ordinands was teaching. The high numbers of teachers led me to do a separate count for them and it was discovered that 38% of women were/are in the teaching profession. Only 4.4% classed themselves as having home responsibilities prior to ordination.

As one might expect there are signs of upward social mobility in the women ordinands when one compares their occupations with that of their parents'. 36.1% of mothers were classed as homemakers with 25.3% in social classes I and II. 38.3% of mothers were in social class III and below compared with 16.7% of the women priests.

This social mobility is also present when one looks at the fathers' occupations. 21.9% of fathers were in social class I and this figure rises to 28.4% when one adds in the fathers who were clergy* (6.8% of women had clergy fathers). This compares with only 6.0% of women in social class I.

The largest signs of social mobility come in social class II where there are over double the amount of women compared to their fathers. 39.4% of fathers where in social class III or below compared to 16.7% of women priests.

When one examines the partners' occupation, 85.9% are in social class I or II. Once again the percentage of men in social class I is higher than the women, 20% of men have occupations in social class I which rises to 47.7% when the numbers of clergy are added in. Over a quarter of the women who were ordained in this period and are married, have clergy husbands. Only 13% of partners were in social class III or below.

(xvii) Marital Status and Childcare

33% of women are single, 54% married, 5.2% are divorced and 6.1% are widowed. 1.4% describe themselves as being in a committed relationship. 43% have no children and, since there were only 1 or 2 single mothers, it can be assumed that 10% of women who are or were married, do not have children. 39.9% have grown up children and of the remaining 16.8%, 10% have responsibility for child care. For 1% childcare is the responsibility of their partner and 4.6% say it is fully shared; 1.3% use professional childcare.

(xviii) Attitudinal Questions

It is not possible to make sense of attitudinal questions in isolation from each other and a more detailed analysis shows underlying themes and patterns. However questions that have responses of over 75% in agreement or disagreement are discussed here briefly.

---

*   In social class classification members of the clergy are usually coded as social class I. For this survey they were coded separately in order to investigate the number of women who had links with the Church through their fathers or husbands.

The sense of call and vocation was a strong element for the women surveyed. 84.5% said that God had spoken directly to them about entering the Church. 81% said their sense of vocation also developed gradually.

There was evidence of a desire to empower congregations with 81.5% saying that they wanted to enable their congregations to get on without them. 87.8% did not agree with the idea that the easiest way to get things done was to tell people what to do and an overwhelming 95.6% said that a collaborative leadership style works best for them.

There appeared to be a contradiction in people's responses concerning the laity. 79% said they did not feel that ordination placed too much distance between clergy and the laity and 75.7% said that only ordained clergy should preside at the eucharist.

The diaconate was an important time for 78.6% of respondents. However only 59.9% felt that the importance of the diaconate had been lost to the Church now that women were ordained automatically after a year, like the men.

88.8% said they felt that when they administered communion they were doing it on behalf of the community.

Despite the opposition women have suffered there is still a very strong allegiance to the Church of England. 90.3% of women said that they would not have left the Church if the vote had gone against them (although only 47.2% said they would have been happy to stay a deacon).

Finally, 60.5% (755) indicated that they would be willing to be interviewed.

BIBLIOGRAPHY

Allport, G., (1954) *The Nature of Prejudice,* Cambridge, Massachutes, Addison-Wesley.
Armstrong, K., (1993) *The End of Silence - Women and the Priesthood,* London, Fourth Estate Ltd.
Austin Baker, J., (1984) "The Right Time", in Furlong, M., (ed.) *Feminine in the Church,* London, SPCK, pp 163-177.
Babbie., E., (1989) *The Practise of Social Research,* California, Wadsworth.
Baber, H., (1999) "What the Ordination of Women Entails: A Logical Investigation", *Theology,* March/April 1999, pp112-121
Balmer, R., (1994) "American Fundamentalism: The Ideal of Femininity", in Stratton Hawley, J., (ed.) *Fundamentalism and Gender,* New York, Oxford University Press, pp 47-62.
Bentley, L., (1998) "At the Grassroots: The Act in the Parishes", in Furlong, M., (ed.) *Act of Synod - Act of Folly?,* London, SCM Press, pp 101-114.
Bernard, J., (1973) "My Four Revolutions: An Autobiographical History of the American Sociological Association", *American Journal of Sociology,* Vol.78, pp 773-791
Bible, New American Standard (1977) New York, Cambridge University Press.
Bórresen, B., (1995) "Women's Studies in the Christian Tradition: New Perspectives" in, King, U., (ed.) *Religion and Gender,* Oxford, Blackwell, pp 245-256.
Brereton, V., Klein, C., (1979) "American Women in Ministry", in Radford Ruether, R., Mclaughlin, E., (eds.) *Women of Spirit: Female Leadership in the Jewish and Christian Traditions,* New York, Simon & Schuster, pp 302-333.
Bruce, M., Duffield, G., (1972) (eds.) *Why Not? Priesthood and the Ministry of Women,* Abingdon, The Marcham Manor Press.
Bruce, M., (1972) *Heresy, Equality and the Rights of Women* in Bruce, M., Duffield, G., (eds.) *Why Not? Priesthood and the Ministry of Women,* Abingdon, The Marcham Manor Press, pp 40-55.
Brunner, J., (1990) *Acts of Meaning,* Cambridge Massachusetts, Harvard University Press.
Bryman, A., (1988) *Quantity and Quality in Social Research,* London, Unwin Hyman.
Bulmer, M., (1982) *The Use of Social Research: Social Investigation in Public Policy Making,* London, George, Allen & Unwin.
Byrne, L., (1994) *Women at the Altar: The Ordination of Women in the Roman Catholic Church* London, Mowbray.
Callaway, H., (1981) "Women's Perspectives: Research as Re-Vision", in Reason, P., Rowan, J., (eds.) *Human Inquiry: A Sourcebook of New Paradigm Research,* Chichester, John Wiley & Sons ltd, pp 457-472.
Carey, G., (1984) "Women and Authority in the Scriptures", in Furlong, M. (ed.) *Feminine in the Church,* London, SPCK, pp 55-55.
Carin Holm, U., (1982) *Hennes Verk Skall Prisa Henne,* Sweden, Plus Ultra.
Carr, A., (1988) *Transforming Grace: Christian Tradition and Women's Experience,* New York, Harper & Row.

Carr, A., Schüssler Fiorenza, E., (1991) *The Special Nature of Women*, Concilium Vol. 6., London, SCM Press.

Chapman, C., (1989) *The Last Bastion: Women Priests - For and Against*, London, Methuen.

Charlton, J., (1987) "Women in Seminary: A Review of Current Social Science Research", *Review of Religious Research*, Vol. 28, No. 4., pp 305-315.

Chaves, M., (1997) *Ordaining Women, Culture and Conflict in Religious Organizations*, Cambridge Massachusetts, Havard University Press.

Chester, G., (1983) "A Woman needs God like a Fish needs a Bicycle", in Garcia, J., Maitland, S., (eds.) *Walking on Water: Women Talk about Spirituality*, London, Virago Press, pp 148-153.

Chittister, J., (1998) *Heart of Flesh: A Feminist Spirituality for Women and Men*, Michigan/Cambridge U.K., William B. Eerdmans Publishing Company.

Chopp, R., (1992) *The Power to Speak: Feminism, Language and God*, New York, Crossroad.

Christ, C., & Plaskow, J., (1979) (eds.) *Womanspirit Rising: A Feminist Reader in Religion* San Francisco, Harper Collins.

Clark, E., (1983) *Women in the Early Church*, Delaware, Michael Glazier Inc.

Clegg, F., (1990) *Simple Statistics*, Cambridge, Cambridge University Press.

Coe, T., (1992) "Unlocking the Barriers to Women in Management", *Executive Development*, Vol. 6, No. 5, pp 15-17.

Cook, T., Reichardt, C., (1979) (eds.) *Qualitative and Quantitative Methods in Evaluation Research*, London, Sage.

Cook, T., Reichardt, C., (1979) *Beyond Qualitative Versus Quantitative Methods*, in Cook, T., Reichardt, C., (eds.) *Qualitative and Quantiative Methods in Evaluation Research*, London, Sage, pp 7 -29.

Craston, C., (1973) *Evangelicals and the Ordination of Women*, Nottingham, Grove Books Ltd.

Craston, C., (1986) *Biblical Headship and the Ordination of Women*, Nottingham, Grove Books Ltd.

Dalen, A. & Almås, K., (1997) "Gender and Church Leadership" in Hansson, P., (ed.) *Church Leadership*, Uppsala, Tro & Tanke, pp 45-56.

Daly, M., (1974) *Beyond God the Father*, Boston, Beacon Press.

Daly, M., (1978) *Gyn/Ecology: The Metaethics of Radical Feminism*, Boston, Beacon Press,.

Daly, M., (1979) "After the Death of God the Father" in in Christ, C., & Plaskow, J., (eds.) *Womanspirit Rising: A Feminist Reader in Religion*, San Francisco, Harper Collins, pp 53-62.

Davie, G., (1994) *Religion in Britain Since 1945*, Oxford, Blackwell.

De Vaus, D., (1986) *Surveys in Social Research*, London, George Allen and Unwin.

Delphy, C., (1981) "Women in Stratification Studies," in Roberts, H., (ed.) *Doing Feminist Research*, London, Routledge & Kegan Paul, pp 114-128.

Dowell, S., Williams, J., (1994) *Bread, Wine, and Women: The Ordination Debate in the Church of England*. London, Virago Press.

Dowell, S., Hurcombe, L., (1987) *Dispossessed Daughters of Eve: Faith and Feminism*, London, SPCK.

Eck, D., Jain, D., (1986) (eds.) *Speaking of Faith: Cross Cultural Perspectives on Women, Religion and Social Change*, London, Women's Press.

Edwards, R, (1989) *The Case For Women's Ministry*, London, SPCK.
Evans, M., (1983) *Women in the Bible*, London, Paternoster Press.
Farren, D., (1990) "'Seeking Susan': Producing Statistical Information on Young People's Leisure", in Stanley, L., (ed.) *Feminist Praxis Research, Theory and Epistemology in Feminist Sociology*, London, Routledge, pp 91-102.
Farrington, C., (1994) "Renewing the Place", in Walrond-Skinner, S., (ed.) *Crossing the Boundary: What will Women Priests Mean?* London, Mowbray pp 67-82.
Fetterman, D., (1988) (ed.) *Qualitative Approaches to Evaluation in Education: The Silent Scientific Revolution*, New York, Praeger.
Field, D (1984) "Headship in Marriage: The Husband's View", in Lees, S.,(ed.) *The Role of Women*, Leicester, Inter-varsity Press, pp 43-63.
Field-Bibb, J., (1991) *Women Towards Priesthood: Ministerial Politics and Feminist Praxis*, Cambridge, Cambridge University Press.
Fielding, N., (1993) "Qualitative Interviewing" in Gilbert, N., (ed.) *Researching Social Life*, London, Sage, pp 135-153.
Fiorenza, F., (1975) "Political Theology and Liberation Theology: An Inquiry into their Fundamental Meaning", in McFadden, T., (ed.) *Liberation, Revolution and Freedom: Theological Perspectives*, New York, Seabury, pp 3- 9.
Finch, J.,(1993) "It's great to have someone to talk to", in M. Hammersley (ed.) *Social Research: Philosophy, Politics and Practice*, London, Sage, pp 166-180.
Fletcher, S., (1989) *Maude Royden: A Life*, Oxford, Blackwell.
Fonow, M., Cook, J., (1991) (eds.) *Beyond Methodology Feminist Scholarship as Lived Research*, Bloomington and Indianapolis, Indiana Universtiy Press.
Fonow, M., Cook, J., (1991) "Back to the Future: A Look at the Second Wave of Feminist Epistemology and Methodology," in Fonow, M., Cook, J., (eds.) *Beyond Methodology: Feminist Scholarship as Lived Research*, Bloomington and Indianapolis, Indiana Universtiy Press, pp 1-15.
Francis, L., (1991) "The Pschology of Gender Differences in Religion: A Review of Empirical Research", *Journal of Religion*, Vol.27, pp 81-96.
Furlong, M., (1984) (ed.) *Feminine in the Church*, London, SPCK.
Furlong, M., (1988) (ed.) *Mirror to the Church*, London, SPCK.
Furlong, M., (1991) *A Dangerous Delight: Women and Power in the Church*, London, SPCK.
Furling, M., (1994) "The Guardian of the Grail" in Waldrond-Skinner, S., (ed.) *Crossing the Boundary - What will Women Priests mean?*, London, Mowbray, pp 17-27.
Furlong, M., (1998) (ed.) *Act of Synod - Act of Folly?* London, SCM Press.
Garcia, J., Maitland, S., (1983) (eds.) *Walking on Water: Women Talk about Spirituality*, London, Virago Press.
Gee, J., (1985) "The Narrativization of Experience in the Oral Style", *The Journal of Education*, Vol 167, no.1, pp 9-35.
Giddens, A., (1977) *Studies in Social and Political Theory*, London, Hutchinson & Co.

Gilbert, N., (1993) (ed.) *Researching Social Life,* Sage, London.
Gilbert, N., (1993) "Research, Theory and Method," in Gilbert, N., (ed.) *Researching Social Life,* London, Sage, pp 18-31.
Gill, S., (1994) *Women and the Church of England: From the Eighteenth Century to the Present,* London, SPCK.
Gillespie, J., (1992) "Gender and Generations in Episcopal Women", in Prelinger, C., (ed.) *Episcopal Women: Gender, Spirituality and Commitment in an American Mainline Denomination,* New York, Oxford University Press, pp 162-222.
Gilligan, C., (1982) *In a Different Voice,* Cambridge, Harvard University Press.
Glaser, B., Strauss, A., (1968) *The Discovery of Grounded Theory,* London, Weidenfield & Nicolson.
Glucksman, M., (1994) "The Work of Knowledge and the Knowledge of Women's Work," in Maynard, M., Purvis, J., (eds.) *Researching Women's Lives from a Feminist Perspective,* London, Taylor & Francis Ltd., pp 149-165.
Goldthorpe, J., Hope, K., (1974) *The Social Grading of Occupations,* Oxford, Clarendon Press.
Greer, G., (1970) *The Female Eunuch,* London, MacGibbon and Kee.
Guba, E., Lincoln, Y., (1988) "Do Enquiry Paradigms Imply Inquiry Methodologies", in Fetterman, D. (ed.) *Qualitative Approaches to Evaluation in Education: The Silent Scientific Revolution,* New York, Praeger, pp 89-115.
Haggis, J., (1990) "The Feminist Research Process: Defining a Topic," in Stanley, L., (ed.) *Feminist Praxis Research, Theory and Epistemology in Feminist Sociology,* London, Routledge, pp 67-79.
Hammersley, M., (1993) (ed.) *Social Research Philosophy, Politics and Practice,* London, Sage.
Hampson, D., (1986) "Women, Ordination and the Christian Church", in Eck, D., Jain, D. (eds.) *Speaking of Faith: Cross Cultural Perspectives on Women, Religion and Social Change,* London, Women's Press, pp129-138.
Hampson, D., (1996) (ed.) *Swallowing a Fishbone,* London, SPCK.
Hampson, D., (1996) "On Autonomy and Heteronomy", in *Swallowing a Fishbone,* Hampson D., (ed.) London, SPCK, pp 1-16.
Hansson, P., (1997) (ed.) *Church Leadership,* Uppsala, Tro & Tanke.
Harding, S., (1987) (ed.) *Feminism and Methodology,* Milton Keynes, Open University Press.
Harrison, P., (1959) *Authority and Power in the Free Church Tradition,* New Jersey, Princeton University Press.
Hayter, M., (1987) *The New Eve in Christ,* London, SPCK
Heeney, B., (1988) *The Women's Movement in the Church of England 1850 - 1930,* Oxford, Clarendon Press.
Henwood, K., Pidgeon, N., (1993) "Qualitative Research and Psychological Theorizing" in Hammersley, M., (ed) *Social Research Philosophy, Politics and Practice,* London, Sage, pp 14-32.
Herbert, C., (1994) "A Resounding Silence", in Waldrond-Skinner, S., (ed.) *Crossing the Boundary - What Will Women Priests Mean?,* London, Mowbray, pp 28-53

Hewitt, C., Hiatt, S., (1973) *Women Priests Yes or No?*, New York, Seabury Press.

Hiatt, S. R., (1996) "Women's Ordination in the Anglican Communion: Can This Church Be Saved?" in Wessinger, C., (ed.) *Religious Institutions and Women's Leadership: New Roles Inside the Mainstream*, South Carolina, University of South Carolina Press, pp 211-227.

Hill, C., (1988) "The Ordination of Women and Anglican-Roman Catholic Dialogue," in Peberdy, A., (ed.) *Women Priests?* Basingstoke, Marshall Pickering, pp 1-11.

Hoad, A., (1984) "Crumbs From the Table: Towards a Whole Priesthood," in Furlong, M., (ed.) *Feminine in the Church*, London, SPCK, pp 100-118.

Hopko, T., (ed.) (1983) *Women and the Priesthood*, New York, St. Vladimirs Seminary Press.

Hornsby-Smith, M., (1989) *The Changing Parish*, London, Routledge.

Hornsby-Smith, M., (1993) "Gaining Access" in Gilbert, N., (ed.) *Researching Social Life*, London, Sage, pp 52-67.

Howard, R., (1949) *Should Women be Priests?* Oxford, Blackwell.

Howe, E., (1982) *Women and Church Leadership*, Michigan, Zondervan Corp.

Hughes, J., (1976) *Sociological Analysis: Methods of Discovery*, London, Thomas Nelson & Sons.

Hughes, J., (1990) *The Philosophy of Social Research*, New York, Longman.

Hunt, M., (1987) "Friends in Deed" in Hurcombe, L.,(ed.) *Sex and God: Some Varieties of Women's Religious Experience*, London, Routledge & Kegan Paul, pp 46-54.

Hurcombe, L., (1987) (ed.) *Sex and God: Some Varieties of Women's Religious Experience*, London, Routledge & Kegan Paul.

Ice, M., (1987) *Clergywomen and Their World Views: Calling For a New Age*, New York, Praeger Publishers.

Jayaratne, T., (1983) "The Value of Quantitative Methodology for Feminist Research" in Hammersley, M., (ed) *Social Research Philosophy, Politics and Practice*, London, Sage, pp 109-123.

Jayaratne, T., Stewart, A., (1991) "Quantitative and Qualitative Methods in the Social Sciences: Current Feminist Issues and Practical Strategies" in Fonow, M., Cook, J., (eds.) *Beyond Methodology: Feminist Scholarship as Lived Research*, Bloomington and Indianapolis, Indiana Universtiy Press, pp 85-106.

Johnson, D., (1998) "Ordained Ministers in Secular Employment", *Journal of Theology*, January/February, pp 22-27.

Keay, K., (1987) (ed.) *Men, Women and God*, Basingstoke, Marshall Morgan and Scott.

Kelly, L., Burton, S., Regan, L., (1994) "Researching Women's Lives or Studying Women's Oppression? Reflections on What Constitutes Feminist Research," in Maynard, M., Purvis, J., (eds.) *Researching Women's Lives from a Feminist Perspective*, London, Taylor & Francis Ltd., pp 27-48.

Kim, J., Mueller, C., (1978a) *Introduction To Factor Analysis: What it is and How to Do it*, California, Sage.

Kim, J., Mueller, C., (1978b) *Factor Analysis: Statistical Methods and Practical Issues,* California, Sage.

King, U., (1989) *Women and Spirituality: Voices of Protest and Promise,* London, Macmillan Press.

King, U., (1994) (ed.) *Feminist Theology from the Third World: A Reader,* London, SPCK.

King, U., (1995) (ed.) *Religion and Gender,* Oxford, Blackwell.

King, U., (1995) "Gender and the Study of Religion", in King, U., (ed.) *Religion and Gender,* Oxford, Blackwell, pp 1-38.

Kirk, G,. (1998) "Editorial", *New Dimensions* vol. 4, pp 4.

Knott, K., (1995) "Women Researching, Women Researched: Gender as an Issue in the Empirical Study of Religion" in King, U., (ed.) *Religion and Gender,* Oxford, Blackwell, pp 199-218.

Kolakowski, L., (1993) "An Overall View of Positivism", in Hammersley, M., (ed) *Social Research Philosophy, Politics and Practice,* London, Sage, pp 1-8.

Krause, E., (1971) *The Sociology of Occupations,* Boston, Little, Brown and Company.

Kroll, U., (1994) "Hope Fulfilled: Hope for the Future", in Walrond-Skinner, S., (ed.) *Crossing the Boundary - What will Women Priests mean,* London, Mowbray, pp 158-172.

Lang, J., (1989) *Ministers of Grace Women in the Early Church,* Slough, St. Paul Publications.

Langley, M., (1987) "The Ordination of Women," in Keay, K., (ed.) *Men, Women and God,* Basingstoke, Marshall Morgan and Scott, pp 79-92.

Layland, J., (1990) "On Conflicts of Doing Feminist Research into Masculinity", in Stanley, L., (ed.) *Feminist Praxis Research, Theory and Epistemology in Feminist Sociology.* London, Routledge, pp 125-133.

Leech, K., (1992) *The Eye of the Storm: Spiritual Resources for the Pursuit of Justice,* London, Darton, Longman & Todd.

Lees, S., (1984) (ed.) *The Role of Women,* Leicester, Inter-varsity Press.

Lehman Jr., E., (1987) *Women Clergy in England: Sexism, Modern Consciousness and Church Viability,* Studies in Religion and Society, Volume 16, New York, The Edwin Mellen Press.

Lehman Jr., E., (1993) *Gender and Work: The Case of the Clergy,* Albany, State University of New York Press.

Li, F., & Harrison, T., (1985) *Much Beloved Daughter,* London, Darton, Longman & Todd.

Litwin, M., (1995) *How to Measure Survey Reliability and Validity,* California, Sage.

Llewellyn, C., (1981) "Occupational Mobility and the Use of the Comparitative Method", in Roberts, H., (ed.) *Doing Feminist Research,* London, Routledge & Kegan Paul, pp 129-158.

Loades, A., (1990) (ed.) *Feminist Theology: A Reader,* London, SPCK.

Lobkowicz, N., (1967) *Theory and Practice: History of a Concept from Aristotle to Marx,* Notre Dame, University of Notre Dame Press.

Lorber, J., Farrell, S., (1991) *The Social Construction of Gender,* California, Sage.

Maitland, S., (1983) *A Map of the New Country - Women and Christianity,* London, Routledge & Kegan Paul Ltd.

Maltby, J., (1998) "One Lord, One Faith, One Baptism, but Two Integrities?" in Furlong, M., (ed.) *Act of Synod - Act of Folly?* London, SCM Press pp 42-58.

Manis, J., Meltzer, B., (1967) (eds.) *Symbolic Interaction,* Boston, Allyn & Bacon.

Mann, P., (1968) *Methods of Sociological Enquiry,* Oxford, Blackwell.

Martin Soskice, J., (1988) "Would the Symbolism Be All Wrong?" in *Women Priests?* Peberdy, A. (ed.) Basingstoke, Marshall Pickering, pp 12-21.

Martin Soskice, J., (1996) "Turning the Symbols" in Hampson, D., (ed.) *Swallowing a Fishbone,* London, SPCK, pp 17-32.

Marty, M., Scott Apleby, R., (1991) (eds.) *Fundamentalism Observed,* Chicago, University of Chicago Press.

Mascall, E., (1972) "Women and the Priesthood of the Church" in Bruce, M., Duffield, G., (eds.) *Why Not? Priesthood and the Ministry of Women,* Abingdon, The Marcham Manor Press, pp 95-120.

May, T., (1993) *Social Research: Issues, Methods and Process,* Buckingham, Open University Press.

Mayland, J., (1998a) *Act of Synod: A Reconsideration,* London, WATCH.

Mayland, J., (1998b) "An Act of Betrayal" in Furlong, M., (ed.) *Act of Synod - Act of Folly?* London, SCM Press, pp 59-75.

Maynard, M., Purvis, J. (1994) (eds.) *Researching Women's Lives from a Feminist Perspective,* London, Taylor & Francis Ltd.

Maynard, M., (1994) "Methods, Practice and Epistemology: The Debate about Feminism and Research", in Maynard, M., Purvis, J., (eds.) *Researching Women's Lives from a Feminist Perspective,* London, Taylor & Francis Ltd., pp10-26

McCarthy Brown, K., (1994) "Fundamentalism and the Control of Women", in *Fundamentalism and Gender,* Stratton Hawley, J., New York, Oxford University Press, pp 175-202.

McFadden, T., (1975) *Liberation, Revolution and Freedom: Theological Perpectives,* New York, Seabury.

Mies, M., (1991) "Women's Research or Feminist Research? The Debate Surrounding Feminist Science and Methodology," in Fonow, M., Cook, J., (eds.) *Beyond Methodology: Feminist Scholarship as Lived Research,* Bloomington and Indianapolis, Indiana Universtiy Press, pp 60-84.

Mies, M., (1993) "Towards a Methodology for Feminist Research" in Hammersley, M., (ed.) *Social Research: Philosophy, Politics and Practice,* London, Sage, pp 64-82.

Millman, M., Moss Kanter R., (1975) (eds.) *Another Voice: Feminist Perspectives on Social Life and Social Science,* New York, Anchor Books.

Millman, M., Moss Kanter R., (1987) "Introduction to Another Voice: Feminist Perspectives on Social Life And Social Science," in Harding, S., (ed.) *Feminism and Methodology,* Milton Keynes, Open University Press, pp 29-36.

Mishler, E., (1986) *Research Interviewing: Context and Narrative,* Cambridge Massachusetts, Harvard University Press.

Moore, P., (1973) (ed.) *Man, Woman, Priesthood,* London, SPCK.

Morgan, D., (1981) "Men, Masculinity and the Process of Sociological Enquiry," in Roberts, H., (ed.) *Doing Feminist Research*, London, Routledge & Kegan Paul, pp 83-113.

Morley, J., (1984) "'The Faltering Words of Men: Exclusive Language in the Liturgy in Furlong, M., (ed.) *Feminine in the Church*, London SPCK, pp 56-70.

Moser, C., Kalton, G., (1971) *Survey Methods in Social Investigation*, London, Heinemann.

Nason-Clark, N., (1987) "Are Women Changing the Image of Ministry? A Comparison of British and American Realities." *Review of Religious Research*, Vol.28, No. 4, pp 330-339.

Nesbitt, P., (1997) *Feminization of the Clergy in America: Occupational and Organizational Perspectives*, New York, Oxford University Press.

Newell, R., (1993) "Questionnaires" in Gilbert, N., (ed.) *Researching Social Life*, London, Sage, pp 94-115.

Norris, Jr, R., (1984) "The Ordination of Women and the 'Maleness' of Christ" in Furlong, M., (ed.) *Feminine in the Church*, London. SPCK, pp 71-85.

Norusis, M., (1991) *SPSS/PC+ Advanced Statistics 4.0*, Chicago, SPSS Inc.

O'Connor, J., (1995) "The Epistemological Significance of Feminist Research in Religion" in King, U., (ed.) *Religion and Gender*, Oxford, Blackwell, pp 45-64.

Oakley, A., (1972) *Sex, Gender and Society*, London, Temple Smith.

Oakley, A., (1974), *The Sociology of Housework*, London, Martin Robertson.

Oakley, A., (1981) "Interviewing Women: A Contradiction in Terms", in Roberts, H., (ed.) *Doing Feminist Research*, London, Routledge & Kegan Paul, pp 30-61.

Oakley, A., (1997) "A Brief History of Gender" in Oakley, A., & Mitchell, J., (eds.) *Who's Afraid of Feminism : Seeing Through the Backlash* London, Hamish Hamilton, pp 29-55.

Oakley, A., & Mitchell, J., (1997) (eds.) *Who's Afraid of Feminism : Seeing Through the Backlash* London, Hamish Hamilton.

Oddie, W., (1984) *What Will Happen to God?*, London, SPCK.

Packer, J., (1972) "Representative Priesthood?" in *Why Not? Priesthood and the Ministry of Women*, Bruce, M., Duffield, G., (eds.) Abingdon, The Marcham Manor Press, pp 78-80.

Parvey, C., (1990) (ed.) *The Ordination of Women in Ecumenical Perspective*, Switzerland, The World Council of Churches.

Patton, M., (1988) "Paradigms and Pragmatism", in Fetterman, D., (ed.) *Qualitative Approaches to Evaluation in Education: The Silent Scientific Revolution*, New York, Praeger, pp116-137.

Pawson, D., (1988) *Leadership is Male*, East Sussex, Highland Books.

Peil, M., (1982) *Social Science Research Methods*, Sevenoaks, Hodder and Stoughton Ltd.

Perberdy, A., (1985) *A Part of Life*, London, MOW.

Perberdy, A., (1988) (ed.) *Women Priests?* Basingstoke, Marshall Pickering.

Prelinger, C., (1992) (ed.) *Episcopal Women: Gender, Spirituality and Commitment in an American Mainline Denomination*, New York, Oxford University Press.

Powell, D., (1978) *The Ordination of Women and the End of Man,* London, The Church Literature Association.

Proctor, M., (1993a) "Measuring Attitudes," in Gilbert, N.,(ed.) *Researching Social Life,* London, Sage, pp 116-134.

Proctor, M., (1993b) "Analysing Survey Data" in Gilbert, N., (ed.) *Researching Social Life,* pp 239-254.

Pugh, A., (1990) "My Statistics and Feminism - a True Story" in Stanley, L. (ed.) *Feminist Praxis: Research, Theory and Epistemology in Feminist Sociology,* London, Routledge, pp 103-112.

Radford Ruether, R., (1972) *Liberation Theology,* New York, Paulist Press.

Radford Ruether, R., (1979) "Motherearth and the Megamachine" in Christ, C. & Plaskow, J., (eds.) *Womanspirit Rising: A Feminist Reader in Religion,* San Francisco, Harper Collins, pp 43-52.

Radford Ruether, R., (1983) *Sexism and God -Talk : Towards a Feminist Theology,* London, SCM Press.

Radford Ruether, R., (1990) "The Preacher and the Priest: Two Typologies of Ministry and the Orination of Women," in Parvey, C., (ed.) *The Ordination of Women in Ecumenical Perspective,* Switzerland, The World Council of Churches, pp 67-74.

Radford Ruether, R., Mclaughlin, E., (1979) (eds.) *Women of Spirit: Female Leadership in the Jewish and Christian Traditions,* New York, Simon & Schuster.

Repstad, P., (1997) "Church, Committees and Gender" in Hansson, P. (ed.) *Church Leadership,* Uppsala, Tro & Tanke, pp 147-161.

Reason, P., Rowan, J., (1981) (eds.) *Human Inquiry: A Sourcebook of New Paradigm Research,* Chichester, John Wiley & Sons ltd.

Reskin, B., and Padavic, I., (1994) *Women and Men at Work,* California, Pineforest Press.

Reissman, C., (1993) *Narrative Analysis,* California, Sage.

Robbins, M., (1998) " A Different Voice: A Different View", *Review of Religious Research,* Vol. 40, No.1, pp75-80.

Roberts, H., (ed.) (1981) *Doing Feminist Research,* London, Routledge & Kegan Paul.

Roberts, H., (1981) "Women and their Doctors: Power and Powerlessness in the Research Process", in Roberts, H., (ed.) *Doing Feminist Research,* London, Routledge & Kegan Paul, pp 7-29.

Robson, B., (1989) *The Turning Tide: Women in Leadership in the House Church,* London, Marshall Pickering

Robson, J., (1988) "Ministry or Profession: Clergy Doubletalk", in Furlong, M., (ed.) *Mirror to the Church,* London, SPCK, pp 106-122.

Romito, P., (1997) "Damned if You Do and Damned if You don't: Psychological and Social Constraints on Motherhood in Contemporary Europe," in Oakley, A., & Mitchell, J., (eds.) *Who's Afraid of Feminism: Seeing Through the Backlash,* London, Hamish Hamilton, pp 162-186.

Rose, H., (1983) "Hand, Brain and Heart: a Feminist Epistemology for the Natural Sciences", *Signs,* Vol 9, pp 73 - 90.

Rosenberg, M., (1968) *The Logic of Survey Analysis,* Basic Books.

Rosenwald, G., Ochberg, R., (1992) (eds.) *Storied Lives: The Cultural Politics of Self-Understanding,* New Haven, Yale University Press.

Russell, B., (1997) "Leadership in Collaborative Ministry in the Church", in Hansson, P., (ed.) *Church Leadership,* Uppsala, Tro & Tanke, pp 162-175.

Russell, L., (1993) *Church in the Round: Feminist Interpretation of the Church,* Louisville, Westminster/John Knox Press.

Saiving, V., (1979) "The Human Situation: A Feminine View" in Christ, C. & Plaskow, J., (eds.) *Womanspirit Rising: A Feminist Reader in Religion,* San Francisco, Harper Collins, pp 25-42.

Santer, H., (1984) " Stereotyping the Sexes in Society and in the Church" in Furlong, M., (ed.) *Feminine in the Church,* London, SPCK, pp 139-149.

Saunders, P., (1990) *Social Class and Stratification,* London, Routledge.

Saward, J., (1978) *The Case Against the Ordination of Women,* London, Church Literature Association.

Schüssler Fiorenza, E., (1979) "Women in the Early Christian Movement" in Christ, C. & Plaskow, J., (eds.) *Womanspirit Rising: A Feminist Reader in Religion,* San Francisco, Harper Collins, pp 84-92.

Schüssler Fiorenza, E., (1983) *In Memory of Her: A Feminist Theological Reconstruction of Christian Origins,* New York, Crossroad.

Schüssler Fiorenza, E., (1990) "Missionaries, Apostles, Co-workers: Romans 16 and the Reconstruction of Women's Early Christian History", in Loades, A., (ed.) *Feminist Theology: A Reader,* London, SPCK, pp 57-71.

Schüssler Fiorenza, E., (1996) (ed.) *The Power of Naming, A Concilium Reader in Feminist Liberation Theology,* MaryKnoll, New York, Orbis Books.

Schüssler Fiorenza, E., (1996) "For Women in Men's World, A Critical Feminist Theology of Liberation", in Schüssler Fiorenza, E., (ed.) *The Power of Naming, A Concilium Reader in Feminist Liberation Theology,* London, SCM Press, pp 3-13.

Scott, M., (1992) *The Role and Ministry of Women,* Milton Keynes, Word (UK) ltd.

Shaw, J., (1998) "Gender and the Act of Synod", in Furlong, M., (ed.) *Act of Synod - Act of Folly?* London, SCM Press, pp 14-26.

Silverman, D., (1993) *Interpreting Qualitative Data: Methods for Analyzing Talk, Text and Interaction* London, Sage.

Simon, R., Scanlon, A., Nadall, P., (1993) "Rabbis and Ministers: Women of the Book and the Cloth." *Sociology of Religion,* Vol. 54, No.1, pp 115-122.

Simon, R., Nadall, P., (1995) "In the Same Voice or is it Different?: Gender and the Clergy", *Sociology of Religion,* Vol.56, No. 1, pp 63-70.

Skultans, V., (1998) *The Testimony of Lives: Narrative and Memory in Post-Soviet Latvia,* London, Routledge.

Slee, N., (1996) "The Power to Remember" in Hampson D., (ed.) *Swallowing a Fishbone,* London, SPCK, pp 33-49.

Smith, S., (1992) *Gender Thinking,* Philadelphia,Temple University Press.

Stanko, E., (1994) "Dancing with Denial: Researching Women and Questioning Men", in Maynard, M., Purvis, J., (eds.) *Researching Women's Lives from a Feminist Perspective,* London, Taylor & Francis Ltd. pp 93-105.

Stanley, L., Wise, S., (1983) *Breaking Out: Feminist Consciousness and Feminist Research,* London, Routledge & Kegan Paul.

Stanley, L., Wise, S., (1990) "Method, Methodology and Epistemology in Feminist Research Processes", in Stanley, L. (ed.) *Feminist Praxis: Research, Theory and Epistemology in Feminist Sociology,* London, Routledge, pp 20-62.

Stanley, L., Wise, S., (1993) *Breaking Out Again: Feminist Ontology and Epistemology*, London, Routledge & Kegan Paul.

Stanley, L., (1990) (ed.) *Feminist Praxis: Research, Theory and Epistemology in Feminist Sociology*, London, Routledge.

Stanley, L., (1990) "Feminist Praxis and the Academic Mode of Production," in Stanley, L. (ed.) Feminist Praxis: Research, Theory and Epistemology in Feminist Sociology, London, Routledge, pp 3-19.

Stark, R., (1996) *The Rise of Christianity - A Sociologist Reconsiders History*, Princeton, Princeton University Press.

Starhawk, (1979) "Witchcraft and Women's Culture" in Christ, C., and Plaskow, J. (eds.) *Womanspirit Rising*, San Francisco, Harper Collins pp 259-268.

Stockard, J., Johnson, M., (1992) *Sex and Gender in Society*, New Jersey, Prentice-Hall, .

Storkey, E., (1985) *What's Right With Feminism,* London, SPCK.

Storkey, E., (1987) "A Feminist Case Against God" in Keay, K., (ed.), *Men, Women and God*, Basingstoke, Marshall Morgan and Scott, pp 3-22.

Storkey, E., (1995) *Contributions to Christian Feminism*, Christian Impact Ltd., London.

Stratton Hawley, J., (1994) *Fundamentalism and Gender*, New York, Oxford University Press, .

Tanner, M., (1984) "Called to the Priesthood: Interpreting Women's Experiences", in Furlong, M. (ed.) *Feminine in the Church*, London, SPCK, pp 150-162.

Tobias, S., (1978), "Women's Studies: its Origins, its Organisation and its Prospects." *Women's Studies International Quarterly*, Vol. 1, pp 85-97.

Tomlinson, D., (1995) *The Post Evangelical*, London, Triangle Press.

Torjesen, K., (1993) *When Women were Priests: Women's Leadership in the Early Church,* SanFrancisco, Harper San Francisco.

Trible, P., (1990) "Feminist Hermeneutics and Biblical Studies", in Loades, A., (ed.) *Feminist Theology: A Reader,* London SPCK, pp 23-28.

Wakeman, H., (1996) *Women Priests: The First Years,* London, Darton, Longman & Todd.

Walrond-Skinner, S., (1994) (ed.) *Crossing the Boundary - What will Women Priests Mean?* London, Mowbray.

Walrond-Skinner, S., (1998) *Double Blessing: Clergy Marriage Since the Ordination of Women as Priests*, London, Cassell plc.

Ward, K., Grant, L., (1991) "Co-authorship, Gender and Publication among Sociologists," in Fonow, M., Cook, J., (eds.) *Beyond Methodology: Feminist Scholarship as Lived Research,* Bloomington and Indianapolis, Indiana Universtiy Press, pp 248-264.

Ward. H., Wild, J., Morley, J., (1995) *Celebrating Women*, London, SPCK

Washbourn, P., (1977) *Becoming Woman,* San Francisco, Harper and Row Publishers Inc.

Webster, M. (1994) *A New Strength, A New Song - The Journey to Women's Priesthood*, London, Mowbray.

Weiss Ozorak, E., (1996) "The Power, but not the Glory: How Women Empower Themselves Through Religion." *Journal for the Scientific Study of Religion*, Vol. 35, No. 1, pp 17 - 29.

Wessinger, C., (1996) *Religious Institutions and Women's Leadership: New Roles Inside the Mainstream*, South Carolina, University of South Carolina Press.

West, A., (1983) "A Faith For Feminists" in Garcia, J., Maitland, S.,(eds.) *Walking on Water: Women Talk about Spirituality*, London, Virago Press, pp 66-91.

Wijngaards, J., (1977) *Did Christ Rule out Women Priests?* Great Wakering, Mayhew & McCrimmon.

Williams, J., (1984) "Jesus the Jew and Women" in Furlong, M., (ed.) *Feminine in the Church*, London, SPCK, pp 86-99.

Williams, J., (1994) "Lady into Fox: Friends into Priests" in Walrond-Skinner, S., (ed.) *Crossing the Boundary: What will Women Priests mean*, London, Mowbray, pp 83-92.

Wilson, N., McClean, S., (1994) *Questionnaire Design: A Practical Introduction*, Co. Antrim, University of Ulster.

Wintle, R., (1996) "What is Priesthood" in Wakeman, H., (ed.) *Women Priests: The First Years*, London, Darton, Longman & Todd, pp 43-58.

Witherington, B., (1984) *Women in the Ministry of Jesus*, Cambridge, Cambridge, University Press.

Wren, B., (1989) *What Language Shall I Borrow? God-Talk in Worship: A Male Response to Feminist Theology*, London, SCM Press.

Yates, P., (1998) "The Social Construcion of Priesthood", *Journal of Theology*, January/February, pp 13-21

Yeaman, P., (1987) "Prophetic Voices: Differences Between Men and Women". *Review of Religious Research*, Vol. 28, No. 4, pp 367-376.

Young, F., (1994) *Presbyteral Ministry in the Catholic Tradition or Why Women Shouldn't be Priests?* Exeter, The Methodist Sacramental Fellowship.

Unpublished Papers and Theses

Avis, P, (1997) "Theological Understandings and Misunderstandings", Unpublished paper given at St. George's House, Windsor, Consultation "In the Light of Experience".

Boulter, H., (1999) "(Ortho)Praxis - A Key Concept in Paul Knitter's Theology of Religions", Unpublished Paper given at the University of Bristol Postgraduate Conference.

Collins, J., (1997) "The Changing Attitude of the Church of England Towards the Ordination of Women to the Priesthood: 1962-1992." Unpublished MA Thesis, De Montfort University.

Field, B., (1992) "A Poststructuralist Analysis of the Discourses of Resistance to the Ordination of Women to the Priesthood in the Anglican Church in Australia." Unpublished PhD. Thesis, University of New England, Australia.

Hudspith, B., (1998) "An Exploration of the Relationships Between Female Rectors in the Anglican Church of Canada and the Laywomen in their Congregations in the Diocese of Niagara", Unpublished Thesis for Master of Religion, Toronto School of Theology.

Roberts, H, (1978) "Women and their Doctors: A Sociological Analysis of Consulting Rates", SSRC Workshop on Qualitative Methodology.

Stanley, L., (1974) "Sexual Politics in Sociology: a Content Analysis of Three Sociology Journals", Unpublished Paper, University of Salford.

Thorne, H., (1996) "My Pastor Says Some of His Best Men are Women: A Study of Gender Differences in Church Leadership", Unpublished MSc. Thesis, University of Surrey.

Reports and Church Publications

Advisory Board of Ministry of the Church of England (1998) "Statistics of Licensed Ministers", London, General Synod.

Church House, (1995) *Crockford's Clerical Directory*, London, Church House Publishing.

Cooper, H., (1972) "The Ordination of Women to the Priesthood: Consultative Document for the General Synod" Advisory Council for the Churches Ministry.

Durston, D., (1997) "Consultation on the Church of England's Response to Women's Ordination," The Edward King Institute for Ministry Development.

Gender and Ministry: Report of the Central Advisory Council for the Ministry", (1962) London, CIO.

Kettle, P., (1997) "Ministry and Marriage: Survey of Women Priests in the Church of England", London, Christian Research.

Lynas, J., (1998) "Are Anglican Women Priests Being Bullied or Harrassed?", MSF Clergy and Churchworkers' Section.

Meakin, T., (1995) *A Basic Church Dictionary and Compendium*, Norwich, The Canterbury Press.

National Association of Diocesan Advisers in Women's Ministry, (1996) "The First Two Years", NADAWM.

Sacred Congregation for Doctrine of the Faith, "Inter Insigniores", (1976).

Sheild, I., (1995) "Marking Out a Base Line".

Sheild, I., (1995), "Opening Season: Women Ordained Priest in the Church of England in 1994."

Sheild, I., (1996) "On Court: A Review of the Deployment of Women Clergy in the Church of England.

St George's House, (1995) "The Journey Continues".

St George's House, (1996b) "Vision and Reality".

St George's House, (1997) "Taking Stock".

St George's House, (1996a) "Holy Saturday People".

The Bonds of Peace: A Statement by the House of Bishops of the Church of England", (1993) General Synod.

The Deaconness Order and the Diaconate", (1981) General Synod.

The Ministry of Women: Report of the Archbishop's Commission", (1935) London, Press and Publications Board of the Church Assembley.

The Ordination of Women to the Priesthood: A Report by the House of Bishops", (1987) General Synod.

The Ministry of Women: Report by a Committee Appointed by the Archbishop of Canterbury", (1919) London, SPCK.

Wellsby, P., (1985) *How the Church of England Works*, London, CIO.

Women and Holy Orders: Report of the Archbishops' Commission", (1966) London, CIO.

Women and the Priesthood", (1930) Presented to Lambeth Conference, Keighley, Rydal Press.